Praise for *Youth Beyond the Developmental Lens*

Wes Ellis is a pastor and theologian who calls youth leaders to look beyond developmental theories to support young people's faith. His view adds to the youth ministry conversation, inviting us to re-see all young people, not merely as human potentials, but as persons made for divine encounter—right now. Take him seriously, and expect your ministry approaches, youth leader role, and view of "successful" youth ministry to change.

—Dr. Steven Argue, associate professor of youth, family, and culture at Fuller Theological Seminary; applied research strategist at the Fuller Youth Institute; author of *Young Adult Ministry Now*; *Sticky Faith Innovation*; and *Growing With: Every Parent's Guide to Helping Teenagers and Young Adults Thrive in Their Faith, Family, and Future*

Youth Beyond the Developmental Lens is ambitious, winsome, sprawling, and convicting—easily establishing Wesley Ellis as a bracing new voice in practical theology. But it is also a love letter to every pastor who has loved a teenager who didn't fit the mold. Challenging youth ministry's exhausting reliance on the "developmental" paradigm of theorists like Erik Erikson, Ellis shows the harm that this paradigm inflicts, theologically and practically, on young people who don't follow Erikson's developmental script. Ellis writes with refreshing clarity and concreteness, with bursts of disarmingly personal storytelling. Reading this book made me rethink my own ministry: I wish I'd spent less time investing in youth's potential and more time embracing their messy humanity, confident that God is already at work in their lives (even without me). Can we refocus youth ministry in this way? It's a tall order—but Ellis makes me want to try.

—Dr. Kenda Creasy Dean, Mary D. Synnott Professor of Youth, Church and Culture, Princeton Theological Seminary; author of *Almost Christian: What the Faith of Our Teenagers Is Telling the American Church* and *The Godbearing Life: The Art of Soul Tending for Youth Ministry*

Wes has opened the door for all of us to reconsider the water we swim in as youth workers: mainly, the assumptions of developmental psychology and the ways in which it has shaped our ministerial imagination. Through thoughtful theological reflection and empathetic storytelling, Wes envisions a new way forward for the church's ministry with young people. Calling for a new vision of friendship instead of benchmarks of development, Wes brings a breath of fresh air into often stagnant and overplayed conversations about ministry. Wes wants us all to start with God's activity rather than seeing the work of youth ministry as pushing young people along from one achievement to the next. Take the time and give this book a read.

—Dr. Justin Forbes, assistant professor of religion, Flagler College

Pastors, lay leaders, and congregants alike are no strangers to the anxiety that accompanies the aging and declining church in the United States. In *Youth Beyond the Developmental Lens*, Wes Ellis offers a generous and freeing alternative to the fevered and frantic practices of ministry that have become commonplace in our spiritual landscape, particularly in the lives of young people.

—Rev. Jessica Vaughan Lower, pastor and head of staff, San Marino Community Church, San Marino, California

Wes Ellis shakes up the youth ministry world of growth-oriented programs, innovative technologies, and even Christian formation with this dogged critique of how developmentalism, with its penchant for positivism, progress, and maturity, lurks even within good theology to dehumanize young people. What's great, though, is that this is a call forward, or even a call back, versus a calling out—a call back to God's action in ministry, our faithful participation in it, and a deep, reorienting reverence toward the youth we seek to serve. Ellis imagines a youth ministry for developmental refugees, lost sheep, and prodigals that offers gospel hope for the church today.

—Rev. Dr. Erin Raffety, lecturer, Princeton Writing Program, Princeton University

American Protestant youth ministry is in a strange place: something is dying, and something new is coming. What that new thing might be, none of us is sure. But I *am* sure that if what's coming is to be faithful, it will need the kind of thinking that Wes Ellis offers in *Youth Beyond the Developmental*

Lens: Being over Becoming. Ellis is a budding star in practical theological reflection on youth ministry, and this book loudly signals his arrival. With great theological depth, sensitivity to the personhood of young people, and a driving appreciation of ministry, Ellis gives us all a gift in this book. Take it, sink your mind and heart into it, and see things differently.

—Dr. Andrew Root, Carrie Olson Baalson Professor
of Youth and Family Ministry, Luther Seminary

Few thinkers challenge my thinking and practice as deeply and consistently as Wes Ellis. This book is a case in point: he makes a compelling argument, infused with personal passion, that youth ministry might have some of its priorities out of order. Ellis offers an illuminating critique of the subconscious attitudes that pervade and guide churches and youth ministries the world over. He argues convincingly that if we focus only on developing young people along some kind of discipleship production line, we risk overlooking the wonder of God's mysterious work among young people even when they don't behave as we're hoping or realize some kind of preestablished potential. After all, if we're called to follow the biblical example that goes after the *one*, why do we so often only make room for the conforming ninety-nine? This challenging book will invite you to reflect deeply on everything you thought you knew youth ministry was for.

—Martin Saunders, director, Youthscape, Luton, United Kingdom

A theologically nuanced approach to youth ministry that moves beyond gimmicks and quick fixes. Ellis's beautifully written book dares the church to act with joy, courage, and conviction that God is already faithfully present in the everyday lives of young people.

—Rev. Dr. Jared Wortman, senior pastor, Plymouth
Congregational Church, Des Moines, Iowa

Youth Beyond the Developmental Lens

WESLEY W. ELLIS

Youth Beyond the Developmental Lens

BEING OVER BECOMING

FORTRESS PRESS
MINNEAPOLIS

YOUTH BEYOND THE DEVELOPMENTAL LENS
Being over Becoming

All Scripture quotations, unless otherwise indicated, are from the New Revised
Standard Version Bible, copyright © 1989 National Council of the Churches of Christ
in the United States of America. Used by permission. All rights reserved worldwide.

Library of Congress Control Number: 2023940376 (print)

Cover design and image: Ashley Muehlbauer

Print ISBN: 978-1-5064-9494-4
eBook ISBN: 978-1-5064-9495-1

To Jesse Ellis

Contents

Acknowledgments

Like any good work of theology—and you will be the judge as to whether this qualifies as such—there is an autobiographical element to this book. These pages are chock full of my own wrestling with not only the perplexing questions that drive the argument but also my own personal doubt and confusion regarding my experience. This project is mine, and therefore it is shaped by the relationships that make me who I am. It is my sincere hope that this will be more than a mere academic achievement but that it will be a blessing to the church—so that those who find themselves concerned about the younger generations and those who work with young people will be liberated and empowered to encounter the living God in the lives of young people.

I want to thank a few of the people who have helped shape me and have thus helped shape this project. First, I want to thank my friend and colleague Dr. Justin Forbes for tolerating countless hours of rambling phone calls and pages of underdeveloped drafts. Perhaps it will be some time now before I need to call him to hash out my swirling confusions regarding developmental psychology and transversal rationality. Justin journeyed—sometimes literally—with me throughout this entire project, and for that I am truly grateful. I also want to thank Marcus Hong for his friendship and mentoring, especially during the germinating stages of the book you are about to read. I am also indebted to Rev. Dr. Ed Davis and the members of First United Methodist Church of Toms River for their unwavering support and friendship throughout the research and writing process. I also want to thank First Congregational Church of Ramona, my church family, for supporting me and nurturing me in my faith journey from childhood until now. Being your pastor has been the great honor of my life.

Several friends and mentors have read and offered feedback on various portions of this book, including Dr. Erin Raffety, Abigail Visco Rusert, Rev. Andrew Esqueda, Rev. Dr. Nate Stucky, and Katie Wall. I also want to thank my friend and mentor Rev. Dr. Kenda Creasy Dean for empowering me, encouraging me, and helping me to keep curiosity and joy at the center of my theological reflection. I owe additional thanks to Dr. Laura Gifford, Rev. Mike Capron, Trey Gillette, Rev. Ryan Irmer, Dr. Mike Langford, and Dr. Amy Jacober.

The bulk of the research behind this book was conducted under the mentoring of my friends Dr. Andrew Root and Prof. John Swinton. I am so humbled to have had the opportunity to talk through this work with two of my heroes, absolute giants in the field of practical theology. I am beyond grateful for their profound insight, their incredible patience, and their persistent encouragement.

Without the unwavering support and encouragement of my mom, Dolores Mortier, who passed to me her obsessive passion for grammatical precision and who believed in me always, even when there was little reason to, I would not have made it through high school, let alone published a book. Thank you, Mom!

Finally, I want to thank my wife, Amanda, and my kids, Bonnie and Henry. The completion of this book would have been truly impossible without the love and support of my family. Amanda loved me and encouraged me through the most difficult seasons in the life of this project, not least the little speed bump we call the COVID-19 pandemic. There were times when her love carried me through my own self-doubt, and the fact that you are reading this now is because of her.

CHAPTER ONE

Developmental Refugees

It seems that "progress" and unhappiness might well be flip sides of the same restless coin . . . . In blindly pursuing progress, our civilization has, in effect, institutionalized frustration.[1]

—Ken Wilber

What good will it be for someone to gain the whole world, yet forfeit their soul? Or what can anyone give in exchange for their soul?

—Matthew 16:26 (NIV)

JESSE'S STORY

We were both raised in the same house, by the same people, in the same church, but our lives were different. When my older brother, Jesse, was into building with Legos, I was into breaking them apart—you can guess how much he enjoyed that. When Jesse was into video games, I found just as much enjoyment in hitting a baseball against the fence in the backyard, pretending to be Tony Gwynn. When Jesse was into playing guitar, I was into wrestling. While Jesse was hanging out with the punk rockers in high school, I was a captain of the football team. Even though we have always shared a lot of the same mannerisms, when we were in high school, one would hardly have guessed we were related at all. We were different. For some years, I thought that might be a good enough reason to explain why church worked for me but just did not seem to work for Jesse.

We were both raised in a mainline Protestant church where the Bible was taught but not with the same *intensity*—for lack of a better term—as it was in the evangelical churches down the road. Our little church did not have much of a youth group to speak of, and when the youth did gather, education and spiritual formation were not its central motivations. I remember bowling trips and progressive dinners, but I do not remember opening the Scriptures or engaging in worship. So it was not until I started going to one of those evangelical churches that I began to really pay attention to the Bible and to my own faith formation.

It was Jesse who brought me to this youth group for the first time. When he was a freshman in high school and I was in the seventh grade, he had become interested in a young woman who happened to frequent one of the youth groups in town. So, naturally, my brother went to the youth group with his new romantic interest. His motivations were mixed, I'm sure. Let's just say he was probably not there just to meet Jesus. But he did find something in that church. To this day, I do not know exactly what it was for him. But whatever he found, it was bigger than a high school crush. It was significant enough to compel him to invite his little brother.

So I went to church with Jesse. He was still feeling it out, trying it on for size, but from my very first visit, I was hooked. I was captivated by the music and spellbound by the youth pastor's messages. I was fascinated by the things I was learning. Looking back, I'm not sure I still believe many of the things I was being taught about the Bible at that time, but it was there and then that I started to become passionate about it. From then on, I took advantage of every opportunity to be the kind of Christian my youth pastor wanted me to be. My youth pastor invited me to read my Bible at home—to do "devotionals"—so I did. My youth pastor invited me to lead prayers at my school campus, so I did. Indeed, one of my first experiences of participating in ministry was reading Matthew 11:28–30 and offering a prayer at an event called "See You at the Pole."[2] My youth pastor invited me to share my faith with my friends, so I did. I was growing in my faith. I was becoming a mature Christian. Yeah, I was *that* church kid.

My brother, on the other hand, was not a church kid. He had no interest in praying in public or "making disciples." I'm pretty sure the phrase itself would have turned him off. He was more skeptical—probably because he was more thoughtful. But after that first time he brought me, even after his love interest had stopped attending, Jesse continued going for a few months.

There was obviously something that brought him back, but the invitations to do devotionals, lead prayers, and evangelize to the high school campus were not it.

Whatever was compelling to my brother about the church and the Christian faith was apparently different from what compelled my youth pastor and his vision of what it looked like to be a mature Christian. When my brother said no thanks to the invitations to develop according to the church's discipleship strategy, the youth pastor's best and only tactic was to start over and ask again, "What about now? *Now* do you wanna be that kind of Christian?" Eventually, Jesse just stopped coming. He must have seen that he and the church had reached an impasse. The church wanted him to become something he wasn't interested in becoming.

When Jesse stopped going to youth group, I am sure the youth pastor simply chalked him and his experience up as collateral damage, just as I would eventually do with my youth group dropouts when I became a youth pastor myself—after all, you can't win 'em all. And I am sure the youth pastor could console himself quite effectively by seeing that his approach "worked" on me. But though I would go on to enter the professional ministry, becoming a pastor myself, I have never been able to see my brother as the collateral damage to an otherwise healthy approach to ministry. My brother's experience has nagged at me throughout my journey of faith. I want to know what my youth pastor missed. What was it that Jesse found in that church that compelled him? What compelled him to bring his little brother to church? If it was not the invitation to grow and become the kind of Christian my youth pastor thought he should be, then what was it? More importantly, perhaps, what kept my youth pastor from being able to figure that out and to participate with whatever it was that God was actually doing in my brother's life?

This book is a project in discerning the answers to these questions and offering a way for pastors, parents, and adults like my youth pastor to participate in God's work in the concrete and lived experiences of young people[3]—not just the ones who respond to our invitations but ones like Jesse too. Let me be clear that the church's failure to "work" for Jesse and my youth pastor's inability to discover God in my brother's lived experience—to participate in that which kept bringing Jesse back to the youth group—are not just *evangelical* problems. Sure, that church was an evangelical church, but the same anxieties drive the practices of mainline churches too. Evangelicalism has been a profoundly influential tradition in shaping how the American church as a whole approaches young people.[4] Indeed, the "youth group model" and youth ministry as a discrete practice in the church was birthed out of the evangelical tradition.[5] But the approach to youth represented in my experience is far reaching in the mainline context as well. While the theology may be different and the practices might look and sound unique, the texture is the same. It is my contention that whatever other factors were at play in my brother's experience, the fundamental problem in the church that has long hindered youth workers, pastors, parents, and leaders from participating in God's action in young people's lives is a deep-seated commitment to developmentalism.

DEVELOPMENTAL REFUGEES: A DAM PROBLEM

"The twentieth century was the century of the megadam," writes Rob Nixon. "In 1900, no dam on our planet was higher than fifteen meters; a hundred years later, there were 36,562 dams that exceeded that height."[6] The rapid construction of megadams worldwide became the iconic symbol of industrialization—the same century and the same industrialization that ushered in the social construction of adolescence. During the Cold War in particular, "the megadam, like the mushroom cloud, made an awesome, cinematic statement of superpower prowess in the race to be the übermaster of natural mastery." In this race for development, "to erect a megadam was literally to concretize the postcolonial nation's modernity, prosperity, and autonomy."[7] As such, the building of these megadams became a sort of "national performance art."[8] They were celebrated by so-called developing nations as monuments of their progress, the realization of their potentiality.

Development dominated the imagination and the socioeconomic narrative of the twentieth century. So, of course, the narrative was told from the vantage point of the developed and the developing. But what is coming into view, however subtly, are the stories of those who are "inundated by development."[9] In the shadow of these colossal monuments of developmentalism stands the collateral damage of development—the millions of people, most often Indigenous people, who are "recast as 'surplus'" and dislocated to "unfamiliar and nonsustaining ecologies."[10] The anthropologist Thayer Scudder, according to Nixon, "estimated the number of people displaced by such dams at somewhere between 30 million to 60 million."[11] This is a precarious reality.

After all, development is supposed to be a positive thing, right? Growth is supposed to be good news. But as it turns out, it is not always good news to everyone. Thus, the paradoxical term *developmental refugees* appropriately holds the tension between the potentiality of progress and the actuality of displacement and marginalization.

It would be inappropriate to draw a comparison between the magnitude of the suffering of displaced peoples and the experience of the youth group dropout. But these stories are marked by analogous imaginative conditions. Stories of national development serve as a metaphor for, and are hermeneutically linked to, stories of individuals' physical, social, psychological, and spiritual development. The stories of displaced peoples, the developmental refugees of industrial society, are marginalized in the same way that my brother's experience is marginalized in the church imaginary—along with the experiences of so many other young people for whom the church has stopped working. In favor of success narratives such as my own, brushed aside are the stories of those who aren't successfully assimilated into civic or spiritual "maturity." In fact, the power of developmental narratives depends on the concealment of failure. As Nixon put it, the stories of development "are partial narratives that depend on energetically inculcated habits of imaginative limit, habits that hide from view communities that inconvenience or disturb the implied trajectory of unitary national ascent."[12]

In the case of the industrial story of progress, long before the bulldozers and the police enter the scene to get people off the land, the "imaginative work of exclusion" is already at hand.[13] Likewise, before Jesse darkened the church doors, his story was buried in expectation and the developmental optimism that demanded he eventually *become* a mature Christian adult. The imaginary path to maturity was already paved with expectations. While some young people do dig their way to the surface of those expectations, developmental refugees are buried under them.

My youth pastor saw his task as that of guiding and walking with young people in the transition to adulthood. God's action, the work God wanted to do in the lives of young people, was located in the *future*, as a *telos* or ultimate goal to be realized. If God was at work at all in the present, it was only to get young people to an *end*. Wayne Rice's metaphor is appropriate: "Like travelers at a busy airport, children arrive at early adolescence looking for the plane to adulthood."[14] If they cannot catch the flight, however, they are simply left at the terminal. When my brother did not accept the invitation to move and improve—to *become*—the ministry no longer resonated with him.

WHAT IS DEVELOPMENTALISM?

Developmentalism is a hermeneutical framework that situates human life—and history itself—on a progressive trajectory and a qualitative scale of improvement.[15] The kind of developmentalism to which we are heirs in the twenty-first century stems in significant ways from nineteenth-century behaviorism, the philosophical basis of which is empiricism.[16] Drawing on the philosophy of John B. Watson, psychologist B. F. Skinner sought to explain human action in terms of observable and measurable behavioral patterns. He rejected elements of depth psychology and other introspective methods that ascribed importance to feeling and internal organization within an "organism." Behaviorists denied unobservable mental activity and reduced human action to impulse and response—to functions of behavior and behavioral patterns, the conditions of which could be altered and manipulated to produce different and preferred behaviors. Although this reductionism was challenged and ultimately rejected by the broader psychological community, the empiricist soil that nurtured its conception is still pervasive and the precepts of behaviorism are still subtly alive in modern education and parenting.

Developmentalism is born of the same soil: it reduces our conception of being human to the achievements of development. The phenomena of love, friendship, and creativity are reduced to their utility as instruments of progress. And this is only exacerbated when anxieties of scarcity and decline are introduced, which makes the church particularly susceptible to the pitfalls of developmentalism. When our motivations are driven by institutional anxiety—fear that there aren't enough young people in church, for example—we reach for technologies to solve our problems—technologies like youth group—and we fix our attention on the effectiveness of our programs. We end up listening to narratives instead of relationships.

Developmentalism interprets human life—and, indeed, history itself—on a scale of improvement. Progress and growth are normative, and *potentiality* sets the terms for an adequate account of what it means to be human. Dawn DeVries refers to this as "instrumental valuation." Things and people are ranked on a scale of how well they contribute or correspond to what we've deemed desirable or "normal." For example, as DeVries puts it, "The child has value because he or she has the potential to become an adult."[17] Value is determined by the outcome. We see children not for who they are in the present but as "pregnant with inevitable development."[18] A person is valued according to their *potential*, and relationships become mere instruments of progress.

If human life itself is pregnant with development, it is interpreted as proceeding according to phases or stages of development, each leading toward the next. Adulthood becomes the interpretive vantage point, providing the metric by which every preceding stage is measured. Even the practical theologian James Fowler admitted, "The most revealing aspect of any theory of human development is the character of the last stages."[19] By hermeneutical necessity, developmentalism values a stage of life according to its potential to reach the next stage because the later stages represent a completion and a fullness that are necessarily absent from the earlier stages. Thus, every stage is defined by deficiency.

We can already begin to point out the influence of this hermeneutical architecture on my brother's experience. My youth pastor looked at Jesse from the vantage point of what he believed to be a *mature* spirituality—namely, one that is "generative" of others' faith experiences through Bible study and evangelism. He saw what he wanted Jesse to become, where he thought my brother should be going, and was thus disinterested in where he actually was except insofar as it could contribute to his spiritual development. In other words, because the vantage point was my brother's potentiality, my youth pastor was obstructed from participating in his *actuality*. Unfortunately, it is likely this was the case not because my youth pastor was ill-trained or undereducated but precisely *because* of his education and training. Developmental psychology has long provided the interpretive scaffolding of the church's intergenerational relationships. So it comes as no surprise that a trained and educated minister of the church would operate on the assumptions of developmentalism and try to capitalize on potentiality rather than participate in actuality.

Developmentalism obscures actuality with potentiality, *being* with *becoming*, and limits adults from true appreciation for the lived experience of youth as anything other than a journey "from here to maturity."[20] In the early 1990s, Allison James and Alan Prout observed that "child development and socialization theories concentrated predominantly on childhood as a sort of 'moonshot', a highly complex and engineered trajectory towards adulthood."[21] This "moonshot" framework is still dominant in the church. Because the metaphors of growth and maturity have dominated our understanding of faith formation in the church, Jesse was valued merely as clay for the potter's wheel. In placing *becoming* at the center, we force *being* into the backseat. From the vantage point of adulthood, youth and the experience of the young person become, as Chris Jenks has put it, "a structured becoming" and not "a location for the Self."[22] Thus, developmental models of ministry, like the one to which my youth pastor was committed, are not about youth at all but rather the adulthood into which it is to be developed. Relationships become tools, not ends in themselves.

Perceptions of "growth" entrenched in developmentalism become even more insidious amid our anxieties about the future of the church. Projects that obsessively concern themselves with institutional "decline"—be they denominational initiatives, grant-funded research endeavors, or missional innovations—are necessarily compelled by improvement and acceleration. The age of developmentalism cannot sit still. It requires "dynamic stabilization," which, according to Hartmut Rosa, "requires constant economic growth, technological acceleration, and cultural innovation in order to maintain its institutional status quo."[23] The collateral damage of developmentalism—anxiety, burnout, church dropouts, my brother—are inherent within the epistemic ecosystem and cannot, therefore, be fixed simply with "better leadership." Developmentalism, as long as we submit to its logic, will inevitably obstruct our ability to minister to young people and to encounter God in their experience, no matter how good the theological packaging may otherwise be.

THE DOMINANCE OF DEVELOPMENTALISM
IN THE CHURCH

The most common source we summon to understand young people is that of developmental psychology—particularly the paradigm of adolescence. Indeed, the very term *youth* has become synonymous with *adolescence*, and this conflation reflects the essentialism and positivism of developmentalism. We categorize the experience of youth as essentially transitory and in need of rectification—sort of like an illness. This has been part of the fabric of the church's interpretive hermeneutic for decades. Some youth ministry thinkers have situated their discipline so firmly in the frame of developmentalism that they have doubled down and constructed the whole project of ministry, as such, into a process of development toward the "maturity" of Christian adulthood. Even Mark DeVries, who has made countless important and positive contributions to the practice of youth ministry and should truly be commended as a sage among American youth ministry practitioners for his practical wisdom and strategic insight,[24] is betrayed by a developmentalist bias. In one of his early and influential books, DeVries claimed that the "crisis" of youth ministry was that "the ways we have been doing youth ministry have not been effective in leading our young people to mature Christian adulthood."[25] Thomas Bergler, another key figure in youth ministry scholarship, attributes the bulk of the problems faced by the church to its "immaturity"—what he calls "juvenilization."[26] For Bergler, the gospel itself is about development into spiritual "maturity," and adolescence is categorically deficient. Development is seen as "common sense"—sometimes even biologically determined.[27]

You don't have to look very far to find a similar bias. If there were still bookstores, and if those bookstores had "Youth Ministry" sections in them, you'd have no trouble finding examples like these in them: "Adolescence is a time of transition," writes Jim Burns.[28] "You are touching lives during the transition years," writes Lawrence O. Richards.[29] Amy Jacober tells us that "teenagers are all about change.... A practical theology of youth ministry requires that we acknowledge and address the change which occurs between childhood and adulthood."[30] Taking cues from developmental theorists—most notably Erik Erikson—youth ministry theologians and youth workers have always viewed the experience of youth and life itself as a "process of differentiation" and "becoming one's own person."[31] Thus, we have seen our primary task as accompanying young people in this transition toward adulthood. "All adolescents need the presence of other individuals," writes Kelly Schwartz, "that will enable them to develop in healthy ways through a potentially challenging developmental transition."[32] We have come to see this adolescence—this diagnosis of experience as transitory—as the commonsense view, simply the way it is. We see adolescence as the *thing* rather than just one *interpretation* of a thing: "*Youth* suddenly became more than a concept: it became a fact."[33]

Of course, young people *do* need supportive intergenerational relationships; we all do. The developmental lens, however, substitutes instrumental ends—guidance into adulthood—for the gifts of companionship. And with few exceptions,[34] developmentalism has seeped into spaces where theology and ministry should be driving our interpretation. It is pervasive even in works that do not center themselves on interpretive categories. Drawing from neuro-scientific sources and referring to recent research, Morgan Schmidt explains young people's behaviors, locating this explanation in the brain.[35] While she tries to elevate the positives of these explanations, the effect of her interpretation is to protect the developmental hierarchy and the commonsense-deficit position of the adolescent. Difference is explained in "natural," "scientific" terms. Young people act like adolescents because they *are* adolescents. What was formerly understood as selfishness and self-consciousness can now be reframed as "identity formation." Young people are not "bad" or "deviant"; they are just developing. This, we tend to think, is the adequate form of compassion for addressing the symptoms of adolescence, but it may in fact only be condescension disguised as understanding. We can rest easy and remain unchallenged by young people's lived experience because, after all, it is just a phase; it is how they are "wired," and they'll get past it someday.

Don't get me wrong. It's true that developmentalism has served us in some positive ways, helping youth workers and parents meet certain developmental needs that some young people indeed have. A developmental lens can provide some guidance and afford some patience. Also, it can allow for some empowerment. It would be unfaithful for me to claim otherwise since, in fact, it was a developmental approach to youth ministry that prompted my youth pastor to encourage me toward the kinds of spiritual experiences and leadership opportunities that have shaped me into the pastor and person I am today. We all have our success stories. But success has a way of paralyzing us. Success stories can hijack the narrative and obscure, even marginalize, the experiences of those on the underside of the narrative. It is deeply dissatisfying for me to applaud my own experience without attending to my brother's experience. While development is real, and meeting developmental needs may be important in specific situations, when we allow developmentalism to be a totalizing, dominant, or even a central motivation, we are bound to leave people behind—to create developmental refugees.

THE INVITATION

As a youth worker and pastor who has worked across multiple denominations and Christian traditions, I have seen the disconnect that exists between young people and adults in the church. I have felt the anxieties of the church in America. Indeed, they are my own anxieties. I have felt the pressure to perform, to produce, to make the budget, to get more money, more programs, and to develop "mature" Christians, all in light of the decline of the church. I have felt the overwhelming anguish of burnout that comes when, despite dedication and the exertion of energy, young people do not develop according to the vision that drives the church's strategy and the pews are still populated (if they're populated at all) exclusively by people older than me. What allows these pressures and the accompanying exhaustion to linger?

It is my contention that the soul of ministry is not growth. The soul of ministry is the encounter of God with creation and especially us: human beings. The soul of ministry is relationships. Ministry is not disclosed in maintaining church affiliations, nor is it discovered through the ability of leaders to produce mature Christian adults. It is not in *becoming* but in our shared *being* that the God revealed in Jesus Christ is encountered. And when every program design, every metric for success, every grant dollar, and the very notion of what it means to be human are oriented toward *becoming*, our vision is obstructed from the *being* of the people with whom we are ministering. The developmental lens cannot bring *being* into view. It only sees *becoming*. When this happens, we become unable to encounter the God in whom we have our *being*.

There is a disconnect between adults, including parents, and young people in churches, a disconnect that contributes to and, more importantly, stems from the adults' obsession with growth and the church's obsession with its own institutional survival. As adults, we struggle to understand why young people are leaving the church, and we struggle to hear what young people are *actually* experiencing. As a result, we are struggling to encounter the God whom young people are experiencing—and I am convinced that, in or out of the church, they *are* experiencing God. It is a mistake to assume that young people leaving the church means that young people are leaving the abundant life that Jesus gives. Just because young people don't express their faith through church programs does not mean they don't have faith. Adults, I propose, are the ones who are truly missing out. We're missing out on the presence of God in *actuality* because we are obsessed with *potentiality*. We are missing out on what God is doing in the lives of young people, especially the ones who aren't part of our church.

The good news of Jesus Christ is good news for all people, or else it is not good news at all. Thus, the "good news" of developmentalism and the developmental lens, which always produces developmental refugees, is far too limited to provide a horizon for the relationships between adults and young people in the church. God is not only in *potentiality* but *actuality*. Developmentalism has a way of limiting our attentions to those places with the greatest potential, blinding us to the faces of "surplus" people, so that interventions might bring about the desired outcome of progress. But God's attention, God's interpretive horizon, is not so limited. When God raised Jesus from the dead, it was not that God resuscitated a body that had the potential to live. God raised a lifeless body, a body with no future, no chance for progress, no potential for development. God raised a broken body. And it is to a broken body that God asks us to look for hope. God is not interested in potential. God's metric for success is not developmental. God's metric is death and resurrection.

One might ask, "What about the call to follow Jesus?" Does that not require growth? And does God not leave us behind if we are not willing to go with Jesus? One oft-quoted story from Scripture that might be employed to argue such a point is that of the so-called rich young ruler. The story tells of a young man who, when he cannot bring himself to meet Jesus's standard, is allowed to walk away. Jesus does not follow after him. He is simply left behind. "If we are not willing to do what Jesus asks," one might argue, "if we're not willing to develop according to Jesus's standard, he will not chase after us; he will let us walk away, just like the rich young ruler." Is that not the simple explanation for what happened with my brother?

But there is more to this story than meets the eye. Found in both Matthew 19 and Mark 10, the story tells us that a man came to Jesus and asked, "Good Teacher, what must I do to inherit eternal life?" (Mark 10:17, NRSV). His question is quite forward-thinking. He is essentially asking how he can "share in the life of the coming world."[36] Without anachronistically presuming too much about what this young person was trying to attain, we can draw some parallels to how we might imagine this question would be conceived today. The young man is trying to understand what his next step must be. What is the next stage of his development? After providing a somewhat perplexing initial response,[37] Jesus refers to the decalogue, the Ten Commandments. The man is not satisfied with Jesus's perhaps somewhat dismissive response. Then the text tells us, "Jesus, looking at him, loved him and said, 'You lack one thing; go, sell what you own, and give the money to the poor, and you will have treasure in heaven; then come, follow me'" (Mark 10:21, NRSV). Imagine how these words might have struck the ears of someone who, it seems, has spent so much of his life trying to *become* someone, to meet the next standard, and to accumulate status. Now he is being invited to sell all he has, all of that for which he has toiled for so long. Now he is being told to basically go the other direction, to abandon his task of accumulation, to stop trying to *become* something and to simply *be*. He is invited to forsake all the symbols of his personal development, every marker by which he has measured himself, and follow Jesus with just his personhood.[38]

Jesus's invitation constitutes a liberation *from* potentiality, a liberation *to* actuality. Can you imagine how this question might be answered in most church settings? If a young person were to ask, "How do I get eternal life?" we would likely respond with something like, "Take the next step in your spiritual journey," "Join our confirmation class," "Pray the following prayer," or "Come with us on the next mission trip." This is not a story of Jesus abandoning someone for the sake of progressive discipleship or growth. Nor is this about Jesus adding a new expectation to a list of expectations. This is the story of a man who is being offered freedom *from* progress and development but cannot help but continue to measure himself by their standards. This is not the story of a rejected invitation to follow Jesus but of the gospel invitation that is extended to all of us, adults and youths alike, which we are given freely without condition—the invitation to depart from developmentalism and to embrace a truly theological horizon for understanding young people's and our own experiences.

Perhaps the greatest biblical image for what we are and what is expected of us is the image of the child.[39] The first thing we should notice about the image of the child is that it is not the image of the adult that we humans have allowed to remain our hermeneutical vantage point. We are children of God. God does not require us to *attain* anything to be called *children of God*: "See what love the Father has given us, that we should be called children of God; and that is what we are" (1 John 3:1, NRSV). The only *becoming* that is appropriate in the kingdom of God is becoming what one truly *is*, which depends decisively on grace alone.

We judge our churches and families by the maturity of the young people in them, by our ability to develop young people into mature Christian adults, and by ensuring young people's affiliation with the church in the future. What God is interested in, however, is not where people are going—what they will accomplish, what they will do—but who they are in the depth of their very being here and now. God places *actuality* over *potentiality*, and it is in the actuality of a young person's experience that God is located. God is not a carrot on a stick; God is closer than the air we breathe. The success of our ministry will be determined not by how we form people but by how we love them.

I am unsure whether Jesse would be a Christian today if my youth pastor had done things differently. That is not the point. The problem is not that my brother did not become a Christian. The problem is that, regardless of his own theological commitments, God was (and is) moving in Jesse's life, and the adults in his life apparently missed it. The concern of this book is not to ensure that young people like my brother will eventually be "won" to the church. It is, however, to construct a theological horizon that can hold the mystery of my brother's experience and enable us not only to heal the intergenerational discord that exists in churches but also to discern and engage in what God is doing in the mystery of lived experience. One of the biggest obstacles to this mystery is the epistemic soil in which developmentalism grows: empiricism.

CHAPTER TWO

The Allure of Empiricism

So-called "soft" forms of knowledge such as spirituality may have their place, but they are only allowed to eat at the table after the hard sciences have finished their meal.[1]

—John Swinton

The secret things belong to the Lord our God, but the revealed things belong to us and to our children forever, to observe all the words of this law.

—Deuteronomy 29:29 (NRSV)

When I was in college, I had every intention of becoming a youth minister, so naturally I took several courses on youth ministry. In fact, for my first year of undergraduate studies, I was a youth ministry major (yes, that's a thing). But I also took a few philosophy and theology courses. While I was passionate about youth ministry, I was also deeply interested in questions of transcendence—theological questions about God's being and action. I was captivated by the readings from my theology and church history classes. I absolutely loved learning from people like Augustine, Athanasius, and Bonhoeffer. I enjoyed reading theology far more than reading about models and strategies for youth group. I quickly discovered this made me a bit of an odd duck in my youth ministry courses. At Azusa Pacific University, the youth ministry students tended to be the types who didn't actually enjoy theology—or perhaps they only cared about theology as long as it was practical. I don't mean to slander them here; I think they'd probably admit it. They rolled their eyes through theology lectures until they could get to the "useful" stuff. They did not have much patience for the more technical and less obviously relevant material of theological reflection on things like doctrine, pneumatology, and soteriology. They wanted whatever would help them lead a Bible study, plan their next youth event, and fend off the expectations of helicopter parents. They were in it for the pragmatic, so my fascination with questions about the nature of divine revelation and the challenge of transcendence puzzled my colleagues.

I remember a particular conversation with one of my fellow youth ministry majors. We were chatting over some cafeteria French fries, and I had a book by Paul Tillich on the table. My friend looked down at the book and then up at me and said, "Does it worry you, Wes?" There was a pause as I struggled to figure out what he meant. He looked down at my book again and said, "Does it worry you that the stuff you think is helpful isn't helpful to anyone else?" He smiled and laughed, as if to ease the tension, and said, "I love that you like theology so much, Wes, but eventually you're gonna have to run a youth group. Maybe pick up a book about youth culture sometime."

My youth ministry courses did discuss youth culture, and, in general, they were focused on adolescent development and figuring out how to keep kids in church. Understanding adolescence seemed to be the primary concern in laying the foreground for doing the work of ministry. In my first semesters as a youth ministry major, I realized that even though I loved young people, if I really wanted to talk about theology—about God's being and action—I would have to switch majors. Theology was just not at the center of my youth ministry courses. So I became a theology major. I did not leave youth ministry. I stayed involved as a volunteer in my local church youth ministry. I still loved the work of encountering God in the lives of young people. But in my context, it seemed that theology and youth ministry had different concerns, and I wanted to be a theologian.

It was not until a couple of years after I'd graduated, after I'd taken a position with a United Church of Christ congregation as the director of youth ministry, that I realized youth ministry itself could be a theological discipline—that through engaging in the concrete and lived experience of young people, I could discover mysteries of God's being and action that simply could not be disclosed any other way. I picked up a book by Andrew Root and then one by Kenda Creasy Dean—and eventually one by Root and Dean together.[2] I began to learn that I could, in fact, be a theologian *as* a youth minister (or a youth minister as a theologian). That is what prompted me to go to seminary.

When I was a first-year seminary student, I took a course called Theological Foundations of Youth Ministry. I was incredibly excited for the course—giddy, actually. Finally, I was going to blend my passions for youth ministry and theology. It was the first youth ministry course I had taken since my first year of undergraduate studies, and I expected it to be completely different. In many ways, it was different. It was certainly more theological than any youth ministry class I'd ever taken. We read books by Andrew Root and articles by Jürgen Moltmann and Catherine Mowry LaCugna. But there was something eerily familiar about it too. The first half of the course was dedicated, almost completely, to questions of adolescent development. I was confused by this. We searched for God's presence, reflecting on our own stories of psychological and spiritual *development*. We read Erik Erikson, as I had done in undergraduate studies, and this time we also read James Fowler, a practical theologian who represented a kind of developmental psycho-theology. While the second half of the course was dedicated to theological reflection and exploring the theological rationale for ministry, this theological exploration was still standing primarily on the interpretive scaffolding of developmentalism and especially developmental psychology. The course was still liberating for me; don't get me wrong. Central to the discussion was the discernment of God's action. My desire to think theologically about youth ministry had been met, but I was still somewhat perplexed.

Throughout my time in seminary, I became interested in exploring why youth ministry took this use of developmental psychology as a matter of course. Why did developmental psychology seem to follow me everywhere I went in the world of youth ministry? Why was adolescence the first and last place we looked to interpret young people's experiences? Why was Erikson in the footnotes of every youth ministry book I read? And why was no one else in the field bothered by these questions?

FERTILE SOIL

Developmental psychology—with youth ministry, I might add, riding conspicuously on its coattails—emerged from the fertile soil of empiricism. Empiricism is the theory that all knowledge is derived from sense experience. It is marked by the conviction that the world lies before us, and that nothing truly exists beyond the reach of knowledge as long as knowledge is aggressive enough to attain it. Existence is immanent. What we do not know is merely what we do not *yet* know. Nothing is a mystery; everything is a puzzle—we can solve it!

Developmental psychology emerges from this very same conviction. However ambiguous we are willing to admit that life really is, we long for shortcuts. We want tidy plumb lines and accounts of normalcy by which we can assess our existence. We want clear-cut and verifiable positions. This is the water we swim in. We are inhabitants of what the philosopher Charles Taylor calls "the immanent frame," wherein "natural" and "immanent" accounts of reality become presupposition, while "supernatural" ones are, by default, suspicious and contested.[3] In reference to transcendent reality—to divine action and the theological—to be situated in the immanent frame is to be predisposed toward doubt instead of belief.

Transcendence, then, is a contested category in the immanent frame. There's really nothing that exists outside of our ability to know it. There are no true mysteries in the immanent frame. And if there are, then we mustn't bother ourselves with them too much because, after all, if you can't know it, how can you use it? Empiricism tells us that everything that matters is *knowable*, that the world is within reach and therefore controllable: "*Our life will be better if we manage to bring more world within our reach.*"[4] This should be difficult to contend with for ministers and theologians because the very focus of our work is a God who transcends knowledge, a God who cannot be *used* or controlled. As Moltmann writes, "Theology has only one problem: *God*. We are theologians *for God's sake*."[5] This is a problem in our modern era. As Andrew Root observes, "Our attention has been drawn away from what our ancestors thought was obvious: that a personal God acts and moves in the world."[6] It is not just that we do not see God anymore; it is that we have a new set of values that has made looking toward God, looking toward the transcendent, seem obsolete and impractical.

The immanent frame compels us to focus on what we can do, what we can use, and what can be manipulated to meet our ends. Its focus is on controllability. Thus, the world becomes a point of development—the world is within control, and therefore we must always improve it, grow it. When our attention is on the development of what is in front of us, we miss the God who looks to interrupt developmental processes and bring about a future that does not issue merely from the potential of the things in front of us. This "distracted" kind of epistemological ecosystem is the immanent frame. Its focus on verifiable knowledge seeks to avoid the ambiguity implicit in a thick description of mysterious reality.[7]

It is important to note that there is a difference between the *empirical* and *empiricist*. The empirical is simply one category or form of knowledge among others. Empirical forms of knowledge are cognitive and nomothetic (generalizable). On their own, they are perfectly capable of saving space for more ideographic (specific) and hermeneutical forms of knowledge.[8] Empirical knowledge need not be exclusive or even prioritized over other ways of constituting and understanding reality. Empiricism comes along when the empirical becomes an ideology, and all knowledge is *reduced* to what we can prove. Empiricism conflates reality with the empirical, generating what's called "the epistemic fallacy."[9]

While not every form of developmental psychology is guilty of reducing reality to the data language of empiricism—indeed, psychology has never *completely* validated itself as a hard science, no matter how hard the behaviorists attempted to do so—there is certainly an impulse to prioritize the empirical over the hermeneutical. In so doing, developmental psychologists dismiss ontology—the nature of *being*—in favor of epistemology, or theories of verifiable knowledge.

If we are honest with ourselves, most of us will see we are prone to empiricism. Even if we consider ourselves to be spiritual people, we usually trust that which is verifiable and replicable over that which is more obviously interpretive and subjective. Something like an encounter with God is a nice thought, but it's difficult to talk about, and thus it's degraded to a kind of secondary realism.[10] Of course, we so privilege our personal experience, too, that we usually choose to embrace subjective experiences as real for ourselves (or even "realer than real").[11] In the realm of discourse, though, we do so with the expectation of suspicion. As Douglas John Hall has observed, "The direction of professional philosophy in the Anglo-American tradition has in fact been so much towards an empiricist-pragmatist approach to reality that the questions of being, meaning, goodness, etc. are frequently relegated to the realm of 'mere poetry.'"[12] This is life in the immanent frame.

As the epistemic landscape turned more and more toward empiricism and as the claims of hard science became the acceptable currency in accounting for human experience, psychology took up the space that had been left vacant by philosophers and theologians who had less "scientific" frames of understanding. Objectivity, falsifiability, and verifiability began to mark the border between serious academic inquiry and subjective speculation. This explains why B. F. Skinner felt the need to establish his discipline as a hard science.[13] If the law of the land is unqualified observability,[14] then it makes sense to focus on concrete behavioral functions and tensions instead of speculating about what it *means* to the inner life of an individual or to what extent that behavior is socially constructed. In the epistemic ecosystem of developmentalism and empiricism, we became preoccupied with charting stages of growth within scientific categories. It was fertile soil to nurture the emergence of developmental psychology.

Empiricist lenses are well designed for acute observance of biological change and corresponding behavior. So, at the turn of the twentieth century, developmental psychology deepened its roots and began the continual stretch of its branches across a plurality of research disciplines including theology, philosophy, and youth ministry—once it came on the scene. As James Fowler pointed out in the 1980s, theorists of developmental change "have begun to play the role in our society that storytellers and myth makers once played in primitive and classical cultures. They have taken on many of the functions that philosophers and theologians performed in the twelfth through nineteenth centuries."[15]

Meanwhile, theologians and philosophers, with their primary focus being on *meaning* and transcendence, could no longer provide the answers to society's questions—at least not in a way that satisfied its epistemic appetite. By focusing on observable changes and zeroing in on progressive development, psychology was establishing itself as a legitimate science over and against philosophy. In a world in which the plausibility of *meaning* and transcendence, or any other such "speculation," had become contested, we were still "cross-pressured," as Taylor puts it, by a longing for meaning and understanding— "on the one hand drawn towards unbelief, while on the other, feeling the solicitations of the spiritual—be they in nature, in art, in some contact with religious faith, or in a sense of God which may break through the membrane."[16] We are "haunted" by transcendence.[17]

With this cross-pressure, we were still asking theology's and philosophy's questions, even while expecting science's answers. Soft data would no longer suffice; nevertheless, we wanted an answer to the questions of human life and experience, even the spiritual questions. Psychology, the bastard child of philosophy and science, promised an answer. It promised to make the soft data of human experience hard enough to wield in the immanent frame. Psychology offered a more "scientific" explanation for why we do the things we do and what our lives are about. The discipline has experimented with varying degrees of empiricism, the behaviorists representing the most extreme experiment. While, overall, the behaviorist experiment seems to have failed, the pressure to prioritize the empirical over the hermeneutical is evident throughout the field of psychology. And since the turn of the twentieth century, there has seemed to be no going back. Even while post-modern and poststructuralist philosophers, including Michel Foucault and Judith Butler, have so thoroughly deconstructed the modernist overreach for universal and positivist structures of rationality, such critiques are situated as a response to the pressure of empiricism.[18] Even postmodern philosophy demands verification. In other words, even if we question modernity, we can only do so *within* modernity.

Once psychology had established itself as a discipline, it became the intuitive field for anyone interested in questions of human existence and experience. Thinkers who, in preceding generations, would likely have been content with philosophical accounts of human life began to join the psychological conversation and frame discussion according to its orders. An exemplar of this changing of the guard is the Swiss philosopher and psychologist Jean Piaget. Piaget's theory of cognitive development is standard reading in developmental psychological education. It was often assigned in my college youth ministry courses.

Piaget was a pioneer in mapping the life cycle through stages of developmental change, and yet Piaget himself was a philosopher—an epistemologist—before he ever thought to be a psychologist. But in the empiricist epistemic landscape, the immanent frame, had Piaget's claims remained strictly philosophical, he may never have been able to break ground. So instead of working around or against the positivist system of psychology, he joined it and expanded it. This likely wasn't even a conscious decision for Piaget. By the time of his writing, psychology was basically the water in which we were swimming when it came to constituting human life and especially youth. So the philosopher Piaget joined the ranks of psychological inquirers and indeed pioneered the very conception of life as development. It was in this way that psychology was reified as the dominant scientific discipline for accounts of human experience in the twentieth century.

STAGES OF CONFUSION: THEOLOGY'S
STRUGGLE FOR EPISTEMIC LEGITIMACY

On the heels of psychology's self-legitimization as a scientific discipline, feeling the gradual waning of their influence, theologians began to seek out ways to reconstruct their own discipline as a legitimate (read: scientific) form of knowledge. Some theologians found deeply creative ways of doing so, some more faithful to the ambiguity and provisionality of their discipline than others. Theologians such as Karl Barth and Dietrich Bonhoeffer argued convincingly for the legitimacy of theological inquiry, although it would be difficult to document their success in the minds of social scientists. One theologian who was perhaps more clearly successful, though he took a greater risk in being so, was Paul Tillich, whose whole theological project was apologetic in shape and form.

Etymologically, theology is *theos* and *logos*, a logic of the divine. Tillich's response to empiricist pressure was to begin theological reflection not with *theos* (the divine), as Barth did, but with the *logos* of it—its logic. In other words, while Barth explicitly began his theological reflection with divine self-revelation,[19] Tillich thought it more apologetically appropriate to begin with human experience, with immanence rather than transcendence, and to reflect on revelation from that starting point. This placed Tillich's work in constant tension between immanence and transcendence.[20] According to Mark Taylor, Tillich's "ways of interpreting these two classic spatial metaphors for relating God and world [immanence and transcendence] were controversial for many. This was due to the radically immanental themes that Tillich played out in his doctrine . . . his transcending God was in fundamental tension with many traditional theisms."[21]

In beginning with immanence, Tillich may have legitimized theology in the minds of some of his colleagues in the social sciences. Unfortunately, his success may have simultaneously set the stage for theology's demise. While Tillich was careful to assign agency to God and priority to the theological, the theologians who adapted and appropriated his method would later become prone to relinquishing interpretive authority—and even theology's distinctive rationality—to disciplines with more immanent and scientific lenses such as psychology. Their actions set aside Tillich's ontology, allowing transcendence to be dissolved all but completely into immanence. Even as scholars such as the German theologian Wolfhart Pannenberg attempted to maintain the distinctive voice of theology and insist on a broader account of knowledge, they were swimming upstream.[22]

In the immanent frame, empiricism continues to set the standard for legitimate forms of knowledge. Reflective of this, other theologians have less successfully navigated these waters, often forfeiting the provisionality and hermeneutical nature of theological reflection to the sciences by outsourcing its interpretive categories to sociology and psychology.[23] Or, in the opposite direction, they have retreated from the challenge to make a case at all and have withdrawn into fundamentalist and secessionist guilds and cohorts, seeing science and empirical knowledge as enemies of theology. According to the rules of the instrumental rationality of the immanent frame, theology must be empirically useful and/or psychologically beneficial before it becomes regarded as legitimate.[24] This is perhaps why much academic theological discourse has shifted from discussion of doctrine and religion to discussion of spirituality and therapy.[25]

PRACTICAL THEOLOGY AND DOWNWARD CONFLATION

Practical theology, which has always concerned itself more specifically and explicitly with human experience as a source for divine revelation than most other theological disciplines, has found a great ally in psychological interpretation. Under intense pressure to legitimize itself, practical theology gravitated toward more objective modes of thinking. Post-Enlightenment moderns centered theological education in the university rather than the monastery. Their work became less about encountering God through prayer and more about making rational claims.[26] Thus, practical theologians struggled to make the hermeneutical and subjective content of their discipline—God's action in lived experience—more accessible, slowly recalibrating and transitioning the focus from divine to human action. The criteria of provability made divine action all but impossible to substantiate, so practical theologians turned their focus toward observable human behaviors such as church governance and spiritual practices.

Seeking to defend theological education from being eradicated altogether from educational curricula in the wake of the empirical turn, Friedrich Schleiermacher produced his *Brief Outline of the Study of Theology*. He defended theology by arguing for its usefulness as a positive science and a kind of tactical form of knowledge. He outlined three chief theological disciplines—philosophical theology, historical theology, and practical theology. Philosophical theology and historical theology, in this outline, both find their true *telos* in practical theology, which in turn justifies their respective endeavors. In other words, practical theology is, by definition, what historical and philosophical theologies look like in practice. Thus, practical theology is reduced to the application of its siblings.

Schleiermacher's understanding of philosophical and historical theologies essentially encompasses what we might now call *systematic, constructive,* and *exegetical theologies* as well as theological approaches to the history of doctrine and the church. Theology, as a unified discipline, finds its legitimacy, according to Schleiermacher, in practical theology—for it is in practical theology that the discipline moves from theory to practice, from vague speculation to observable and verifiable behaviors and the practices of church governance.[27] With one hand, he places practical theology in the prominent position of being the true purpose of the whole theological enterprise, but with the other hand, he reduces it to a mere technique and "craft of church governance."[28] In so doing, Schleiermacher essentially subjects practical theology to the whims of social and ecclesial interest. Only when the *real* theology has been done, when the theoretical grounding has already been laid by other disciplines, can practical theology engage in its task.

Schleiermacher, then, simultaneously invented *and* emasculated the discipline of practical theology. While practical theologians have pressed against this proposal throughout the discipline's history,[29] in large part it has continued to suffer from this pattern, often being reduced, in one way or another, to the practical application of inherited and/or imbedded theologies. For practical theology to avoid these reductions, it must not only provide scholastic methodologies that maintain the distinctiveness of its own theoretical content but it must also offer a theological account of rationality itself. We will begin toward such an account in chapter 4.

One of the major shapes this pattern has taken in contemporary practical theology is an approach known as the *revised critical correlational method* of interdisciplinarity. Proponents of this methodology have not reduced practical theology to applied theology, but they have, by and large, risked outsourcing theology's theoretical content to their interdisciplinary conversation partners, forfeiting its distinctive rationality. This methodology is an adaptation of Paul Tillich's method of correlation. It was Tillich's endeavor to make theological language and propositions palatable to the modern (Western) intellectual landscape by explaining and reconceptualizing theology in avoidance of the "absurdities" of supernaturalism.[30] While it would be a great misreading of Tillich to paint him as an empiricist, his theological starting point in human experience kept him grounded in the observable and the immanent. According to Ray Anderson, "Tillich posits an 'out-and-out' transcendence, but it can only be a symbolization of that to which [humankind's] question about ultimate reality points."[31] His theological methodology began with human experience, or "culture," and allowed it to set the standards for theological reflection. Culture raises the questions, and theology gives its answers. As Tillich put it, "The answers implied in the event of revelation are meaningful only in so far as they are in correlation with questions concerning the whole of our existence, with existential questions."[32]

Tillich saw this not as an imperative so much as an observation. "Systematic theology," he wrote, "uses the method of correlation. It has always done so, sometimes more, sometimes less, consciously, and must do so consciously and outspokenly, especially if the apologetic point of view is to prevail."[33] The method was implicit according to the limitations of human epistemology, so he believed that it must be made explicit for the sake of epistemic integrity, if nothing else. Similar to Schleiermacher's scheme for practical theology, however, in making this assertion—if only by reception—Tillich risked limiting the theoretical content of theological reflection to "culture" and to the natural and social sciences. He risked prioritizing epistemology over ontology, even if he personally wished to save space for divine action. For if theology can only answer the questions posed to it by culture, it loses its ability to pose its own questions. Tillich did maintain, in his systematic theology, the discipline's ability to offer its own distinctive normative claims, stating that the true answers to culture's questions emerge from "the symbols used in the Christian message."[34] But the revised critical correlational method, according to Andrew Root, "strips all ontology from the Tillichian correlation, leading the revised critical correlation method into an antirealist perspective."[35] In other words, where Tillich made room for theology to make distinctive normative claims about ontology and the transcendent reality of God, the revised critical correlation model does not.[36]

Taking up and developing Tillich's method of correlation, theologian David Tracy developed a revised critical correlational method wherein "not just the questions from human experience are considered but also the various answers that arise from the situation. The answers are then considered alongside those that come from 'the message.'"[37] Rather than mining human experience for questions to which theology can offer answers, Tracy sought to explore the answers offered by the situation itself, offered through the social sciences and the arts, and to correlate them with questions and answers from theology: "The revision states that the job of the social sciences is not simply and only to surface the questions—it can also answer them."[38]

From Tillich to Tracy, social sciences have slowly emerged to greater and greater prominence in the theoretical content of practical theology. The theologian's job, in this framework, is to examine problems faced by people in society, to refer to the interpretations and solutions offered by the social sciences, and to essentially theologize those answers—to give them a theological texture and determine their various levels of theological appropriateness to the situation. In the end, the social sciences offer the real picture, and, like Instagram, theology can only change the filter. This method has become dominant in the discipline, and given the empiricist epistemic landscape, there is no wonder. Where theology, in its ideographic and hermeneutical commitments, has become less and less convincing on its own, it has slowly but surely had to sacrifice its own ontological persuasions on the altar of empiricism—outsourcing its legitimacy to social sciences, which, as it is perceived, offer more "reliable" explanations and more "pragmatic" solutions to modern problems. This is problematic for practical theology as a field that must concern itself *primarily* with divine action—a perceivably subjective phenomenon.[39] As Andrew Root has put it, this is "a debilitating move for practical theology, for while it gives the field the sense of scientific rigor, it is a reduction of reality that keeps it from speaking of divine action. But it does more, because an overempiricism is a downward conflation that keeps the field of practical theology from speaking of reality and leads it to settle for measuring the regularity of events rather than exploring the layered and emergent meanings of the events."[40] In other words, this "epistemic fallacy"[41] has led practical theologians to put empirical social sciences in the driver's seat of theological reflection, especially when it turns to the task of interpretation, and driven the discipline off its own rails. While not every practical theologian has chosen to take up the full mantle of the revised critical correlational method, the impulses that constitute the conditions of its emergence have profoundly impacted the way all practical theologians conduct their tasks; it has been integral to the church's ministry with young people and the adolescent paradigm of interpretation.

THE REIFICATION OF DEVELOPMENTALISM

James Fowler, the renowned Emory University practical theologian, was not known for occupying himself with naming and categorizing his interdisciplinary methodology. But the empirical impulses of Tracy's revised critical correlational model are strong throughout his work. Though he was committed to practical theology's "difficult but central focus on constructive and critical discerning of and responding to the *praxis* of God," Fowler saw practical theology as "needful of the dialectic involved in what David Tracy and Don Browning call the 'mutually critical correlation' between theological and social scientific interpretations."[42] Fowler's most noteworthy contribution to practical theology and to youth ministry is the developmental schema of the growth of faith he laid out in his work *Stages of Faith*. While Fowler addresses the tension between the ambiguity of actual human experience and the theories we use to name and categorize them—calling them "blinders" that limit us to "see to only those features or phenomena that we can name and account for"[43]—his project is essentially to name and categorize faith development alongside psychological models of human development.

Using the developmental theories of Jean Piaget, Lawrence Kohlberg, Daniel Levinson, and especially Erik Erikson, Fowler constructs a developmental theory of faith. While he desired to offer a theology of "faith" itself, Fowler built his normative claims on the descriptive and interpretive scaffolding of developmental psychology. Fowler correlated his theological claims with the interpretive claims of developmental psychology, essentially laying his theology of faith over the positivist template of stage theory. Fowler wanted to maintain a focus on transcendence and divine action. Yet, while occasionally he did nuance and critique the psychological schemas he employed, Fowler's acceptance of developmental psychology as a baseline for interpretation served to reify the dominance of developmentalism in practical theology. By the time it reached the imaginations of youth workers and youth ministry theologians, the approach seemed to constitute a matter-of-fact account of reality and the commonsense approach to understanding not only psychological development but spiritual and faith development as well. This gave unprecedented authority to the psychological disciplines. Thus, it is considered common sense in youth ministry to apply the term *adolescence*—a term that finds its origin in psychology and its epistemic shape in developmentalism—to the experience of the young people with whom we work.

Psychology provides practically all the language we have for understanding young people's experiences.[44] This psychological regime reflects the larger epistemic landscape to which theologians and scholars of the church have been accountable since the turn of the century. And not unlike psychology itself, youth ministry has been trying to establish itself as a legitimate empirical discipline. Thus, in our descriptive and interpretive endeavors, we have bonded ourselves to the discipline of developmental psychology, parasitically drawing our own empirical legitimacy from its veins.

CHAPTER THREE

King Erikson

Life is not a problem to be solved, but a reality to be experienced.
                                        —Søren Kierkegaard[1]

Truly I tell you, whoever does not receive the kingdom of God as a little child will never enter it.
                                        —Mark 10:15

Few theorists have been as influential to the church as Erik Erikson.[2] Youth ministry scholar Nancy Going has gone as far as to suggest that "perhaps Erikson has influenced practical theology more than any theologian."[3] Anecdotal as Going's comment may be, it certainly testifies to the weight of Erikson's influence. Whether implicitly or explicitly, most who draw from the categories of adolescence and identity formation are influenced by Erikson's thought. Kara Powell, Jake Mulder, and Brad Griffin, for example, engaged in a broad-reaching sociological study of churches' engagement with young people. In their book, *Growing Young: 6 Essential Strategies to Help Young People Discover and Love Your Church*, they claim that "every young person" asks three questions, respectively, regarding identity, belonging, and purpose: "Who am I?" "Where do I fit?" and "What difference do I make?"[4] While Erikson is nowhere to be found in the citations of the study,[5] the contribution is observable to anyone familiar with his work. Not only was Erikson responsible for the concept of identity formation—the "Who am I?" question—especially as it pertains to adolescence;[6] his constructions thereof were profoundly oriented toward notions of *belonging* and *purpose,* or "generativity." The "vital strength" that develops in adolescence, according to Erikson, is fidelity, which is about deciding which ideologies and occupations will teleologically define the individual in society. Erikson writes, "Young people must become whole people in their own right, and this during a developmental stage characterized by a diversity of changes in physical growth . . . and social awareness [*identity*]. . . . The young person, in order to experience wholeness, must feel a progressive continuity . . . between that which he conceives himself to be and that which he perceives others to see in him and to expect of him [*belonging*]."[7] All of this, according to Erikson, is oriented toward the "opportunity to decide with free assent on one of the available or unavoidable avenues of duty and service [*purpose*]."[8] This is not to say that Powell, Mulder, and Griffin were in any way concealing Erikson's influence on their thinking. Indeed, they are not the only ones whose conceptions of youth can be implicitly traced to Erikson. What I am suggesting is that Erikson is so prevalent in our imaginary as youth workers that his thinking has become the water we swim in when it comes to interpreting young people's experiences.

Even scholars such as Kenda Creasy Dean, who have sought to break beyond the developmental lens, have fallen short. While Dean pushed theology back to the center of youth ministry scholarship, she did so on the flimsy interpretive scaffolding of Eriksonian developmental psychology. In short, Erikson's influence is pervasive in youth ministry.

SMUGGLING NORMALCY

At a time when youth ministry was especially bound to the rules of developmental psychology in its horizon for understanding young people, Kenda Dean sought to break beyond that horizon and turn the focus from resolving the crises of development to discovering the mysterious God who is present in the lived experience of young people. In her early work, Dean was a pioneer, paving the way for others to follow behind her in the theological turn in youth ministry.[9] But, like Piaget, she did not operate out of an alternative interpretive framework. Instead, she only expanded the developmental model, which she had inherited.

According to Richard Osmer—one of Dean's teachers—there are essentially four movements in practical theological reflection, and whether implicitly or explicitly, all practical theologians engage in them. These are the descriptive, interpretive, normative, and pragmatic movements.[10] When attending to a situation or practice in human experience, the descriptive movement asks, "What is going on?" The interpretive movement asks, "Why is it happening?" This is often where methods of interdisciplinarity become most relevant. The normative movement asks, "In light of who God is and what God is like, what should be going on?" This is where overt normative claims regarding divine action become most relevant. And finally, Schleiermacher's vision for practical theology gets to go to work in the pragmatic task—this is where new practices and strategies emerge from what has been learned in the preceding three movements. Dean's work in *Practicing Passion* was a masterpiece in its attention to the normative movement, a movement too often neglected by her more pragmatic predecessors. She provided a way forward for youth workers to attend to God's action in young people's experiences, redefining youth ministry as ministry for generations of youth workers to come.

But, like Fowler and Piaget, it did not occur to Dean to engage alternative interpretive scaffolding to bolster her normative claims. Evidently, no one at the time saw it necessary to depart from the developmental model of youth ministry. So Dean took her cues from Erikson. Making references to concepts such as the adolescent brain and the life cycle, she constructed her arguments on the framework of Eriksonian developmental psychology.[11] She followed Erikson in determining what she believed were the three main "longings" of adolescents within which the church can discover God and relearn its own passion for Christ—the longing for "fidelity" (an explicitly Eriksonian category), "transcendence" (or *locomotion*, for Erikson),[12] and "communion" (for which she draws more subtly on Erikson but clearly embraces a developmental psychological framework for conceiving of the human need for intimacy). In so doing, Dean built her interpretive house on the sand, not nearly a strong enough foundation for the normative claims she was making. This is not to say her argument did not stand; indeed, in its own regard, it certainly did—and effectively so. She introduced new ways of understanding youth ministry. Meanwhile, dubious conceptions were smuggled in with these new ideas—conceptions that threaten the reader's ability to fully embrace a theological turn in youth ministry.

Dean succeeded in changing youth ministry forever. By transforming people's thinking from a pathographic hermeneutic of youth to a rehabilitated and hopeful view, she launched forward a theological vision for youth ministry that has, by and large, swept through the field.[13] She believed that youth was not a problem to be solved but a human experience in which to participate. She saw adolescence as something to be "exegeted" rather than "endured."[14] But by leaving the interpretive door cracked open to psychological and psychoanalytic modes of thought without proper interpretive critique, norms are smuggled in—particularly a kind of condescension disguised as understanding. Young people's passion is understood as a symptom of an ego that is "in flux."[15] They are not quite themselves, and so they feel more acutely the needs felt by adults. The condescension that gets smuggled in under Dean's nose is manifest in the assumption that there is always an explanation beneath the surface, if only we know where to look, and that as adults and by virtue of our maturity, we are positioned to apprehend that explanation. Young people are a puzzle to be solved, and youth is a "stage" that must be resolved through developmental change.

Most importantly, what gets smuggled in is an essentialism of *normalcy*. Even though she insists that "we can no longer view youth as incomplete adults"[16] and that adolescence is socially constructed, Dean's account of youth naturalizes *passion*, projecting an image of the normal and healthy young person as the one who longs for a particular vibrancy and meaning. Her robust and otherwise nimble theological arguments teeter on the foundation of an optimistic cosmology of youth that cannot adequately hold the stories of those young people who do not conform to her image of health and normalcy. In other words, Dean's interpretive framework necessarily marginalizes young people who are not *passionate:* its horizon cannot hold the stories of young people who are burnt out and feeling trapped, the stories of young people who do not have anything to offer, or the stories of young people who simply are not developing according to the Eriksonian itinerary for development.[17] Built on the interpretive scaffolding of developmental psychology, Dean's horizon risks forsaking the stories of developmental refugees like my brother, Jesse. She offers the profound reminder that "Christian theology challenges Erikson's concept of identity 'achievement' by proclaiming true humanity as God's gift, obscured by sin but restored by Christ."[18] Even so, Dean's work reflects a cross-pressure she may have inherited from Erikson himself.

ERIKSON'S BOUNDARY EXISTENCE

Like Piaget, Erikson expanded the field of psychoanalysis and developmental psychology. He, far more than the Freuds (Sigmund and Anna) before him, was interested in more subjective and nuanced approaches to understanding human life. He was more open to mystery. In this sense, he was himself profoundly cross-pressured—he was deeply compelled by art and anthropology. Although he knew and recognized the ambiguity of human life, he was pressured by the demand for verifiable and replicable descriptions. Crisis is a common theme in Erikson's theory, as it was in his own life. The transitions in Erikson's eight stages of human development are characterized by the crises of trust versus mistrust, autonomy versus shame, and so forth, as each stage moves forward toward maturity—the most critical crisis being that of identity formation, a crisis that Erikson saw as particularly situated in adolescence. Each stage of development inhabits a boundary that must be navigated. Likewise, according to his biographer Lawrence Friedman, Erikson saw his own life as one of the inhabiting boundaries, "As an old man, Erik saw special significance in the fact that the Karlsruhe of his childhood was just on the German side of the Rhine. He noted that his whole childhood involved learning to navigate borders—between Judaism and Christianity; Denmark and Germany; mother, stepfather, and biological father."[19] Erikson was never completely at home, even in his own theoretical framework. Indeed, many of his followers and interpreters, including those who work with youths, might have become more comfortable with the eight-stage framework than Erikson was himself.

Likely due to the ambiguity of his own childhood, Erikson recognized the ambiguity of human life and how it eludes empirical explanation. Throughout his work, according to one of his biographers, "One can sense a man struggling to make his case, to use the chart [the crude illustration of his eight stages of development] as a means of highlighting his views (for himself as much as anyone else), yet all the while fearing the very fate some of Freud's ideas came to have."[20] According to another account, Erikson "felt that he was only beginning to get a sense of the vast complexity of the human life cycle, and he was irritated by popularizers who cast it in overly finite form."[21] Erikson knew that people would take his theories and strip them of their hermeneutical and ambiguous qualities, making them more literal and positivistic than he ever intended them to be. As Robert Coles put it, "It is quite clear from his various writings that [Erikson] worried about what would come of his own search for clarity and precision once literal-minded readers got the message."[22] In other words, Erikson never intended his ideas to be reduced to a formula. But it is clear, nevertheless, that he was responding to an overt pressure to represent his findings in broadly universal terms and language. Erikson felt the cross-pressure that many feel in the immanent frame: the pressure to find universal precision and replicable principles, even amid the haunting ambiguity of lived experience. We want puzzles, not mysteries.

Despite his boundary existence between subjective and objective interpretive frames, Erikson did not escape the totalizing allure of empiricism. An admirer of Kierkegaard,[23] he knew that human life is shot through with mystery, but he, too, desperately desired a measuring stick. Just as Dean jeopardized her theological claims with an overreliance on Erikson, Erikson jeopardized the ambiguity and nuance of his project with empiricist impulses. So, despite his best intentions, youth ministry has inherited from Erikson a profoundly essentializing and positivist—thus, reductionistic—interpretation of young people's experiences. Despite his laments and cautions, by constructing a scheme of "normal" human development, he left his readers, and himself, with a thoroughly gerontocentric and hierarchical interpretive framework, which turns out to be inadequate not only for youth ministry but for theological anthropology as well.

THE CROSS-PRESSURED ERIKSON

As it turns out, Erikson's own experience is a testament to the inadequacy of the empiricist impulse of developmentalism. Before Erik was Erikson, he was Erik Salomonsen. His early childhood was quite complicated—so complicated, in fact, that just sorting out the genealogy of his surnames will give you a headache. Very little is known about the identity of his biological father. All we really know is that, unlike his mother, his father was a Dane. His mother, Karla Abrahamsen, on the other hand, came from a "prominent Jewish family in Copenhagen that traced its genealogy back to the seventeenth century and the north of Germany."[24] Karla was brilliant in her own right. It was she, in fact, who introduced Erik to the writings of Kierkegaard and sparked his interest in interrogating the depths of the human mind and experience. In 1898, four years prior to Erik's birth, Karla married a Jewish stockbroker by the name of Valdemar Isidor Salomonsen. According to Friedman, "Karla's marriage to Valdemar did not last a night and was probably not consummated."[25] Valdemar fled to America, leaving his wife in their honeymoon suite in Rome, never to be seen or heard from again.[26] The family maintained the appearance of propriety throughout the ordeal, even though no one was ever really certain who Erik's biological father was, including Erik himself. This presentation of outer propriety became a common theme in Erik's life.[27] When Erik was born, Karla retained the surname Salomonsen and passed it on to her child. But Erik would not be a Salomonsen for long. When he was still very young, Karla fell in love with Erik's pediatrician, Theodor Homberger. The two were married on Erik's third birthday, and Erik became a Homberger. Theodor committed himself to being Erik's father.

In fact, Erik was raised to believe that Theodor was his biological father. "All through my earlier childhood," Erikson later recalled, "they kept secret from me the fact that my mother had been married previously and that I was the son of a Dane who had abandoned her before my birth."[28] In short, Erik spent his childhood being lied to by his parents about his paternity. With its actual dubiety concealed from him, Erikson forgot—or suppressed—those first three years without Theodor and basically accepted him as a father. However, Erikson was able to recall some real tension as a child and the feeling of being "different." He struggled with difference.

Erikson's childhood was checkered with struggles, including the death of his one-year-old sister, Elna. Biographers have speculated that Elna was born with a disability of some kind. The only photograph of her that remains, taken only months before her death, is of her leaning against a stoic four-year-old Erik. As Friedman recounts, "For Erik, the trauma of her passing was accented by the sense that he did not quite belong within the family."[29] He struggled in school, taking more interest in art than in science.[30] It was not until he was almost an adolescent, after he observed clue after clue, that he discovered, and Karla confessed, that Theodor was not his father. Throughout his youth, Erik collected further suspicions that his mother was still concealing information from him. He never waned in his love for his mother, but the discovery that she was dishonest with him certainly contributed to some further identity crises in his life. He remained a sort of wanderer, never really belonging here or there. Eventually he would even go on to change his name to Erik Erikson, metaphorically deeming himself his own father and the true modern "self-made man."[31]

After a fairly drawn-out moratorium, and after dabbling in the arts, Erik went on to receive psychoanalytic training from Sigmund Freud's daughter, Anna Freud, at the Vienna Psychoanalytic Institute. Despite his poor performance as a student in previous contexts, he was a promising young scholar who often followed, but sometimes rebelled against, his more orthodox tutors, including Anna. The wandering Erik might not have stayed in Vienna for so long had it not been for a certain Serson. He met a young woman named Joan Serson and swiftly fell in love with her.[32] The two did not wait long before marrying and starting a family. By 1933, they had two children, Kai and Jon.

While training in Vienna, Erikson always resisted the full gravitational force of Freudian psychoanalytic orthodoxy. He was torn between his admiration for Anna Freud and for his more free-spirited and artistic wife, Joan. In a sense, these two strong women in his life represented competing ideologies that had always troubled and would continue to torment Erikson.[33] While Sigmund Freud's—and by extension, Anna's—attention to the role of social influences in psychological development was not nearly as closed off as some of his critics might wish to contend, Erikson was even more open to society's role in forming human beings. Erikson, again, was cross-pressured by the solicitations of two dynamics, that of the social—and subjective—and that of the more biological and universal data language in human development. He wandered between ideographic and nomothetic forms of knowledge. Eventually, he came to believe that the Freudian ideology of his mentors and colleagues in Vienna focused too strongly on the "inner world" of the ego and did not reflect heavily enough on the "outer world." With encouragement from Joan, and despite discouragement from Anna, Erik decided that it was time to depart from Vienna and find his "own way" of doing psychoanalysis. The young Erikson family left Vienna, Sigmund Freud himself seeing them off at the railroad station.[34]

Though Erikson's earliest work was focused on ego development and the life cycle, his love for the external and social elements of psychoanalysis—a love that Anna Freud discouraged in favor of Freudian orthodoxy—brought him to America. In the United States, he began new approaches to psychoanalysis that were more sociological and idiographic in nature. Erikson obtained joint positions at Harvard Medical School and Massachusetts General Hospital, which were among the most prestigious appointments one could receive in the United States at the time.[35] At Harvard, he met anthropologists like Margaret Mead, Gregory Bateson, Ruth Benedict, and Scudder Mekeel, who would encourage him to venture out from the rigidly positivist Freudian paradigm in which he was previously nurtured.[36] But after only three years, Erikson moved on again. He spent time at Yale, where he became further enthralled by the works of anthropologists until eventually, at the prompting of Mekeel, Erikson went to South Dakota to study the Indigenous people living on the Pine Ridge Reservation and the Yurok people farther West.[37] For a psychoanalyst, taking interest in anthropology and the study of culture was a statement. Erikson's interests and the types of projects he undertook sent a clear message regarding his beliefs about the role of society in the shaping of human development. These studies were the investigative fodder for what would become his chief contribution to developmental psychology.

Erikson was in search of that which was common among human beings in their developmental trajectories across cultures and contexts. He was committed to a view of the biological, social, and ego processes wherein each were interdependent,[38] admitting that social science and psychology were together necessary for charting the "course of individual life in the setting of a changing community."[39] His interests in art and culture were nurturing in him a suspicion that pure psychology was not enough to account for the meaning of human life. Nonetheless, Erikson remained committed to a sort of Cartesian privilege for the ego process as universal and normative. He continued to see the ego process as primal, only secondarily in "relation" to social processes.[40] As Erica Burman describes this kind of mechanistic thought process, "Cultural issues are treated as informing the 'content' of development rather than entering into its structure in any more fundamental way."[41] The outer and material world's role, for Erikson, was instrumental—not dynamically constructive of the ego identity but only "guiding and narrowing of the individual's choices."[42] Erik was cross-pressured by a strong commitment to his field and a haunting suspicion that life itself is too mysterious to be contained within epistemic framing. From his own experience of being lied to throughout childhood and tossed about between identities as the perpetual wanderer, he knew that life could only be wrestled with, never mastered. Even so, that knowledge never completely stopped him from trying to master it. Perhaps because of his own troubled upbringing, Erikson continued his search for healthy—and therefore "normal"—human development.

THE CHILD ANALYST'S UNWANTED CHILD

By the 1940s, Erikson had made a name for himself and built a respectable career in his field. His family was the picture of health—a happy marriage with three children (Kai, Jon, and Sue), headed by a young, up-and-coming child analyst. Joan felt fulfilled, a confident mother, and Erik was making strides in his research. Despite Erik's sordid upbringing, it seemed that through psychoanalysis, he found a way to create a happy and healthy family. Erik and the Eriksons were finally settled. That is, until Neil was born.

Joan's previous three deliveries were natural and uncomplicated; her fourth was anything but. Because the obstetrician was late in arriving to the hospital, Joan had to be "immobilized and drugged."[43] They could not have her giving birth without the appropriate medical attention. After a long delivery, followed by a routine post-birth surgery, she finally awoke from the anesthesia dizzy, disoriented, and asking to hold her child, Neil, whom she had waited and labored so long to meet. But before she could even see his face, Erik and the doctors had sent him to a special facility. The doctors informed her, as they had already informed Erik, that their child was a "Mongolian idiot"—the term used at the time to describe children with Down syndrome.

Down syndrome was a fairly new diagnosis. It would still be roughly a decade until karyotype techniques, which help identify the shape and number of chromosomes, were even discovered.[44] It was still conventional wisdom to institutionalize children with Down syndrome, though it was not a compulsory practice. Even with the doctors' encouragement, Erikson felt compelled to seek insight from his friends. Though it seems that he could have called one of his friends in pediatrics, like Benjamin Spock who was on the cutting edge of Down syndrome research at the time, his first call was to Margaret Mead. Claiming that keeping the child with the family would be disruptive to the otherwise healthy upbringing of the other children, Mead did not hesitate in advising Erik to send Neil away. Had he called Dr. Spock, perhaps the advice may have been different, and Neil may have indeed felt the warm embrace of his mother's arms on his first day of life.[45] Unfortunately for Neil, that is not what happened. With the doctors' and Mead's advice, the great child analyst dismissed his infant child to an institution, in the likes of which Neil would spend the rest of his days, isolated from his parents and siblings.

Erik decided to conceal the truth from his other children, not dissimilarly from the way the truth had been concealed from him in his own childhood. Believing the loss of their brother in death would be less disruptive than having a brother with Down syndrome, he told Kai, Jon, and Sue that Neil had tragically died in childbirth. He tried to bury the memory of Neil in preservation of the success story he wanted to project. But these decisions—both that of institutionalizing her son and concealing the truth from her other children—never sat well with Joan, though she agreed to comply with Erik's lie. She cared at least as much for appearances as her husband, but she could not lie to herself. Although she was bedridden, she still insisted on visiting her son.[46] She eventually had Neil transferred closer to home so she could make more frequent visits, on which Erik seldom joined her.

Their decision to institutionalize their son turned out to be the very disruption the Eriksons so desperately wanted to avoid. Joan blamed herself for their plight, and the tension in the family grew with each passing day. The children could sense that not all was well, and their suspicions abounded, just as Erik's suspicions had concerning his paternity during his own childhood.[47] Erik, unable to keep the secret completely to himself, did eventually tell his eldest son, Kai, that his brother was indeed alive, had Down syndrome, and was living in an institution. Now Kai was burdened with keeping the secret from his siblings. These tensions—a corrosive concoction of guilt, shame, grief, secrecy, and resentment—filled the Erikson household. Though they struggled to maintain the image of a healthy family of five, their true family of six was far from healthy. Neil's doctors believed the boy would pass within two years of his birth—much like Erik's sister, Elna. In fact, Neil would live for more than twenty years, and he lived every one of those years in segregation from his family.[48]

While Joan took up her art as an almost frenetic compulsion, Erik's respite from the crisis constituted by Neil's existence was his academic work. He returned to his earliest curiosities, diving headlong into developmental theory again. In response to his guilt and shame, he essentially locked himself in a room and wrote his most groundbreaking work, *Childhood and Society*, giving to the world the eight stages of the life cycle. Ironically, then, it was Neil who inspired Erikson's return to his earlier work and its renewed orientation toward healthy psychosocial development. Even before Neil was moved closer to the family, he was integral to Erik's personal and professional formation.[49]

Erik Erikson's universe had been thrown into turmoil. The great child analyst failed to produce a "normal" and "healthy" child. His feelings of inadequacy would go on to haunt him throughout his lifetime.[50] He decided to return to the comfort of his positivist psychological roots and retreat into an epistemic world that he could more easily control. The self-made man couldn't quite bear the uncontrollability of his situation. His developmental scheme was his attempt to reorder his universe, to take control where he had none, and to bury Neil's story, once and for all, beneath the concrete foundation of his developmental model. Cross-pressured by the weight of the significance of his own son and his need to empirically account for what it is to be a healthy human being, Erikson took up the mantle of positivism and developmentalism. In so doing, he staked his lasting claim on his field and on the Western imaginary.

Erikson's eight stages were his escape from having to look face to face at the unfathomable mystery of Neil Erikson. As Craig Dykstra has put it, "We really do want a measuring stick. We want to be relieved of the hard, inconclusive, exhaustingly concrete and complex work of looking closely, and of the responsibility for our own being and acting that is placed on us."[51] Developmentalism and instrumentalism are comforting ideologies insofar as they give our world a sense of purpose and possibility. We do not need to accept that reality is fundamentally mysterious—we can solve the puzzle; we can discover the future.

NEIL ERIKSON: THE QUINTESSENTIAL DEVELOPMENTAL REFUGEE

As Erikson biographer Friedman put it, "A life cycle framework for the development of 'normal' people that comported with the lives in the 'normal' Erikson family of five required Neil's disappearance—at least physically but perhaps from memory as well."[52] In short, there was no room for someone like Neil in the developmental model that Erik was constructing. In a previous chapter, we discussed developmental refugees—those who are left behind and marginalized by the success narratives of progress in developmentalism. Be it economic, psychosocial, or adolescent development, stories of passionate progress and development are incapable of holding the stories of those on the underside of the narrative. The stories of Indigenous people are flooded by the waters of the megadam, and the stories of burnt-out or disabled young people are painted over by narratives of growth and maturity. In our imagination of developmentalism, Neil's story is swept under the rug of the story of Erikson's perfect family of five and buried under the concrete slab of the eight stages of development.

This is problematic enough for the developmental psychologist or the social scientist. But for theologians, and particularly practical theologians, this represents a sort of modern-day heresy that must be corrected not through better social scientific research but by deeper and more committed theological reflection. After all, as John Swinton has provocatively suggested, "the body of Christ has Down Syndrome."[53]

As theologians, ours is the work of doxology—speaking praise to God—directed toward the mystery of a crucified Christ. We worship a refugee. And we are called not only to make room for Neil Erikson in our ministry and our account of what it means to be human but we are also called to expect God's presence in the lives of those who have been marginalized and rejected. When we are obstructed from holding the stories of developmental refugees, when we are denied communion with the "least of these" Jesus mentions in Matthew 25 through our narratives of progress, we are obstructed from communion with the very life and being of God. For, as John Swinton has put it, "God is with the poor, not in triumphalistic revolution, but in the weakness and vulnerability that is experienced in the everyday tasks of living together in community."[54] Neil Erikson's story and the stories of young people everywhere who are not conforming to the prescriptions of developmental diagnostic interpretations are God's stories. God's story includes people like my brother, Jesse, too—people who do not spiritually develop according to the best-laid plans of their youth pastors. And those stories, the experiences of developmental refugees, are illuminated—not obscured—by the eschatological light of God's in-breaking Spirit and hope.

A BROADER HORIZON:
TOWARD THE EMBRACE OF MYSTERY

Therefore, we need a theological vision not only of what it means to be human but also a vision of what it means to hope. This is a vision in which developmental psychology's theoretical horizon, in its commitment to essentialism and empiricism, falls terribly short. The kind of trust we in practical theology have placed in epistemic frameworks of developmental psychology and correlational methods of interdisciplinarity have put us at a severe disadvantage. Our downward conflation has compelled us to limit ourselves to a framework that proves itself, even in its very origins in Erikson's personal life, to be suspect. What practical theologians are obliged to investigate—even in our cross-pressured state—is not just epistemological frames of explanation but also the ontological and transcendent reality of the Holy Spirit, who acts and lives and moves in the lived experience of actual human beings. In short, we are to dive to the depths of reality itself, its meaning included, and developmental psychology on its own is simply an inadequate tool for this investigation.

Our theological vision must embrace, not resolve, the mystery of God's presence in human experience. And that is precisely the problem with the psychological and developmental model. Its fundamental disposition is that of control, and thus its necessary orientation is toward solving problems, not embracing mystery. For Erik, Neil was a problem to be solved, not a mystery to be embraced. In his book *The Mystery of the Child*, Martin Marty makes the helpful distinction between problem and mystery. For him, a problem is something we can solve, resolve, or control. A mystery, on the other hand, is something in which we can only participate and never really solve. One cannot *solve* a mystery like Sherlock Holmes solves cases. Rather, as Marty writes, "to propose a solution means that one has not been working with a genuine mystery."[55] A mystery draws one into itself and draws all who approach it into a kind of understanding but never a comprehension. God's reality, and thus the depth of lived human experience, is a mystery—always beyond the reach of epistemology.

Empiricism teaches us to see the world as a set of problems to be solved and dismisses true mystery. Practical theology and ministry itself are not, at their core, about solving puzzles or problems, however. They are about participating in God's mystery. "A Problem," according to Gabriel Marcel, "is something which I meet, which I find complete before me, but which I can lay siege to and reduce."[56] The interpretations of young people's experiences with which we have contented ourselves over the past several decades, including the adolescent paradigm, are reductionistic. As Marty writes, "The child [or young person] seen first and fundamentally or even only in the context of her problems is, in Marcel's world, 'complete' before us. Who she is and what she represents can be 'laid siege to' by physicians, psychologists, ministers, or coaches, or 'reduced' by psychological analysts. The adult who conceives of the child as mystery, however, is involved with that child on a different set of terms."[57]

In the following chapters, we will seek to construct a theological interpretation of young people's experiences—one that is capable of holding the mystery of God in the stories of people like Neil Erikson and, indeed, my brother, Jesse. In this, we will move toward the kind of ministry that participates in the action of the crucified Christ, moving not toward progress, control, or development but toward hopes for resurrection. I hope through this work that leaders working with youths will learn not only to understand the young people with whom they minister but also to embrace them as mystery—to expect the disruption of God's presence, even in the experiences of those who are not "developing" as Erikson's model might lead us to expect.

CHAPTER FOUR

A Ministerial Theology of Interpretation

We cannot talk abstractly and theoretically about the phenomenon of rationality anymore: it is only as individual human beings, living with other human beings in concrete situations and contexts, that we can claim some form of rationality.[1]

—J. Wentzel van Huyssteen

It is the glory of God to conceal things, but the glory of kings is to search things out.

—Proverbs 25:2 (NRSV)

In a previous chapter, we saw how practical theology, and particularly youth ministry, was affected—in some ways shaped—by the empiricist turn in the epistemic landscape of Western scholasticism. As the criteria for legitimacy of knowledge shifted toward harder sciences—as verifiability, falsifiability, and replicability became normative in accounting for reality—theology became more and more dependent on outside sources for its own legitimacy as a form of knowledge. Theology, along with philosophy, had to learn to speak the language of the sciences to be logically persuasive. Theology turned to correlational methods of interdisciplinarity; the sciences set the standards for interpretation. Psychology emerged as a happy medium between hard sciences and philosophical accounts of meaning. Youth ministry, taking up its own—often ad hoc—correlational approaches, rode the wave of developmental psychology right onto the sandy beach of epistemic legitimacy. This epistemic landscape—the immanent frame, as Charles Taylor calls it—set limits on the horizons of ministerial interpretation. Consequently, certain experiences have not been adequately included in theory or practice. Acquiring legitimacy in the immanent frame meant, at key points, outsourcing or sacrificing practical theology's own distinctive theological voice and, in relying on an exclusive interpretive framework, rendering itself unable to hold the stories of those on the underside of developmental psychological interpretation—those developmental refugees such as Neil Erikson.

In this chapter, we will begin to move toward an interpretive methodology that embraces the cross-pressure of ambiguity and rationality yet does not reduce itself to abstractions of normalcy. We will look for an interpretive framework that empowers us not to solve the problem of human experience but to participate in the mystery of personhood. In order to construct a broad enough horizon to attend to the mystery of lived experience in youth ministry, we must outline the parameters of a theological anthropology of youth.

I have to admit that it has happened, on more than one occasion, that I have used the wrong interpretive lens to approach conversation with my wife, Amanda. It is a recurring pattern really. Amanda begins to tell me about something that is on her mind—some problem she is having or an anxiety she has—and I come to her with the full force of instrumental rationality, immediately diagnosing the problem and prescribing a solution. "Wes, I'm really worried about getting Henry (our son) into the right school next fall." And before she can really finish, I offer my response: "Well, did you schedule that meeting with the school district? Do you need me to call them? We will just have to get him enrolled and see how it goes (etc.)." The conversation doesn't usually advance very well from there. "I don't want you to fix it," she will say. "I just want you to listen." I do not usually recognize the problem in the moment—thank God that Amanda is so patient with me—but from the vantage point of my desk right now, I know that in those conversations I am employing the wrong interpretive framework, or lens, in my encounter with Amanda. I take the fix-it lens, interpreting the conversation as the presentation of a problem in need of a solution. However, though I am always too dense to see it in the moment, the correct lens would be to see the conversation as an opportunity to comfort and be present with Amanda. The lens I take with me into the conversation always determines whether I rise to the occasion or miss the opportunity and leave Amanda feeling unseen and unheard.

Not only is it problematic to take the wrong interpretive lens into a situation but it is also problematic to take the wrong interpretive posture. Indeed, the posture often determines the lens. By *posture*, I am talking about the way we carry ourselves into the task of interpretation. Even if we're using what might be the right *lens*, our posture may predispose us against interpreting the right *thing*. In my brother's life, as we discussed in chapter 1, our youth pastor's posture was an important element in how he approached the situation. My brother *was* experiencing something. Had my youth pastor chosen to investigate that experience, he may have discovered it to be God's action—ministry in which he himself was being called to participate. But my youth pastor's interpretive posture was oriented not toward my brother's lived experience, as such, but toward a particular and perennial outcome that preoccupied his attention. What he was interpreting was not how and if my brother was experiencing God. He was interpreting how and if my brother's potential for a particular brand of spiritual maturity could be developed. His posture obstructed him from seeing what God was doing in the actuality of my brother's experience.

Part of the problem at hand is that we do not usually think of interpretation as a theological task. It can be tempting for practical theologians to restrict theology to the normative task of practical theology—to assume that description and interpretation are somehow theologically neutral. But this is problematic, to say the least. When we apply ourselves to any of the tasks of practical theology, we are to apply ourselves *as theologians*, and thus every task is a theological task, including, if not especially, the task of interpretation. In our interpretive and descriptive tasks under the auspices of developmentalism and empiricism, we practical theologians and youth ministers have been far too content with affirming and *endorsing* the questions and answers offered by the social sciences, especially developmental psychology, through critical correlational methodologies. We have lost the distinctiveness of theological knowledge by submitting it to the authority of empiricism and developmentalism. This has left us in what Douglas John Hall has referred to as a "methodological cul-de-sac," stuck arguing for the legitimacy of our knowledge yet unable "to advance beyond the how of knowing to the what."[2]

Theological knowledge is not, after all, knowledge that can be contained in immanent structures of verifiability because theological knowledge is fundamentally relational knowledge. On the continuum of empirical rationality, where objectivity is king, theology sits firmly on the subjective end of the spectrum. "What" we know in theology "is not properly designated 'it' but only 'Thou.'"[3] And the "Thou" of our knowledge—God—is one who has engaged the world as a minister, inviting us to participate in ministry. *Revelation*, as

Hall says, *is the basic epistemological presupposition of Christian belief and theology.*[4] This is fundamental to the theological mode of knowing. Theology's quest to "make itself agreeable to a view of reason which insists that whatever one claims to 'know' must be capable of empirical verification," then, is an act of self-negation.[5] What we need is a mode of interpretation that maintains the distinctive rationality of theology as ministerial and relational, even as we engage the sciences to help interpret the situations we are trying to address.[6] We need an interpretive posture that helps us interpret the right thing.

Practical theology must also maintain the distinctiveness of its voice among the theological disciplines. For those worried about this, my previous statements may be cause for concern. Some have seen interdisciplinarity as the distinctive feature that sets practical theology apart from, for example, systematic and constructive theologies. What makes practical theology different is its turn to verifiable sciences to support the application of theological doctrine, ethos, or critique. But as John Swinton has put it,

> It is not simply a matter of practical theology *applying* insights drawn from the other theological disciplines. . . . Practical theology makes its own interpretations of Scripture and tradition in the light of the contemporary practice of the church, which it then brings into dialogue with those disciplines who approach this data with different hermeneutical criteria. . . . Thus, it does not merely receive theology and then merely pass it on. It has a constructive, critical and analytical part to play in the process of developing theological understandings.[7]

Practical theology is theology and not merely its application to situations previously addressed by the social sciences. What sets practical theology apart from other disciplines is not its interdisciplinarity; interdisciplinarity is penultimate. The ultimate concern of practical theology, the quality that sets it apart from other theological disciplines, is the disclosure of God's action in and through human experience and the practices of the church. God is our ultimate research subject, not human experience or anything else. By investigating human experience, practical theology expects to be able to say things about God that could not otherwise be said. Interdisciplinarity is simply a means to that end, and therefore, if it turns out to be obstructive rather than productive, practical theology must be able to work without it. Social sciences are important tools to the practical theologian, but they do not provide the validity of its theological knowledge.

So what sort of interpretive posture must the practical theologian, and particularly those of us working with young people, take to encounter God's action in the experiences of developmental refugees while continuing to serve those for whom our methods have already proved successful? What we need at this juncture, I propose, is what Andrew Root calls a *ministerial transversal rationality*.

A MINISTERIAL POSTURE

One of the key issues of interpretation is judgment. How do we judge which interpretive lens to take with us into a situation, practice, or encounter? Who will be our conversation partners? There are various interdisciplinary models, including the correlational models we have already mentioned above, all designed to help. But judgment generally remains an open question. Are practical theologians simply to cherry-pick other disciplines for their interpretive questions and answers? How do we know which framework we should take up and when?

As Root has suggested, ministry itself must inform our interdisciplinary judgment. What guides our interdisciplinarity is our orientation to the experience of the others and particularly their experience of God—a posture indigenous to ministry. We do not choose our interpretive categories or dialogue partners prior to engaging in the work of ministry. Rather, our interpretive paradigms must emerge from the work of ministry itself. Root has explained this point by saying that ministry calls the practical theologian into "events of convergence with other (scientific) epistemologies. But she uses these epistemologies only so long as they assist her ministry."[8] This, however, is somewhat misleading. The language of *use* and *assistance* here implies an instrumental relationship between the theologian and the sciences. The point is not, however, to reduce interdisciplinarity to the mere choosing of a tool from a toolkit. Indeed, the intersections into which we are called as ministers are relational intersections in and of themselves. We should revere interpretive intersections as sacred spaces and not merely as instruments for reaching our own ends. The point is that rather than relinquishing interpretive control to the sciences and to empiricist forms of knowledge, we must relinquish control to the experience of ministry itself. We allow experience to dictate which interpretive framework is appropriate for understanding. This is not to say that experience is normative for practical theology. In allowing interpretive frameworks for interdisciplinarity to emerge from experience, we must not allow ourselves to end here, nor should we let the situation do all our thinking for us. Rather, we must discern experience honestly and thoroughly enough so that the *kerygma*—cataphatic, or affirmative, proclamation—of divine action can honestly and thoroughly penetrate and even transform the situation.[9] In other words, we need to let ministry do the driving. It is ministry that sets the standard, an action of God in which humans participate through *attending to human experience*. What really guides our interdisciplinarity, then, is not what "assists" us in ministry so much as our orientation to the experience of the other and what is indigenous to ministry itself.[10]

Now this is not to impose a kind of "pure" phenomenology by assuming that the criteria for our interpretive judgments will fall from the sky. Reality is not somewhere behind the curtain of interpretation in some pure form of experience. Reality, however, is in Christ. What saves us from pure phenomenology and from merely using mystery as a cop-out is the insistence that there is indeed an agent in ministry and that there is discernible action. God is the actor. So when we suggest that categories of interpretation will emerge from ministry itself, we are not dealing in abstraction. It is God who acts in concrete events. Because the biblical witness reveals God in Jesus Christ in works of love, the criteria for interpretation are before us. We can look to the "fruit of the spirit" for our understanding as we participate in the work of God in the lives of young people. God is mystery, but God is also an agent—an agent who cultivates "love, joy, peace, patience, kindness, generosity, faithfulness, gentleness, and self-control" (Gal. 5:22–23, NIV). It is for these fruits that we must search as we participate in and interpret young people's experiences.

According to Hall, theology is definitively contextual precisely because the community that is engaged in its practice is a "disciple community"—a community not only of thinkers but of agents, a community of *disciples*.[11] Interdisciplinarity is guided by *actual* engagement in dialogue, not just theoretical engagement. Hall writes,

> True contextuality means the initiating and nurturing of a *dialogue* with one's culture, a genuine give-and-take, in which the world is permitted to speak for itself, and in which therefore the Christian community opens itself to the *risk* of hearing things that it had not anticipated and to which it cannot *readily* respond. In other words, in a fully contextual approach to its subject, the disciple community sees its sociohistorical habitat, not only as a field to be investigated but as a partner in the investigation—and therefore as a contributor to the theological task itself.[12]

A similar kind of dialogue originally motivated the emergence of the correlational methods criticized in the previous chapter and above. But a key guiding principle missing from its most prominent articulations was that of discipleship. Ministry and practical theology are not merely *fides quaerens intellectum* (faith seeking understanding), Anselm's famous motto, but faith seeking participation in the life and being of God. Therefore, the cost of theological interpretation is as high as the cost of discipleship—"Thinking the faith implies suffering."[13] Discipleship protects theology from losing or outsourcing its theoretical content and distinctive rationality to the safety of the laboratory. What we are after are not just answers but ministry— participation in the life and being of God, the minister.

Whenever theology loses discipleship, it is always at risk of allowing the forces of alien epistemologies to determine its shape and form.[14] Indeed, this is precisely what has happened in youth ministry in its interpretation of young people's experiences. We allow the presuppositions of a psychological paradigm—namely, adolescence—to precede actual engagement in young people's experiences. Hall points out the subsequent dangers: "Christian theology must entertain the deepest suspicions of any account of reality which underestimates or defies the dimensions of time and space and offers finality." Indeed, "the disciple community . . . must warn susceptible humanity against putting its trust in domesticated absolutes."[15] There are few examples that are more deceptively defiant of the dimensions of time and space than that of Erikson's model of the eight stages of the life cycle. When confronted face to face with the ambiguity of conditioned existence—indeed, face to face with his son Neil—Erikson turned to the absolute for comfort and sought finality as an escape from his situation. He clearly missed an opportunity for ministry, not to suggest he was necessarily interested in one. And yet in youth ministry, this model of development and its paradigm of adolescence persists. How is this so?

We have always been faced with the challenge of deciding just whom we should turn toward to help us interpret our situation. When legitimacy of knowledge is determined by utility for development and verifiability of data, then absolutes and finality have a certain appeal: "Subject at every turn to the unpredictable and the chaotic, the human psyche reaches out for order, certitude, and stability wherever they can be found—and finds them, regularly, in many places where they cannot, in reality be found!"[16]

Empiricism is an opiate. It offers false security by presuming a kind of objectivity and, through positivist accounts of reality, believes itself to transcend contexts of time and place. But, as Hall suggests, "When the church permits its theology to transcend time and place . . . it is always contributing to evil, sometimes to spectacular evil."[17] One need only notice the complicity of the church in the ecological crisis to see the kind of evil that can be done when theology relegates itself to the "spiritual" and ignores the world in which we actually live. When theology operates in abstraction, it's easy to baptize the objectification of creation. As theologians, we must recover our suspicions of finality and universality. In doing so, we will have to abandon our default prioritization of hard sciences and empiricist claims on reality in the immanent frame. We must return to discipleship—the ministerial—as our guiding principle for discerning the frameworks of interpretation and interdisciplinarity. Indeed, we will need to anticipate not the fruit of our investigative labor but the fruit of the Spirit as it is disclosed to us in the lived experiences of the young people with whom we are ministering.

As practical theologians, we will become ministers. Our participation in ministry, and solidarity with the community and individuals with whom we minister, will precede the assumptions with which we engage in the interpretive task. This does not mean we can "bracket"[18] our experience—suspending our personal preconceptions altogether—or adopt a pure objectivity. On the contrary, interpretation is always a reflexive practice. Nor does it mean we must give in to a flat-footed relativism, allowing the situation to do all our thinking for us. Either of these options would represent a monologue rather than a genuine *dialogue* with the situation. Interpretive categories will still be important. But our selection of which category—whether it be psychological, anthropological, biological, or poetic—will emerge from participation and all the vulnerability associated therewith.

The *ministerial* element of ministerial transversal rationality, then, is definitely not a positivist science. We might describe it as ethnographic in nature. Just as ethnography demands that the researcher take a subjective posture toward the situation they are interpreting, the ministerial assumes subjective and active participation. According to Erin Raffety, "By engaging in sustained, long-term fieldwork, the ethnographer immerses him or herself in the host country and culture, learning about culture by way of relationship."[19] Quite distinct from the objective approach of positivist sciences, the immersive posture of ethnography involves a "defamiliarization" with cultural assumptions and the relinquishing of control regarding interpretive categories to the research subject(s).

One key distinction, however, between ethnography and ministry is that the goal of ministry is not mere understanding but *participation*—namely, participation in God's action in the concrete and lived experience of persons. The minister must not become an ethnographer, even if there are helpful analogies between the two practices. In ministry, it is God's action, not human action, that is of central interest and importance. In this sense, Kenda Dean is right in suggesting that, in fact, youth ministry is not primarily about youth but Jesus Christ.[20]

This participatory posture is necessary for us if we are to construct a horizon capable of holding the stories of developmental refugees. Whenever and wherever an interpretation is wrongly imposed on a situation, there will always be casualties. This is especially true in regard to developmentalism. Ministry is our best mechanism for subverting the abstract optimism of developmentalism. In our context, participation with the God who associates Godself with the least of these (Matt. 25) is the only way we will be able to hear the voices of the crushed and the persecuted over the noise of achievement and progress.

This, then, is what Andrew Root means by the "ministerial" in *ministerial transversal rationality*—a prevenient participation in God's ministry in the lived experience of particular human beings as *the* catalyst for the determination of interpretive paradigms and categories for understanding and indwelling that same lived experience. Our interpretation of a situation presumes our participation with God in the situation. Interpretation, therefore, is not an abstraction but flows from the concrete and lived experiences of actual human beings, precluding an *a priori* privileging of potentiality over actuality. The ministerial is the guiding principle that will remedy not only our interdisciplinary confusion regarding what and whom we, as disciples, should take as interdisciplinary interlocutors but also the theoretical resignation to empiricism and developmentalism that has plagued the family of correlational methodologies so prevalent in youth ministry.

APPROACHING RATIONALITY

Transversal rationality is usually introduced as a model—among others—for interdisciplinary collaboration and dialogue. Typically, it is offered as an alternative to critical correlational and Chalcedonian methods of interdisciplinarity.[21] While transversal rationality certainly does constitute a method of interdisciplinarity—and, as such, represents an alternative to traditional methods—it first represents an alternative *epistemological structure* and should be treated as such before it is treated as a methodology. In other words, transversal rationality does not merely deal in strategies or methods, but, primarily, it deals with the question of rationality, of understanding itself. This—before anything else—is what makes it unique. Transversal rationality is also postfoundationalist: rationality emerges in a transverse space between various modes and forms of knowledge. How can transversal rationality help us develop a ministerial theology of interpretation?

Universal Rationality

The best way to understand postfoundationalism and transversal rationality is to contrast it with modern foundationalism—with its classical and universal conception of rationality—on one hand and the nonfoundationalism of postmodernity—with its radically relativistic and pluralistic conception of rationality—on the other.[22] Foundationalism, for example, sees rationality as a single continuum of more and less rational forms of knowledge. This spectrum can prioritize different forms of knowledge; what makes it foundationalist is its universal structure of rationality. For example, the empiricist regime of epistemology in the immanent frame prioritizes objectivity, placing sciences like psychology—with their fidelity to the rules of verifiability and falsifiability—further along the spectrum than other more subjective forms of knowledge, such as theologies and philosophies, which may take reason to be a source of knowledge but do not hold it as normative. As I have tried to illustrate in figure 1, the universal rationality of modernism sees understanding and rationality essentially as a monolith—one thing, one spectrum, in which various disciplines exists and converse.

One *could* try to flip the script by prioritizing something other than objectivity. This, as it turns out, is how some conservative Christian apologists try to respond to the challenge of empiricism. Rather than prioritizing objectivity, they might prioritize something like divine revelation, Scripture, or even doctrine, plotting theology onto a more prominent end of the spectrum than psychology and giving it logical priority (see fig. 2).

In the Chalcedonian model, as offered by Deborah van Deusen Hunsinger, theology engages in interdisciplinary dialogue in differentiated unity,

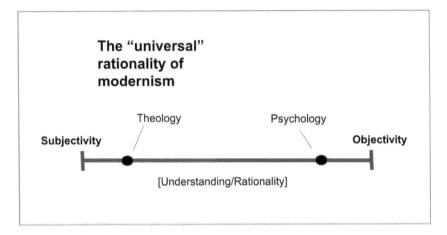

Figure 1: The "universal" rationality of modernism

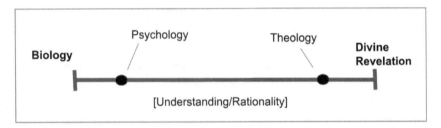

Figure 2: Theology's attempt at flipping the script without changing the rules of modernism

expressing a true and "inseparable unity" in the economy of address yet an "indissoluble differentiation" between the disciplines, as such.[23] This conception of differentiated unity actually sits well in the postfoundationalist account of rationality, which will be outlined below, but the conception of rationality that accompanies this Chalcedonian approach implies a universal rationality wherein theology is given a predetermined logical priority. As Swinton and Harriet Mowat explain, "Within the process of practical-theological research, qualitative research data *does* acquire its significance from theology. Theology's significance is therefore logically prior to and independent of qualitative research data."[24] Even in their differentiated unity, the interplay between the disciplines is characterized as a spectrum, but now theological disciplines are asymmetrically privileged because they are seen as moving further toward the pinnacle of rationality—in this case, divine revelation. This asymmetry is certainly appropriate in reference to the divine and human natures of Christ in the hypostatic union. However, *theology is not divinity*, grasp as it might to apprehend it. Theology is but a human endeavor—a discipline among others. In giving it a logical priority, the Chalcedonian model repairs the wrong leak, neglecting to address the problem of rationality itself by trying to keep theological interdisciplinarity and legitimacy afloat on the waters of empiricism.

As long as rationality is perceived as "one thing"—a universal spectrum on which every discipline is a point to be plotted—our empiricist impulses will continue to revert to the elusive yet comforting allure of objectivity. We saw this illustrated in the intellectual career of Erikson, who, though he was drawn to the arts and had a growing interest in anthropology, found his comfort in the ordered and precise language of developmentalism, which grew in the fertile soil of empiricism.

In any case, a universal rationality is an inadequate horizon for holding the stories of developmental refugees. Even while questions of meaning and transcendence might have a place on the spectrum, there is a trajectory toward abstraction, for abstract principles are the pillars that uphold the universalist structure. Essence precedes existence, categories of interpretation precede experience, and "the pre-delineated markers of certitude guide the quest for the justification of our beliefs"[25]—this is the epistemic landscape of the subject-centered and universal rationality of modernity. This structure is definitively characterized by the enforcement of abstract rules and an essentialism that cannot help but cultivate victims, for abstraction breeds hegemony. As van Huyssteen writes, "The classical model of rationality's claims to universality and necessity is very closely connected to a commitment to 'appropriate, objective rules.'"[26] Some of these include rules about time and its passing. As Schrag points out, drawing from Jean Baudrillard, modernity brought with it a construction of time as having three distinct characteristics—the *"chronometric, linear,* and *historic,* respectively."[27] It will be helpful to quote Schrag at length to explain this:

> The chronometric dimension provides the matrix for a quantitative measurement of time. The linear dimension fixes time as an irreversible succession of instants moving across a continuum of past, present, and future. The historic dimension . . . portrays time as a dialectical becoming that actualizes the potentialities of a beginning in a consummatory end. It was the imprint of the historic dimension of time that directed the gaze of modernity to the future and to the envisionment of perfectibility.[28]

Essentially, universal rationality brings developmentalism with it—as a total-izing rule and criteria for interpreting experience, history, and time itself—and imprints developmentalism implicitly but inexorably onto the very fabric of epistemology. Thus, to move beyond developmentalism—and I hope chapter 2 demonstrated that, for the sake of ministry, we must—it is necessary for us to address rationality itself and oppose the hegemony of empiricism and developmentalism inherent within classical universal accounts.

Pluralist Rationality

Nonfoundationalism represents an alternative, but it also poses problems of its own. It does not turn out that we can adequately escape our problems by dispensing with the structure of rationality altogether. In its opposition to a universal rationality, nonfoundationalism adopts a pluralist account of rationality—or, better yet, *rationalities*: "Instead of a model where knowledge is seen as an entity resting on fixed and immutable foundations, nonfoun-dationalists offer a picture of human knowledge as an evolving social phe-nomenon shaped by the practical implications of ideas within larger webs of belief."[29] No mode of rationality can adequately indwell another to afford a hierarchical association of one discipline or approach over another. Nor is there room for critique between disciplines on mutual grounds. Indeed, there is *no rationality* in nonfoundationalism; only various rational*ities*. So while we may still find correlations—while neighboring rationalities might still borrow sugar from one another, so to speak—there is truly no unifying or intersecting foundation for the construction of knowledge. They cannot inhabit the same dwelling. There is no understanding, only understandings. In figure 3, for example, psychology and theology are two different rationali-ties and two alternative understandings. While conversation between them is still possible, they do not converge or intersect.

It is dubious to speak of divine revelation in nonfoundationalist plural-ism. For in abandoning any *a priori* criteria for rationality and rejecting any universal referent of disclosure (contra realism), it must also disavow God's self-disclosure as emerging from outside the structures of epistemol-ogy. In other words, we are restricted, in this nonfoundationalism, from any normative ontological claims about the nature of being. We must limit ourselves to epistemology as such. While the rules of foundationalism are

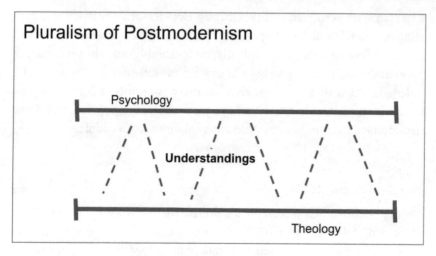

Figure 3: Postmodern pluralism

universal laws of governance and justification, nonfoundationalism has a predetermined pluralist cosmology. In other words, since everyone has their own rationality, we cannot make ontological normative claims.[30] Forms of knowledge like theology that are fundamentally committed to questions of ontology are permitted to maintain their own distinctive rules and criteria for rationality, but they are marginalized. Those sciences and disciplines whose rules and criteria adhere to the epistemic limitations delineated by the pluralist ideology are permitted a more authoritative voice. Thus, in interdisciplinary discussions, even where a critical correlational method is adopted, theology must essentially follow the rules of more "objective" rationalities. This is how interdisciplinarity has played out in the context of interpretation in youth ministry. If totalization is the sin of universalism, then the sin of pluralism is resignation. And, with resignation, a reduction of ontology to epistemology.[31]

TRANSVERSAL RATIONALITY

Transversal rationality offers an alternative not only to the totalizing ideology of a universal rationality but also to the resignation of a pluralist conception of rationali*ties*.[32] Rather than being *uni*versal—wherein rationality is "one thing" constituting a spectrum on which various disciplines and sciences can be plotted—this conception of rationality is *trans*versal, emerging from the concrete interplay of the "crossing of perspectives."[33] Transversal rationality maintains that understanding is not one thing, but nor is it a plurality of isolated rationalities. Transversal rationality accepts the postmodern critique of pluralism insofar as it affirms the fact that disciplines cannot eliminate their distinctiveness enough to indwell another on a universal spectrum of rationality. The disciplines are affirmed in their integrity. Theology has its distinctive voice, and so does psychology. The theologian does not have to become the psychologist, nor is the psychologist expected to become a theologian. However, this does not mean that rationality is isolated to disciplines. It is not the lines of reason themselves that make up the shape of rationality but the intersections of various disciplines in the dialogical economy of human experience: "[Transversal rationality is] . . . a lying across, an extending over, a lining together, and an intersecting of various forms of discourse, modes of thought and attitudes."[34] We can concede the fact that all human knowledge is historically, socially, and even geographically *situated* knowledge. Whether we are postmodernist or not, we are living within postmodernity. But where rationality emerges in this transversal account is in the rubbing of shoulders and the conversations themselves. Rationality is in the intersection of disciplines, not in the rules and laws of the disciplines themselves. This is befuddling to those in search of ontological certitude, but it does not reduce reality to epistemology, either. We can pursue the notion, and even the exploration, of ontology even as we admit that epistemology never apprehends it and that, in the end, we are always engaged in interpretation.

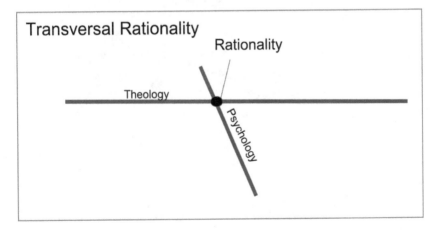

Figure 4: Transversal rationality

Rationality emerges at these crossroads precisely because it is concrete and not abstract (see fig. 4). Because rationality is not a Platonic ideal or a predetermined law, it must be interdisciplinary and intersubjective. Rationality belongs to human beings, embodied creatures, who live and move in the world. No totalizing abstraction will ever replace or account for concrete lived experience. No "universal truth" will ever govern human knowledge and hold the stories of these creatures who live in the world. They must be held in real life, through actual encounter, precisely what Erikson meant to avoid when he constructed his abstract theory of the life cycle. Human knowledge is not a spectrum or a collection of spectrums. Rather, it is a lacing of intersecting modes of knowledge and experience (see fig. 5). It is a web of actual encounters. Thus, not only are the connections between various modes of knowledge honored—as they are, to a fault, in universalism—but so are the divergences and differences between disciplines, as they are in pluralism. Figure 5 demonstrates why Osmer asked us in explaining this concept to "think of the ways surfaces both intersect and diverge when the sticks are thrown in a game of pick-up sticks."[35]

Because transversal rationality is concrete and not abstract, no singular discipline or mode of knowledge is awarded logical priority. Theology—though it has its distinctive voice and cannot be expected to fully indwell another discipline—is a human discipline, not to be confused with the object

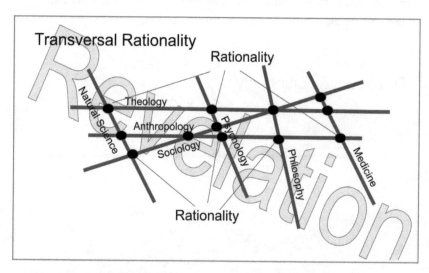

Figure 5: The bigger picture of transversal rationality

of its study (i.e., God).[36] The theologian necessarily, and rightly, privileges theology by virtue of their vocation as theologian—preserving its distinctive interdisciplinary voice—but *not* by virtue of some special status or logical priority among the disciplines. Divine revelation is not something the theologian *discovers*, as though God stands waiting at the end of a path called *theology*. Figure 5 illustrates the location of divine revelation not in any one intersection but behind the web itself so that no one discipline—not even theology—has the market cornered on God's self-disclosure. Theological knowledge is something definitely *disclosed* according to God's action. It does not occur through human action, especially not the action of a theologian. Instead, it comes from outside the structures and rules of human rationality. Revelation stands beneath the concrete interplay of human encounters and, though we cannot guarantee their efficacy, is at times received in the transversal intersections of rationality as God communicates Godself to the world.

THE SHAPE OF TRANSVERSAL RATIONALITY

Transversal rationality is characterized by three basic descriptors, not rules. These characterizations—or "coefficient dynamics"[37]—of rationality form the basic shape of an epistemological structure that provides theologians with the interpretive posture to hold the stories of the people with whom we are engaged in ministry, including people living with disabilities, people from varying cultural contexts and social classes, and young people inside and outside of our churches.

Praxial Critique

The first characterization that forms the shape of transversal rationality is that of praxial critique. Rationality emerges in true dialogue, when interpretations and ideas are genuinely engaged. Thus, critique is indigenous to rationality. But in transversal rationality, critique is not based on preconceived ideas. The "criteria" for critique do not come from rules or abstractions. Rationality itself, and the epistemology on which it is situated, emerges from praxis. It is important to note that praxial critique is not merely a "practical" critique, as though all that matters is actionable information and the things that are immediately applicable to strategy. Praxis and practice are different. Practice simply corresponds to the things people do with certain intentions; it does not govern the intentions themselves. When we allow the practical to govern intention, we devalue thought and analysis. In other words, those concerned only with what is practical will disregard more theoretical contemplation and display impatience with theory in general—thus, the undergraduate student of practical theology may be disappointed to discover that they have to read Kierkegaard after all. Praxis, on the other hand, holds no opposition to theory. As Hall helpfully clarifies, "The point of praxis is not to substitute act for thought, deed for word, but to ensure that thinking is rooted in existence—and committed to its transformation. . . . It means . . . to pledge oneself to the overcoming of the (after all, artificial) gap between thought and act, and so to become more serious *about both*."[38] Praxial critique means critical and *theoretical* dialogue with a variety of perspectives—it means critique in the context of praxis such as ministry, particularly for the theologian and Christian youth worker.

According to Schrag, "Praxial critique is critique *in* the community, *by* the community, and *for* the community."[39] Community is the ground on which we walk whenever we endeavor to think, know, rationalize, or encounter reality. We never do so as isolated subjects who engage the external world according to mechanistic theory. As Jürgen Moltmann put it, "According to mechanistic theory, things are primary, and their relations to one another are determined secondarily, through 'natural laws.' But in reality relationships are just as primal as the things themselves. . . . Nothing in the world exists, lives and moves of itself. Everything exists, lives and moves in others, in one another, with one another, for one another in the cosmic interrelations of the divine Spirit."[40] Praxial critique rejects the idea that ideas can be forged in isolation. Rationality is a communal and interdependent reality. It is situated knowledge. Thus, it "enjoys neither modernity's zeal for foundations nor its hopes for the attainment of certainty. It rests content to discern and assess the play of forms of thought and action against the background of changing and historically conditioned patterns of signification."[41] Our epistemic structures never presume to reach the horizon of ontology. Reality is bigger than what we can know.

Interactive Articulation

This discussion of the communal element of critique quite naturally leads us to the second dynamic of traversal rationality—its "communicative turn."[42]

Because rationality is communal, it is also rhetorical. Along with critique, articulation is a necessary dynamic of rationality. In other words, transversal rationality must be persuasively expressed in the community. Rationality, as praxial, cannot exist outside of communication. Rationality does not float above us. It can only exist between us. Rationality is not only inaccessible but inexplicable unless it is communicated.[43]

Communication need not be textual or even verbal. Since rationality is, after all, "alive and well in *all* the domains of our human lives" and not only in the cognitive domains,[44] we must not presume a definition of rationality that would exclude those without the powers of verbal or traditionally linguistic forms of self-expression. Indeed, we only discover what rationality is once we have adequately engaged the other, no matter who the other may be. This is what is meant by *interactive* articulation. If your articulation cannot be interactive, then you must seek another articulation. Rationality is concrete, not abstract. It does not exist merely as a theory but as an interactive, relational experience.

Incursive Disclosure

Rationality, and thus understanding, is fundamentally "shaped by its interactions with the world."[45] What are opened to us through these interactions and praxial intersections are new features of reality to which we did not formerly have access. But because rationality is both praxial and communicative, understanding of reality is not the product of our bold discovery. It is, rather, something that comes to us. It is *disclosed*, not *discovered*. We will say more about this distinction below, but suffice it to say that disclosure is *incursive*. It invades and penetrates the immanent frame, transcending the rules and cognitive legislation of positivism and empiricism. It comes not from within but rather from without our epistemic frames of reference. As such, the referent of disclosure maintains itself as a mystery that cannot be solved but can only be encountered. Reality includes both immanence and transcendence. Reality cannot be upwardly conflated with the transcendent so as to lose place, context, and conditionality or downwardly conflated with immanence so as to foreclose on the reality that sits beyond the horizon of what human knowledge can ascertain. The horizon of human knowledge must remain open to mystery. We can only hope to participate in the mystery, for we cannot possess it or lay it bare. Ontology always overspills epistemology.

This becomes the distinctive point of departure for the *ministerial transversal rationality* of practical theology, for God, as person, is not known merely intellectually but experientially.[46] From this vantage point, we can begin to outline the distinctively theological epistemology on which a transversal rationality must sit in theological reflection.

A THEOLOGICAL EPISTEMOLOGY—"WHO?" NOT "HOW?"

Theological epistemology begins and ends in disclosure, not discovery. According to Dietrich Bonhoeffer, "There is no general blind seeking after God."[47] We do not *discover* or reveal God. Only God can reveal God, and God's disclosure is not something we can will or conjure through discursive practices. Ministry is always God's work, to which we are always and everywhere responsible as participants. God is the transcendent and wholly other to whom we are responsible. Thus, theological disclosure is necessarily incursive; it is dependent on the "act-character of God's being," which constitutes the very *real* horizon of theological knowledge, even if it is a horizon beyond which we cannot travel on our own volition, and derives its rationality not from the world in which God interacts but ultimately by the God who acts.[48] When God acts and is revealed to us in this incursive disclosure, God is always revealed as subject or person, not object. Therefore, there is always an element of mystery and concealment—*even* in disclosure. God remains other even as God draws near and becomes familiar to us. The knowledge of God is not apprehended through data but always through relationship, always through ministry. As Ray Anderson has put it, "Ministry precedes and creates theology."[49] It is through God's interaction with us—"all of God's actions in history"[50]—that human beings are granted knowledge of God. God is a person and, as such, a minister.[51]

The logic of developmentalism, with its instrumental rationality, is compelled to ask the question "how?" because it sees reality itself as progressing or regressing on a scale of improvement. If everything is developmental, if the world exists only on a scale of improvement and decline, then even God must be valued according to the standards of optimization. But God is not an idol or an object; God is a living subject within the event and network of relational encounter. As Anderson states, "To claim a revelation of God apart from the ministry of God is to violate the first commandment and to clothe ourselves in fig leaves."[52] Therefore, no knowledge *about* God will ever amount to *knowing God*. "Human knowledge," as John Swinton wrote, "is useless in the quest for knowing God. Having a profound intellectual disability is no different from being Albert Einstein when it comes to what it means to know God. It is all a gift."[53] Where positivist rationality and empiricist epistemology are compelled to ask "what?" and "how?," the question of *theological* epistemology is "who?" Who is this God that encounters us? That is the question of disclosure, the question of transcendence, the question of faith seeking understanding. In the immanent frame, hypercognitivist epistemologies— epistemologies privileging powers of cognition and thus marginalizing those whose cognitive abilities diverge from the dominant standard—can never account for the kind of knowledge to which theology, as such, must witness. Theological epistemology is not centered on the ability of the inquisitor but on the ministry of God.

Getting Warmer: Wesley's Story

When the young John Wesley first traveled to the United States as a missionary of the Church of England, he took with him not only an ambitious spirit but a mind full of knowledge. Having been educated at Oxford University by some of the elite theological thinkers of his time, Wesley knew plenty *about* God. But when he courageously crossed the Atlantic Ocean with the ambitious goal of "converting the natives" there, the ship on which he traveled hit a squall, and all the things he knew about God ended up counting for a lot less than he had expected. He was gripped by fear, paralyzed by it. He was not faithfully trusting in God's protection. No. He was scared out of his mind!

Yet, amid his fear, he noticed some Moravians. They were not crying in fear; they were praying together and singing songs to God in praise. He must have known more about God than those Moravians—after all, he was Oxford-educated! But in his moment of crisis, none of that knowledge seemed to make a difference. He did eventually make it to the United States, where he was less than completely successful in his missionary endeavor. But he had to rush back to Oxford—that is another story in itself—to work alongside his brother, Charles. He continued in ministry for years, haunted by a sense of failure, a subtle but unassailable sense of doubt, and his memory of the storm.

What was it about those Moravians? How were they able to trust God, while he, the great evangelist, was paralyzed by fear and doubt?

Wesley carried these things with him throughout his ministry, and he determined to preach the gospel regardless of his own doubt, even in his despair. He spent much of his time in Bible study gatherings, reading theology and learning about God. These gatherings were mainly routine until at one of them in a place called Aldersgate Street—one that Wesley was reluctant to attend—something was different. Wesley was reading Martin Luther's commentary on the Epistle to the Romans—nothing outside the ordinary for Wesley—and as he put it, "While [Luther] was describing the change which God works in the heart through faith in Christ, I felt my heart strangely warmed. I felt I did trust in Christ, Christ alone for salvation; and an assurance was given me that He had taken away my sins, even mine, and saved me from the law of sin and death."[54] Even with all his knowledge *about* God, it was not until Wesley was grasped by an encounter *with* God that his heart was "strangely warmed." It was at Aldersgate, not at Oxford, that he felt the blessed assurance of knowing God. It was not in the discovery of new ideas or philosophical knowledge but in revelation—the "disclosure of a presence"[55]—that Wesley came to know the mystery of God.

The interpretive posture of theology and of Christian practices more broadly, especially the practice of ministry, cannot be that of discovery. The posture of discovery is one of conquest: the ambitious, if not arrogant, posture of going out into the world to apprehend and, in many cases, to control it. The posture of theological interpretation and of Christian practices must be that of disclosure. Knowledge of God does not come through examination, as in a laboratory, but through encounter and communion—indeed, through worship—wherein God arrives among us.[56] Therefore, a theological epistemology must be a relational epistemology. John Calvin made the point when he wrote, "We know the most perfect way of seeking God, and the most suitable order, is not for us to attempt with bold curiosity to penetrate to the investigation of [God's] essence, which we ought more to adore than meticulously to search out, but for us to contemplate [God] in [God's] works whereby [God] renders [Godself] near and familiar to us, and in some manner communicates [Godself]."[57]

Rather than going forth to discover God through a kind of research practice or even the practice of ministry itself—rather than attempt to conjure God by tearing the veil from God's face—we must humbly set ourselves before God, placing ourselves in a position to receive God's self-disclosure and to allow God to reveal whatever God wills. We must "be still" before we can "know" (Ps. 46:10, NRSV). We might describe this as a kerygmatic epistemology, an epistemology of proclamation—an account of knowing that is fundamentally dependent not on investigation or discovery but on our being addressed by God and oriented toward fellowship with God in communion, prayer, and worship. This is an account of knowledge that is more fundamentally relational than cognitive. Indeed, it is *only* in relationship and *never* through cognition that we can claim to know God. To know God is to love God, one might say. Or, to put it perhaps more precisely, "Whoever does not love does not know God, for God is love" (1 John 4:8, NRSV).

Knowledge of God, then, is not the result of an ambitious pursuit of discovery but of a humble reception of God's gracious self-disclosure as God meets us and knows us. The primary distinction between discovery and disclosure is a distinction of agency. In discovery, the agency primarily belongs to the human interpreter. In disclosure, the agency is always that of the subject. In theological interpretation, the agency is always primarily God's and not our own. God discloses Godself to us; God reveals God: "We do not approach God like we engage in the study of objects around us, namely, in an objective, scientific manner or at the whim of our own human will . . . God, and not the human person, is the active agent."[58] We, as interpreters, can never grasp for God. We can only open our hands, hearts, and minds—placing ourselves in a position to receive: "The Emmanuel who will be '*with* us' will *not* be possessed *by* us."[59] Theological knowledge is always a product of God's grace through God's coming to us as a person, as a minister.

ENCOUNTERING MYSTERY

Under the auspices of this theological epistemology, we must now conclude by turning to the question of rationality in the interpretation of human experience. Our investigation of human experience as theologians has as its true object and concern not the experience itself but its referent—namely, God. So we cannot content ourselves with any account of interpretation that reduces or resolves the mystery of divine and human encounter. All our human interactions are holy, for God encounters all human beings and indwells their experience, even as human beings are invited to indwell divine reality through reception. While there are certainly ways of knowing *about* human experience through scientific discovery—be it neurobiological, psychological, or even sociological—*theological* knowledge of the human being is distinctly ministerial insofar as it is disclosed to us by God through the encounter of ministry. No human experience can be discovered or possessed but only disclosed and engaged through participation. Thus, as theologians, we must reject any presumption of universality, finality, or totality in any interpretive framework. The tools of "objective" frameworks may become helpful to us but only *after* we have encountered the other through praxial critique, interactive articulation, and incursive disclosure.

Ministerial transversal rationality, as I have outlined it here, aids the theologian by offering them a posture of interpretation that can receive God's self-disclosure because it sees the intersection of rationality as both motivated by and generated in the practice of ministry itself—God's practice into which we are invited as participants. As interpreters, rather than bringing our own presupposed theses to be proven or reducing their experience to positivistic frameworks, we encounter the human being as a mystery in which we must participate, a mystery that cannot be discovered but only disclosed to us: "When we think that the human beings with whom our lives are most closely bound are fully comprehended by us ('Now I know what makes you "tick!"'), we have in that moment violated them, reduced them to objects, made of the mystery of their being a graven image."[60]

This kind of rationality will not allow us to continue to engage with abstractions. For example, being an expert on "adolescence" will bring us no closer to actually knowing young people than being experts on geology will bring us to the Grand Canyon. In the end, we have to actually go there. We have to actually encounter young people. We have to be curious. Church leaders and adults will no longer be able to speculate about what makes young people tick. We are instead compelled to meet them and to be open to the disclosure of who they are through our relationships with them.

CHAPTER FIVE

From Curing Adolescence to Caring for Young People

Care is something other than cure. Cure means "change." A doctor, a lawyer, a minister, a social worker—they all want to use their professional skills to bring about changes in people's lives. They get paid for whatever kind of cure they can bring about. But cure, desirable as it may be, can easily become violent, manipulative, and even destructive if it does not grow out of care. Care is being with, crying out with, suffering with, feeling with. Care is compassion. It is claiming the truth that the other person is my brother or sister, human, mortal, vulnerable, like I am.[1]

—Henri J. M. Nouwen

But Jesus said, "Let the little children come to me, and do not stop them; for it is to such as these that the kingdom of heaven belongs."

—Matthew 19:14 (NRSV)

Adolescence has been the dominant, if not exclusive, interpretive paradigm for understanding young people's experiences since the early 1900s. Adolescence is understood as a stage in the process of development from childhood to adulthood. Practical theologian Chap Clark has noted, "The earliest person to give developmental prominence to the notion of modern adolescence was G. Stanley Hall."[2] Though in recent years, Clark may have backtracked somewhat on this claim,[3] which represents a basic consensus in the field,[4] he was right to make it—especially in this way. Hall was indeed the first to give "developmental prominence" to "modern" adolescence because, prior to the psychological revolution that came with the emergence of modernity and the empiricist regime in the epistemic landscape of Western society, such a developmental interpretive framework did not exist. Although adolescence certainly had its precursors and early relatives, the paradigm that currently bears the name *adolescence* is fundamentally a twentieth-century invention, not a biologically determined stage of human existence. And as I hope to show throughout this chapter, it remains anything but normative.

Blame for the pervasiveness of adolescence as a paradigm for interpretation belongs not merely to developmental psychology but to the broader ideological governance of developmentalism itself. Cynthia Lightfoot writes that adolescence's "widespread acceptance had as much to do with larger social and economic processes as it did with the nature of teenagers themselves."[5] We can certainly "reach back," as Lightfoot puts it, "to a time before 'adolescence' became embodied in school curricula, youth organizations, and judicial systems, that is, before it became institutionalized, and find references to individuals with a foot on each side of whatever it means to be fully mature."[6] Lightfoot points out that young people, or "adolescents," have been viewed as deviant in their behavior throughout history: "Chaucer, Shakespeare, Milton, Wordsworth—all present a vision of youth as characteristically excessive, passionate, proud, and sensual, and contrast it with the clear-eyed sobriety of adulthood. . . . These images penetrate deeply into the literary and philosophical canons of Western thought."[7] All of these accounts of young people's experiences represent precursors to the adolescent paradigm.[8]

Adolescence—whether it is seen as problem or opportunity—emerged as an interpretation of young people's experience, built fundamentally on empiricist epistemic scaffolding, that sees youth as something to be resolved through a process of maturation toward adulthood. The word *adolescence* itself is "derived from the Latin root word *adolescere*, 'to grow up.'"[9] As such, the most appropriate metaphor for understanding the function of the word and its application—the sort of interpretive activity in which ministers and theologians engage when they use the term—is that of *diagnosis*.

While the debate has commonly been characterized as one between biological determinism and social construction, the metaphor of diagnosis cuts closer to the heart of the issue. For diagnosis addresses not only where adolescence comes from and what characterizes the *experience* but how it is applied in the first place. By addressing adolescence as a diagnosis, we can cast new light on our theological assumptions regarding adolescence and the church's ministry with young people.

Diagnosis is typically directed toward the activity of curing; we identify an illness or a pathology to discern the best interventions toward the eradication of the illness or resolution of the pathology. The central activity of youth ministry in the theological epistemology we outlined in the previous chapter, however, is not cure but care. *Diagnosis orients us toward problems and resolutions, while ministry orients us toward persons*—and thus to God's self-disclosure in relationship.

Adolescence is an interpretation, or reinterpretation, of a person's experience.[10] In other words, as Swinton has put it, "Diagnoses have an epistemology but no ontology. They are pencil sketches of human experiences that are frequently being erased and altered."[11] They can tell us things that may be important to our description of a person's experience, but they cannot stand in for the experience itself. As we've previously seen, adolescence is a historically new concept.[12] Although the existence of the word predates its current meaning, it did not emerge as *a discrete interpretive category within the larger itinerary of human growth and development* until the early 1900s, beginning with the publication of Hall's *Adolescence* in 1904.[13] But psychologists and sociologists didn't invent a new experience; rather, the interpretation changed as a new orientation emerged.

When human life is interpreted on a scale of improvement, as development from simplicity to complexity, then society naturally structures and orients itself toward such development, conditioning the experience of youth or childhood in ways specific to that interpretation. Progress becomes king, and those who cannot serve progress—including children, young people, and people with disabilities—experience life in a deficit position.[14] It is no longer sufficient to merely say that adolescence is a "social construct." This bears the risk of obscuring the differentiation between diagnosis and experience.

While we can get stuck in the weeds of the debate around the social construction of adolescence, what is most important is not whether it was constructed in the 1900s, during the Renaissance, or in the divine work of creation itself but *how* our interpretive assumptions bear on young people's experience here and now. It is the *current* construction of youth, not the historical construction of adolescence, that we must address. If interpreters ignore the social construction of adolescence or dismiss it in favor of biological determinism, they will fail to address their own complicity in, and responsibility toward, young people's experience in society. And if ministry is our main concern, then experience is of utmost importance.

While the categories for diagnosing illness are taken primarily from medicine, the categories for diagnosing adolescence are taken primarily from developmental psychology, even with notable interest in neurobiological approaches to developmentalism.[15] Often, physiological factors are taken into account, including puberty and "genital maturity,"[16] but the key category for this interpretation is that of the task—the achievement of certain performances in the transition from childhood to adulthood. One of the defining features of modernity is its presumption that identity is an achievement. The referent of the social construction of identity is an "object," a "goal" that we must reach rather than a divine subject who reaches toward us.

According to Erikson, the chief architect of the adolescent paradigm, "The adolescent mind is essentially a mind of the *moratorium*, a psychosocial stage between childhood and adulthood."[17] What marks this transitional stage is the task of identity formation, or the closely related concept of individuation. According to Peter Blos, "Individuation implies that the growing person takes increasing responsibility for what he does and what he is."[18] The process of identity formation is characterized by transition toward individuality, autonomy, and belonging. Within this framework, the traits of identity are essentially the traits associated with *adulthood*—rationality, productivity, status, and, chiefly, generativity. The adolescent, by contrast, is framed either explicitly or implicitly as one who is, as yet, without identity.

The philosophical bases for this interpretation are apparent, though they often go unquestioned. Commitments to individualism, empiricism, and behaviorism are all operative. Most significantly, what is necessary for such an interpretive orientation to exist is a particular anthropology that sees human life as a "natural" progression on a scale of improvement. Under the auspices of developmentalism, maturity is normative, and whatever does not bear the marks of maturity—including cognitive complexity, productivity, and independence—is interpreted as deficient, even pathological. The more *mature* a person is, the closer they are to God.[19] To achieve identity is to achieve adulthood. This presents a problem for interpreters operating out of more hermeneutical frameworks such as ethnography[20] or childhood studies.[21] For these interpreters, allowing adulthood to hold the kind of normative authority it is granted by the adolescent paradigm becomes a kind of ethnocentrism, or, if you like, "gerontocentrism."[22]

THE DIAGNOSTIC BACKDROP

Practical theologian Jeremy Paul Myers asserts that the adolescent paradigm of interpretation, this diagnosis of young people's experiences, renders young people as *undeveloped, identity-less, self-centered, commodified consumers.*[23] He rightly attributes this account to the larger cultural forces of consumerism and commodification at play in Western societies. As Julie Elman has put it, "When high school became compulsory by the 1940s, teenagers emerged as a distinct social group, while adolescence (at least for members of the white middle and elite classes) increasingly became defined as a period of suspended maturation devoted to schooling prior to employment and adult responsibility."[24] However, it is important to note that these cultural realities go beyond the surface of the sort of "assembly line" approach to understanding human development.[25] The backdrop of the adolescent paradigm of interpretation, as with any diagnostic approach to interpretation, is a normative definition of health and normalcy.

Have you heard any of those "X implies the existence of Y" jokes? It's a trend I've noticed on social media lately—one, I suspect, that will already be old news by the time you read this. It's a bit of observational humor where you point out that one thing implies the existence of another. For example, one might point out that "fun-sized" candy bars imply the existence of "boring-sized" candy bars. Or "content creator" implies the existence of "content destroyers." "Top Ramen" implies the existence of "Bottom Ramen." *Space Jam* implies the existence of "Space Peanut Butter." Or, one of my favorites, "reading for pleasure" implies the existence of "reading for pain"—hopefully that's not a concept with which you're currently relating. These jokes rely on the basic idea that every positive has a negative image and vice versa. "Up" implies "down," "east" implies "west," "light" implies "darkness," and so on. The coherence of one concept relies on an understanding of another.

Instability implies stability. Development implies the existence of that which needs development. Pathology implies the existence of health and normalcy. In the case of adolescence, the archetype is adulthood.[26] Adulthood is "normal," and childhood or adolescence is in need of resolution.[27] As Chris Jenks put it, "Childhood receives treatment through its archetypal image; it is conceptualized as a structured *becoming*, not as a social practice nor as a location for the Self (however elusive poststructuralism may have rendered this concept)."[28] Children's social worlds are studied not on their own account but for their magnetic connection to adulthood. By this scheme, society itself is "identical with adult society."[29]

"Besieged by raging hormones while at the mercy of an incomplete brain," young people stand against the backdrop of "normal" adulthood.[30] Since, under the new empiricist regime in epistemology, where reality is self-evident, biological and psychological categories set the terms for interpretation because of their perceived verifiability and relative objectivity, it was clear that adolescents were no longer children but also not yet adults. They were physically and intellectually capable of work and productivity, but they were yet unfinished. Despite their maturity beyond childhood, they had not yet achieved adulthood. Adulthood set the standard for what it means to be human, rendering young "adolescents" as incomplete, potential adults.

It is important to understand that it is not just adolescence that is socially constructed but the entirety of the so-called life course. According to James, "The precise chronologization of aging, regarded as a 'natural and unremarkable feature of contemporary representations of the life course,' is in fact a relatively recent social phenomenon, a by-product of the rationalization of all aspects of life which industrialization brought with it."[31] This is especially true in the West.[32] The value of economic productivity has significantly ordered our interpretations of human life and its value. Status and *telos* are directed toward and ordered according to the human being's ability to generate, produce, and contribute to society's industrial expansion. Indeed, if *telos* is the standard—if life is indeed "goal oriented"—then there's no time to sit still. Life becomes synonymous with activity and *being* is subordinate to *becoming*. In the developmental age, being is a waste of time. These values powerfully construct adulthood as a stage of "generativity" (per Erikson) and independence.

The "adult" in an industrial society is one who actively produces—no longer merely as an apprentice—and contributes to society through work or in support of work.[33] It now becomes important, according to this social construction of adulthood, to socialize youth, to move them through their adolescence and into productive adulthood so they can in turn contribute to the socialization of following generations. Development perpetuates development. This view of the life course, and indeed of the meaning of human life more generally, is a distinctly modern social construct. Adolescence, as such, cannot exist outside the matrix of the value systems associated with modern, industrial, secular, and developmental conceptions of reality.

The hermeneutical vantage points of health and normalcy, then, are what set the standards for diagnosis. In the case of adolescence, it is adulthood that constitutes health and normalcy. Young people's stories are reduced to "symptom stories," and the symptom stories of young people are set against the backdrop of the social practice of adulthood, of what is considered normal. We determine appropriate interventions for correcting or curing that which deviates from or is deficient of "maturity." Under the logic of instrumental rationality in the immanent frame, diagnosis is a powerful interpretive reflex. Set against the picture of health, the interpreter can diagnose and "treat" adolescence, making up the deficit and calming the storm of adolescence. This is the power of diagnosis: it gives the interpreter a clear way forward. This is, perhaps, what drew Erikson to stage theory and what compelled him to eventually construct what would be the most robust interpretive framework of developmental stages in history.

THE INTERPRETIVE VANTAGE POINT

Psychology begins with adulthood. The basic presupposition of developmental stage theory is that life itself can be understood as development through stages. The implicit epistemological starting point for determining these stages is their potentiality. Building on the work of Jean Piaget and Sigmund Freud, Erikson proposed that life consists of eight stages, with each one leading to the next on the way into the "integrity" of "mature adulthood."[34] Every stage serves in the development of maturity and is thereby definitively determined as *im*maturity.[35] Every stage leads to the next until adulthood is achieved, and as Donald Capps observes, "Good progress at one stage increases our chances for good progress at the next stage, for positive growth is cumulative."[36] In Erikson's model, "each stage is linked with physiological maturation and framed as an either/or dichotomy, with the primary task listed first and the threat posed if resolution is not obtained presented second."[37] Youth is really only of concern in reference to adulthood, and thus it is judged according to the standards of adulthood.

Young people, then, are characterized by our expectations that they will become adults. According to the childhood studies scholar Jens Qvortrup, "Colloquial expressions such as 'children are the future of society', 'children are the next generation' and 'children are our most precious resource' tend to deprive them of an existence as human *beings* in favor of an image of them as human *becomings*."[38] Young people are commodified as things in which we are to "invest"—kinda like the stock market. We put in time, or energy, or resources so something will come out. This is substantiated by developmentalism's portrayal of youth as "progressive towards completeness." In other words, they are "regressively incomplete."[39]

With adulthood as the interpretive vantage point for every preceding stage of development, the child is not even considered an authority on the interpretation of their own experience. As Erica Burman puts it, "The child exists in relation to the category 'adult.'"[40] "Research into children's lives," writes Martin Woodhead, "has been largely shaped by adult agendas for children, and reflected dominant power relationships between expert [read: adult] researchers and innocent, vulnerable, developing children."[41] According to Robert Wuthnow—not a psychologist but an established scholar in the study of American religion—"accounts of childhood can only be given by people who are no longer children" because adults are the only ones able to make judgments about "what is actually of value" in the interpretation of young people's experience.[42]

By this logic, children and adolescents are not active interpreters or social agents in their own experience. They are passive consumers of a world ultimately shaped by adults, mere "receptacles of adult teaching."[43] The aspiration of objectivity and the instrumental rationality of empiricism compel the researcher toward control, resolution, and universalization in order to propose a valid form of knowledge, thus obscuring the subjectivity of actual young people. As James points out, "For developmental psychology"—and for the child studied in the laboratory of the early-stage theorists—"the individual child . . . was ironically only of interest for what that child revealed about children's thinking *in general*."[44]

There's a kind of solace in positivism. It provides the interpreter a standard, a backdrop of normalcy, and a corresponding sense of the universal against which they can measure subjective experience. This is where developmentalism becomes particularly dangerous to a person working with young people. When a youth worker or pastor, who often knows just enough about developmental psychology to be dangerous, encounters the young people with whom they are working with a foregone conclusion regarding their experience—or perhaps, in a better-case scenario, with a thesis (i.e., adolescence) to be proven, via the "symptom stories" of the young people—they are immediately at risk of obscuring the experiences of those to whom the diagnosis does not relevantly apply. In my brother's case, my youth pastor had a preconceived idea of what maturity looked like. The youth pastor's foregone conclusion regarding Christian maturity, however, did not apply to my brother. So Jesse was marginalized from the outset as a developmental refugee.

Developmentalism gives the interpreter an archetypal narrative to order all the symptom stories of life, and thus it offers a sense of control. Now the interpreter can become the author; they can move and direct the narrative to match the archetype. They can account for illness and move toward health. They can see an adolescent and move them toward adulthood. The youth worker can make it their mission to "disciple" adolescents toward mature Christian adulthood.

In churches, we adults are excited to see young people when they do decide to darken the doors of the church. Sometimes, maybe all the time, we over-react and can risk smothering young people when they show up—it's okay to be excited, but chill out! What is our excitement all about? Is it really about encountering young people as bearers of the image of God and as people who can teach us and transform our lives and ministries? Or are we just excited to feel validated in what we're already doing? Who do we see as the object of change? Us or them? I submit that we're a lot less excited about how young people can transform us—aside from injecting some energy into what's already happening—than how we might transform them. Developmentalism gives us the illusion of holding all the cards. It tricks us into thinking *we* have what *they* need. And it orients our ministries, indeed even our ministry of welcome on a Sunday morning, toward moving young people toward our vision of Christian maturity and adulthood rather than a true openness to including *them* in our "*us*" and thus being changed.

NO ABSTRACTIONS

One of the main issues of the diagnostic adolescent paradigm of interpretation is its essentializing impulse. In essentialism, things are presumed to have a set of universal characteristics that determines what they are, and knowledge is constituted by the discovery of those characteristics. It is built on the doctrine that essence precedes existence. As Martin Woodhead has pointed out, despite some developmental psychologists' attention to children's subjectivity in their own fieldwork, "the scientific paradigm continues to expect developmental researchers to adopt an objective stance. Their subject—the child—is transformed into a de-personalized object of systemic enquiry, their individuality evaporated into a set of measurable independent and dependent variables, condensed into data sets that can address the hypothesis being tested, and abstracted into a general developmental pattern."[45] In other words, personhood is reduced to data.

Erikson's work is no exception to this, even though he was influenced by hermeneutical and phenomenological frames of interpretation. When he presumed to chart the life course in its eight stages, he was, quite explicitly, offering a picture of the essence of healthy development against which all deviations therewith—including someone like Neil—could be analyzed and even "treated." He was not content with the concrete reality of his own child, so he retreated to the abstraction of "childhood." He wanted to discover the "normal" child amid his own personal struggle with his very real but apparently "abnormal" child.

Barring a few notable exceptions,[46] the psychological project has remained in the empirical and positivist business of discovering the "real" person, the "normal" child. The field is still, by and large, under the spell of the assumption that real childhood is somehow at the end of the path of scientific discovery—that if only their science were complete, a normative picture of the child and of human existence would be revealed. But as William Kessen eloquently asserted as far back as 1979, "It may be wise for us child psychologists . . . to peer into the abyss of the positivistic nightmare—that the child is essentially and eternally a cultural invention and that the variety of the child's definition is not the removable error of an incomplete science."[47] In search of *childhood*, developmental psychology has often missed actual *children*. In the search for "adolescence," actual young people have fallen to the wayside, marginalized as developmental refugees.

Theologians, then, would do well to look to alternative interdisciplinary conversation partners in interpreting young people's experiences. As I have suggested elsewhere, the field of childhood studies presents one helpful alternative to developmental psychology in interdisciplinarity.[48] Childhood studies differentiates itself from developmental psychology in part "through a systematic differentiation between children and childhood."[49]

Theological knowledge is disclosure, not discovery. The theologian does not make discoveries; they humbly receive that which is disclosed through encounter—they embrace revelation. And because it is praxial and not merely theoretical, theology clearly distinguishes interpretation from reality itself. Thus, essentialism and its "discoveries" can only be understood as abstraction. Theology is not content with abstraction because abstraction always produces outliers and exceptions. Because Jesus himself was a refugee and a victim of torture and execution in the name of Roman progress—because of Jesus's association with "the least of these" (Matt. 25, NRSV), ultimately "crucified between two thieves in the place of the skull, where the outcasts belong, outside the gates of the city"[50]—the "outlier" must be at the center of theological reflection and interpretation, not at its periphery as some unfortunate exception. There can be no collateral damage in Christian practical theology.

Both Matthew (18:12–14) and Luke (15:3–7) record that Jesus asked his disciples an important rhetorical question: "If someone has one hundred sheep, and one of the sheep runs away, what will they do?"[51] It is a rhetorical question because, at least from Jesus's perspective, the answer is obvious. Of course, the shepherd would leave the ninety-nine sheep and go rescue the one. On finding the lost sheep, Jesus insists the shepherd would invite "his friends and neighbors, saying to them, 'Rejoice with me, for I have found my sheep that was lost'" (Luke 15:6). Throughout the Hebrew Scriptures, God is described as Israel's shepherd—for example, see Isaiah 40:11 and Psalm 23:1–4.[52] Here, Jesus leaves it to the imagination of the listener to discern who the shepherd might be, but the references to God as the shepherd throughout their religious tradition certainly would not have been far from hearers' imagination. Whether the listener is to infer that the shepherd is explicitly the God of Israel or just a general theological exemplar, it is quite clear what Jesus is saying. God is not content with 99 percent. God's dominion is not just for most people. It is for all. If there is even one who finds themselves on the outside of the gates of God's city, God will go after them. In theology, and particularly in practical theology—which has the normative task as one of its central motivations—the normative task is not to protect and interpret the experience of the ninety-nine but to include and centralize even the one. As Jürgen Moltmann so eloquently put it, "There is no 'outside the gate' with God . . . God himself is the one who died outside the gate on Golgotha for those who are outside."[53]

YOUTH AS DIFFERENCE

Even though the diagnosis of adolescence has provided a helpful frame of interpretation for the ninety-nine, then, for theologians, the paradigm presents fundamental challenges. When it has been allowed to occupy the space of normativity, it produces developmental refugees for whom the paradigm is not only unhelpful but even oppressive. The one lost sheep is not embraced by adolescence; it is pathologized by it. And even for the ninety-nine, adolescence, as such, has had a dehumanizing effect. As Ben Conner put it, adolescence "is a construction that characterizes young people as pathological—a biologically inferior group of disordered people with temporary brain damage facing a crisis who need to be protected from themselves and rehabilitated to be contributing citizens in the future."[54] This is no surprise, given the practices of diagnosis are essentially oriented toward treating pathology and curing illness. But the theological practice of ministry is oriented directly and intentionally toward the one lost sheep, not the ninety-nine. It is more fundamentally interested in caring for people in a way that reflects the care of God than it is in curing a pathology against the diagnostic backdrop of developmental normalcy. Ministry is, at base, the disclosure of God's friendship with humanity, which refuses to objectify the individual, reduce personhood to pathology, or otherwise operate with abstraction rather than lived experience. Theologically, youth ministry cannot be about resolving or curing adolescence. It cannot merely be about creating mature Christian adults. It must be about caring for and *healing* young people in the way of Jesus.

While adolescence constitutes a stage of development between childhood and adulthood—a transitional period marked decisively by its provisionality and its potentiality—youth, from a theological perspective, constitutes a category of human difference. As such, youth represents a full expression of humanity, created in the image of God. According to Michael Langford, "In response to the medical model of youth . . . the theological model would assert that, rather than understanding the young as deficient adults, we should see them as merely *different* than adults."[55] Like disability, race, or gender, youth is not to be addressed as a deficit but as an authentic and authoritative account of what it means to be human. For the theologian, then, youth is not just a problem to be solved through scientific discovery but a source of new knowledge through the praxial and incursive disclosure of God's very being. Jesus did not become the "image of the invisible God" (Col. 1:15, NRSV) on achieving adulthood. Rather, from birth to death, to resurrection and ascension, Jesus is "Emmanuel," God with us (Matt. 1:23, NRSV). Youth is taken into the life and being of God and becomes an authentic location for God's self-disclosure through ministry. *That is, then, what youth ministry means: not disciplining adolescents to becoming mature Christian "adults" but encountering God-as-minister in the being and lived experiences of young people.* Healing, then, for the youth minister, must not be about curing adolescence but rather about affirming young people's being, the full humanity of young people, by deconstructing the hegemony of the adolescent paradigm.

INTERPRETATION AND CHRISTOLOGY

According to Friedrich Gogarten, "The central question of Christology is that of the unity of God and man [*sic*] in Jesus Christ. . . . This unity must be such that neither God nor man [sic] forfeits anything at all, the one of his [sic] deity and the other of his [sic] humanity."[56] The Christological rationale for ministry, then, is embedded in the theology of the incarnation—specifically the relationship among healing, curing, and God's desire to be *with* us. To understand the incarnation as the central problem of Christology is to understand that the incarnation is not just a mechanism for curing the pathology of sin or solving the "sin problem" but is also a genuine disclosure of the reality of God. The incarnation is an authentic revelation and expression of God's friendship with the world, which is fundamental to the God who creates in freedom and goodness.[57] Therefore, incarnation is not a means to an end but an end in itself.[58] Whereas diagnosis is oriented toward *curing* pathology and illness, the incarnation is oriented toward *caring* and the *healing* that comes through the affirmation of humanity in community.

We must explore Christology, the question of Jesus's divinity, then, as it relates to soteriology, or the question of "salvation" from sin. As Wolfhart Pannenberg has written, soteriology and Christology cannot be neatly separated, but nevertheless soteriology is not the "reason" for the incarnation.[59] Incarnation is the presupposition of soteriology, not the other way around. "Christology," writes Pannenberg, "must start from Jesus of Nazareth, not from his significance for us."[60] Christ, in Christ's very being in the man from Nazareth, is not *determined* by history, including the history of human sin. Indeed, Jesus is history's origin and end. God's being is concrete and historical, not static and ethereal. Indeed, God's being is *in* history—in gracious orientation to human beings in their lived experience—and "the self-revelation of God . . . is never purely contingent to history."[61] No external logic—nothing about human life or creation—compels the incarnation as a matter of necessity, as though it would not otherwise be the life and being of God. What *determines* Jesus, if we are to use such language, is his *personal* and *perichoretic* trinitarian relationship: "The Son is the image of the invisible God" (Col. 1:15, NIV). As such, there is nothing true of Jesus that has not been true of God from the very beginning.[62] Only God can reveal God. The incarnation does not represent a change in God. Nor, more importantly, does it represent a mere reaction to the reality of human sin. There is no speculative reality in which God is not revealed in Jesus Christ. There is no God but Jesus.

When God became a human being in Jesus Christ, what was revealed was the being of God as such, in both end and origin.[63] Bonaventure, the great thirteenth-century Christian mystic, understood this. He sometimes referred to Christ as "the Divine Art."[64] According to Elaine A. Heath, "Bonaventure asserts that the incarnation of Christ was not brought about by sin. Rather, the incarnation is the final perfection of creation, the completion of the universe. '. . . .The Incarnation is willed for its own sake, and not for the sake of any lesser good.'"[65] God is Jesus Christ, and Jesus Christ is God, not merely as an intervention but as revelation. God is revealed in the whole history of Christ, including Christ's participation in the history of the completion and redemption of the universe. This history, which is yet unfinished, includes the future of Christ as well, namely, Christ's resurrection from death.[66] The rationale for the incarnation—since incarnation constitutes an authentic revelation of God—precedes the existence of sin just as grace itself precedes sin.[67]

"It is God who justifies" declares the apostle Paul (Rom. 8:33, NRSV). But what is it that constitutes our need for justification in the first place? It is the prospect of separation. As we made clear in chapter 4, God is a person, not merely an idea. God's being is concrete and relational. In the incarnation, God is a human person who encounters human beings in relationship. It is in Christ's humanity that Christ is known as God. As Moltmann put it, Jesus "has to be [human] and nothing but [human]; and it is only in this way that he is completely God. So God's divinity is not cut off from his humanity, and his humanity is not cut off from his divinity."[68] The affirmation of personhood begins and ends not in the affirmation of individuals, as such, but particularly in the affirmation of the one person, Jesus Christ, in relation to other persons.

Salvation depends not on some mechanism or treatment but only on Christ's being with us, on our encounter with the love of God and our communion with the person of Christ. As Paul proclaims, "I am convinced that neither death, nor life, nor angels, nor rulers, nor things present, nor things to come, nor powers, nor height, nor depth, nor anything else in all creation, will be able to separate us from the love of God in Christ Jesus our Lord" (Rom. 8:38–39, NRSV). Christ came to be with us so that nothing will separate us, so that not even sin can keep us from the love of God in Jesus Christ. In Christ, God knows us and embraces us just as we are.[69]

Jesus did not come to save us from sin, to cure us, or to justify us. God came to us in Christ to be God-with-us, to affirm our personhood by lovingly relating to us as person—*thereby* saving us from sin. "God becomes incarnate in Christ," writes Root, "not because it meets God's goals or desires, but rather because God's heart yearns to be near to humanity."[70] Jesus came, in essence, not to *cure* us but to *care* for us. It is precisely because Jesus came to be with us, regardless of necessity, that nothing can separate us from God.

The reason we cannot help but think about salvation when we think about Christ, however, is that Jesus, in taking on the full weight of human experience, must take on the history of sin and brokenness as well. In being God-with-us—the priority of the incarnation—Jesus saved us from sin and healed us. God is revealed as love in Jesus, and God, as love, must suffer alongside suffering human beings: "God must pass through pain at the sight of the evil which works such havoc in that world which [God] so infinitely loves."[71] This is why the cross becomes the logical outcome of the incarnation, even if it is not proper to consider his death as the principal motivation or "cause" of Christology. As Moltmann put it, "It is true that love is brought to its act of mercy through the need of the beloved; but as love it precedes this form of mercy—precedes even the pitiable state of the beloved. The beloved's need is only the occasion (*occasio*) for the love, not its reason (*causa*)."[72] This distinction between cause and occasion helps us understand the proper place of soteriology in our conception of the incarnation. The cause of incarnation, God's love for and friendship with creation, is independent from the condition of human sin and brokenness. God's love would have caused the incarnation whether or not sin existed. Yet because the incarnation occurs under the conditions of the human reality of sin and death, God's care for creation leads to the salvation of creation from sin and death. If we are to conceptualize the relationship between cause and condition as similar to that of care and healing, we can say that care precedes healing and exists independent from the possibility of healing in a formal sense, even as God's care indeed leads to healing. God did not become human in Jesus to *cure* the world of sin. God came to *care* for and love the world.

It is through this caring and loving that healing comes, which includes the eradication of the oppressive power of sin. "Incarnation is anything but indifferent";[73] it is God's *fidelity* in action. But it is not Erikson's kind of fidelity, motivated by generativity. It is not fidelity for the sake of salvation. It is fidelity for love's sake, for Christ's sake, the only kind of fidelity that *can* lead to salvation.

So we should, with Phillip Ziegler, "resist any strong separation between the 'essential' and 'economic' modes of Christ's royal office."[74] In other words, God's being is revealed in Christ's action. But we must also resist any flat-footed reduction of Christology to salvation. The person and work of Christ cannot be separated, but there is a logical priority given to the person of Christ insofar as the work of Christ is mediated by the person of Christ. God does not merely have a function. God is not a job description. The work of Christ *is* the person of Christ. The "saving act" is where "God concretely exegetes his own identity and purpose."[75] God is not oriented toward human beings merely as objects of salvation, as problems to be solved. God is a person who desires to know and be known as a friend.[76]

The church cannot afford any longer to see young people merely as objects of ministry, and we cannot afford to see people—anyone in our congregations—as merely existing to be formed by our ministries. Ministry and formation are not synonymous. Ministry must be first and foremost about connection, resonance, friendship—being with and for our people and our communities. Only then can the church begin to think about "salvation," getting people from point A to point B. Ministry is not developmental. Discipleship is not progressive.

"Man [sic] does not have to deceive himself about himself," wrote Paul Tillich, "because he is accepted as he is, in the total perversion of his existence. But being accepted by God means also being transformed by God—not in terms of a tangible change but in terms of 'anticipation.'"[77] Healing involves the affirmation of personhood, not merely the eradication of pathology. It is not transformation in some tangible form that we can control. It is transformation that only comes through sharing and waiting on God—namely, anticipation. Swinton writes, "Healing is much more than simply ridding a person of particular difficulties. Healing relates to that aspect of care which attends to the inner structures of meaning, value and purpose that form the infrastructure of all human experience, irrespective of the presence or absence of distress and illness."[78] So much of youth ministry has been about resolving—or surviving!—adolescence. The objective has been to develop adolescents into mature Christian adults. But, according to a christological rationale for youth ministry, our objective should be to "share in the concrete and lived experience of young people as the very place to share in the act and being of God."[79]

PERSONHOOD OVER PATHOLOGY

Ministry is about participating with God in healing the world and, as Swinton so eloquently put it, "healing is possible even if cure is not."[80] *Real healing does not necessarily make us "able" where once we were "disabled." It renders inability irrelevant.* We will celebrate cure, of course, and celebrate "the ways the technological alters our world, but not if it opposes or crushes personhood and the environments in which people live."[81] When adolescence as a diagnosis is helpful in the practice of healing, in affirming the full personhood of young people in their lived experiences without an ulterior motive, then we should apply it. But when it hijacks the narrative, when personhood is reduced to pathology, and when we as theologians and youth workers are merely oriented to abstract problems rather than actual persons, then we need to rethink how we are using the term *adolescence*. If diagnosis orients us toward *curing* adolescents, ministry for Christ's sake orients us toward *caring* for young people.

Therefore, we must move from pathology to personhood: "Persons are more than their diagnoses; they cannot be totalized into problems to solve."[82] We transgress the christological rationale of youth ministry when we are oriented toward diagnosing and treating the symptoms of adolescence. The normative authority that we have granted to "adolescence" as the paradigm for interpreting young people's experience has limited our focus and fundamentally oriented us toward pathology and intervention rather than caring and healing. When we can see just how medicalized and diagnostic our approach to young people has become, we will be able to open ourselves to broader horizons—interpretations that consider the whole person and not just their symptom stories. By reimagining young people's experience, we might begin to learn from it, encounter God in it, and allow our sense of the normalcy and superiority of adulthood to be disrupted for Christ's sake.

CHAPTER SIX

From Effectiveness to Faithfulness

When religion, church, and faith are considered only from the standpoint of their expediency and usefulness for society, they are bound to vanish as soon as the purposes of society can be served by other means.[1]

—Jürgen Moltmann

Progress is never satisfied.[2]

—Audi

"Martha, Martha," the Lord answered, "you are worried and upset about many things."

—Luke 10:41

The Sunday school movement flourished during the Industrial Revolution, especially in urban settings with high levels of child labor. In a new industrial society where children were confined to the factories six days a week, Sunday school was adopted as a solution to a social problem out of the anxiety that children might not be adequately socialized without proper education. It was not so much that Sunday school provided the best space for children's own spiritual exploration or that Sunday, as a day of worship, was a day for children to learn theological truths. Rather, Sunday was the most *pragmatic* choice in the new industrial society. As William Kessen explains, "The Sunday school at its origin was not today's pale extension of secular training; Sunday was chosen for the working child's *only* education because it was the day on which blue laws kept the factories closed."[3] Within industrial society's developmentalist framework, children themselves were seen as deficient, in need of resolution through socialization into productive adulthood. Education seemed to be the best technology for meeting that end. Sunday school did provide some theological education, but its primary purposes, its goals, were essentially to meet the problems of industrialization through socialization. To be fair, socialization was basically seen as a theological category at the time. Secularization had not yet fully parsed socialization from what we now call *spiritual formation*. Spiritual formation and Christian education were part and parcel of socialization because Christianity, or at least theism, was a cultural staple. Sunday school founders saw the work of socialization as a spiritual obligation, the very process by which people were "saved to God."[4] To the advantage of these early architects, theologies of children and childhood preceded the Sunday school movement within the Christian tradition, so they had these theologies in their toolbox. Consequently, even though the adoption of this approach hinged squarely on the sociological phenomena of early industrialization and new child labor legislation, Sunday school architects did articulate some theological rationale for their practices, for better or worse. For example, many early adopters of the Sunday school movement believed that a major justification for Sunday school was not only that children needed a place to be when they were not working in the factories but that children are born into sin and that education provides a pathway to sanctification. Thomas Martin, a Methodist pastor and one of the early theorists of the Sunday school movement, put it quite explicitly: "*Native depravity* is certainly the source of all moral evil in the conduct of mankind; and as we bring with us into the world a nature replete with evil propensities, and as these propensities begin to manifest themselves as soon as the mind is capable of expression or action, so the first emotions of a mind, in such a state, will be evil: And hence it will be easy to trace the follies of youth."[5] The Sunday school movement was built from latent theological understandings of childhood such as this.

Whether or not the theological rationale for the Sunday school movement was central or even beneficial, it was there. The later practical iteration we now know as "youth ministry," however, was not influenced by latent theologies of youth the way the Sunday school movement was influenced by theologies of childhood. Youth ministry rose out of the diagnostic and scientific discovery of adolescence. With the emergence of a new adolescent paradigm of interpretation, the theological impulse remained dormant, to say the least, within youth ministry. There were no precedent theologies of adolescence from which to build. So strategies for youth ministries, driven by practical concerns, were not imbued with significant theological reflection. After all, theology had taken a backseat in the epistemic landscape by the time adolescence emerged.

In any case, the early architects of youth ministry found that in light of these new sociological and psychological phenomena, they would need to find a new direction. However late the church was in coming to the realization, they did discern they had to do something different and innovative to address this new phenomenon and appeal to a new demographic. Congregations began to form youth ministries and youth groups, even hiring people to be youth ministers. Because youth ministry was birthed out of a psychological discovery and its corresponding sociological impact, the questions that drove its inception were psychological and sociological, not primarily theological. How do we address the new problem of adolescence? The church's impact on the lives of young people is waning; how can we correct that? The motivating question was, unfortunately, not about how the church and its ministers might encounter the Holy Spirit in the lived experience of young people or open young people to the good news of Jesus Christ. Theology's role was to provide justification for conclusions that were already drawn from pragmatic concerns and a deeper commitment to the social sciences.

As Kenda Dean pointed out, "Youth workers are famously impatient with theological abstractions."[6] This makes sense in light of youth ministry's more pragmatic origins. More recently, though, we can document a new trend, a trend that Dean has referred to as a "new era" in youth ministry and that Dean and Root have called a "theological turn in youth ministry."[7] In 2011, Dean observed that "theological reflection is becoming the norm in youth ministry instead of the exception," going on to say that "while the practice of youth ministry has been with us for quite a while now (70 to 120 years or so, depending on how you count), it has not always been concerned with theological reflection."[8] Looking back on the decade of youth ministry since Dean's observation, one might conclude her outlook was a bit optimistic. Certainly, attention to theology has become more common among youth ministers as the academic field has evolved and the practice has been more professionalized. Large conferences that were formerly designed to offer merely pragmatic resources for youth workers have turned some attention to theology. Dean's own legacy in youth ministry is marked by the work of her students, who represent a generation of youth workers creatively attentive to divine action in the practice of youth ministry and a generation of scholars who think about youth ministry as theologians.[9]

But to say we have reached a new era in youth ministry might be an over-statement. Even with youth workers paying more attention to theological insight, theology has remained somewhat peripheral to the strategic con-struction of the practice of youth ministry, still operating more as justifica-tion than as rationale for the strategies adopted by many youth workers. In the following pages, we will explore just what has provided the rationale for youth ministry and how theology might begin to not only receive lip service but actually become primary to the church's work with and for young people.

SLAVES IN EGYPT

Many scholars maintain that Exodus is truly the first book of the Bible insofar as it provides the starting point for the larger biblical narrative. It is out of the memory of being liberated that the entire story of the Bible emerges.[10] Even the Genesis account, which precedes it in the order of the canon, was writ-ten out of the memory of the Israelites' exodus from the captivity of Egypt.

Prior to liberation, the Israelites were enslaved in Egypt for generations, made to "serve with rigor" (Exod. 1:13, KJV) until they forgot the meaning of freedom. Their very existence was reduced to productivity, to building up Pharaoh's "treasure cities" (Exod. 1:11, KJV). They were slaves, not only by vocation but by identity as well; when they were finally free, they needed instructions on how to live as free people (Exod. 19:5–6). It was at Sinai that God met with Moses to offer these instructions and to give the law that would guide the people in their freedom. Grounded in the priority of God's action—"I carried you on eagles' wings, and brought you to Myself" (Exod. 19:4, NASB)—the people were given a picture of what it means to be the people of God, a theological rationale for living as "a priestly kingdom and a holy nation" (Exod. 19:6, NRSV) in response to the salvation they received by the grace of God.

God's picture begins with the image of what it means to love God: "you shall have no other gods before me" (Exod. 20:3, NRSV). It ends with the picture of what it means to love one another, to encounter other human beings as persons and not as slaves: "You shall not murder. You shall not commit adultery. You shall not steal. You shall not bear false witness against your neighbor. You shall not covet your neighbor's house" (Exod. 20:13–17, NRSV). But between those two images, there is an image that may seem strange to our modern sensibilities and, if we are honest, unfamiliar to many of us who grew up in the church. God tells the people to "remember the sabbath day, and keep it holy" (Exod. 20:8, NRSV). The text paints the image:

> Six days you shall labor and do all your work. But the seventh day is a sabbath to the Lord your God; you shall not do any work—you, your son or your daughter, your male or female slave, your livestock, or the alien resident in your towns. For in six days the Lord made heaven and earth, the sea, and all that is in them, but rested the seventh day; therefore the Lord blessed the sabbath day and consecrated it. (Exod. 20:9–11, NRSV)

Central—quite literally, in fact—to the image God paints of the rationale for being God's people, for responding to and participating in God's ministry, is a command to stop. God tells the people that if they are to live into their identity as God's people, they must rest and allow those around them to rest. This may seem counterintuitive. The people are finally free; should they not be getting busy being holy and doing priestly things? It is just as counterintuitive as the seventh day of creation, when just after they had been given "dominion over the fish of the sea, and over the birds of the air, and over the cattle, and over all the wild animals of the earth, and over every creeping thing that creeps upon the earth" (Gen. 1:26, NRSV), human beings' first task on their first day on the job is to rest with God in the garden (Gen. 2:1–3). It is certainly backward to our modern sensibilities in industrial society, which tell us we should only rest in order to be more productive, and to make better use of our time once we are able to get back to work.[11] But once we remember what this law is really about, once we remember these are instructions for people who have been slaves for longer than they can remember, the reason for the centrality of such an image comes to light. These are people who have been programmed to believe their value and their identity as human beings rested solely in their work, their productivity, their contribution to the larger scheme of Pharaoh's progress. God is telling them that in their freedom, they are no longer slaves. They are not merely what they do. They are human beings and not just human becomings. They are who they are, even and especially in their rest with God. They not only need to be freed from slavery but also from the rationale of slavery: "You are no longer a slave but a child, and if a child then also an heir, through God" (Gal. 4:7, NRSV).

As we discover from the rest of the story, the rationale of slavery is seductive throughout the history of Israel. Indeed, this is why the Pharisees in the New Testament take so seriously the call to keep the Sabbath holy when living under Roman authority. The threat of reverting to a mechanistic identity is ever looming. Youth ministry, I am afraid, has a history of its own kind of rationale of slavery. Please don't read this as an absurd comparison between the plight of actual slaves and the work of youth ministry. But the rationale of slave identity that conflates human identity with social productivity is prevalent in the church's intergenerational relationships. As youth workers and youth ministry theologians, our history of instrumentalism, of reducing our ministerial identity to productivity and seeing our ministry merely as a means to an end, is a seductive image. We need to embrace a new image of ministry not as a means to an end but as a theological task of encountering and resting with God as a response to God's creative and redemptive work. We are not slaves to the outcomes or survival of institutions; we are free to encounter God as we encounter one another and to make God's coming to us, God's taking us "on eagles' wings" (Exod. 19:4, NRSV), an end in itself.

MINISTRY AS TECHNOLOGY

Root notes that "since its inception in the mid-twentieth century, American youth ministry has been entrenched in a technological mindset. North American youth ministry has been *a technology*."[12] Developmentalism brought with it a kind of drive for progress in which development became the essential *telos*, the ultimate goal of history. To bring about the next big thing, the next advancement, was the normative end of which industrialization and technologization were only natural means. In other words, when progress became king, everything else became its servant. As John Swinton demonstrates in his important work *Becoming Friends of Time*, time itself became an instrument for advancement: "This changing cosmological background combined with increasing human knowledge of science and technology provided the backdrop for the development of industrialization and its accompanying perspective on time: industrial time."[13] Industrial time sees everything as moving forward and thus sees the human being as one who must keep up.

"If you cannot keep up and use time productively," writes Swinton, "you will become an economic and social burden on the state, on your family, and on society; you will become a 'handicap' to progress."[14] If, as I have argued, the notion of adolescence we have inherited from the Eriksonian tradition was birthed out of Erikson's own crisis regarding the birth of his son Neil, who certainly represented a "handicap" in Erikson's mind, then it will come as no surprise that this industrial view of time profoundly corresponds to the construction of adolescence as "undeveloped, identity-less, self-centered, commodified, consumers."[15] Like the Israelites in Egypt, young people are reduced to their becoming, their achievement, and their development.

This instrumentalist reductionism is at the heart of the technological. "Technology is science," as Root argues, "used for functional ends."[16] When science is instrumentalized and applied to a problem, the intervention is called *technology*. A problem arises and is diagnosed, and then science creates a tool or medicine to solve the problem. Aspirin is a technology to solve the problem of pain, an umbrella is a technology to solve the problem of rain, a chair is a technology to solve the problem of standing for too long, and a spoon is a technology for solving the problem of soup. It is science used for functional ends. We had a problem, and we needed a solution, so we employed an instrument.

Technology, of course, is not always so crude or innocent as spoons and umbrellas. The twentieth century brought with it a kind of technological revolution. With the new drive for progress that came with developmentalism and the new faith in verifiability and replicability, people turned to science to get them the progress they now saw as the normative *telos* of human life. Progress, the development of industry and society, was the problem of the twentieth century, and as we saw it, technology was going to solve all of our problems. By the mid-twentieth century, our faith in technology reached a peak. This was exacerbated by the World Wars. Our salvation depended on making more and better bombs and planes. In Root's words, "After World War II the battlefield moved from the fronts of Europe and the Pacific to the consumer marketplace."[17] The same technology and technological thinking that allowed us to eat soup and defeat the Germans would now provide the new appliances and TVs that shape the capitalism that would eventually win the Cold War and allow Elon Musk to buy Twitter: "If technology provided the magic to win the war, then technology could solve all our problems, whether those problems be medical, engineering, or even the decline in religious involvement."[18] It is this same principle that birthed youth ministry in the church.

As our faith in technology grew in strides through the 1950s, '60s, and '70s—the same years in which Western youth ministry as we know it was being conceived—we began to place such trust in it that public interest in *how* technology worked began to decline, superseded by a less-than-rational assurance that it "just works." This rift between trust in technology and knowledge of its functioning is partly what Root, drawing on the work of Richard Stivers,[19] calls the "magical" element of technology: "We have little idea how the apps on our phones actually work, for instance, but they do, giving us the efficiency we want as they magically summon a taxi before we even think to need one."[20] Technology, unlike the relics of religion, demands our fidelity in the empiricist landscape of the immanent frame because even if we do not know how it works, we can rest assured that it is scientific— replicable, verifiable, and "real." Thus, technology also, like magic, demands a certain respect—even fear. Because we know it works and can be wielded, we also know it can be wielded against us. Our trust in technology leads to our fear of it. And this is exacerbated by the less-than-rational rift between knowledge and trust.

IS MY PHONE SPYING ON ME?

In light of foreign interference in the 2016 US presidential elections, concerns over internet data security were a theme throughout 2018. Executives from two of the country's largest internet companies, Facebook and Google, were summoned before Congress. These hearings were organized to determine the companies' liability in potential data privacy infractions and the future of government regulation of internet security policy. What most Americans will remember from these hearings, however, will not be their bearing on federal legislation or investigation but the comedy of the apparent ignorance that so many of the lawmakers seemed to display in the odd and anxious questions they put before the tech executives. Highlights from these hearings became fodder for late-night television sketches and viral videos, highlighting the irony of representatives who seemed to be in the dark about how the internet actually works posing questions to experts in the industry.[21]

When Mark Zuckerberg, the founder and CEO of Facebook, sat before representatives, he was on more than one occasion asked to answer what many regarded as basic questions about the technology of the internet and how it works. One senator asked if emailing through one cross-platform messaging service, which is not an email service, would "inform" Facebook's advertisers. Zuckerberg had to calmly resist the temptation to correct the representative regarding what the application to which he was referring was actually for in the first place and simply explain, "No, we [Facebook] don't see any of the content" from that application.[22] To another senator, Zuckerberg was compelled to try to explain how cookies work during internet browsing. One representative asked the question, "Will Facebook offer to all of its users a blanket opt-in to share their privacy data with any third-party users?" to which Zuckerberg promptly answered, "Congresswoman, yes. That's how our platform works."[23]

In a similar hearing, in a somewhat awkward exchange, a representative asked Google's CEO, Sundar Pichai, "I have an iPhone, and if I move from here and go over there . . . does Google track my movement? Does Google, through this phone, know that I have moved here and moved over to the left?" Pichai began to offer a more complicated answer than the representative was apparently expecting, explaining that his location would not be tracked, "not by default," but that he could not answer the question without knowing which location services had been "opted into use" on the device. In other words, Pichai cannot know the answer to the question without knowing more about the device in question.[24] What was a pretty straightforward answer, at least by the standards of those who actually understand how these things work, did not satisfy the representative: "It's not a trick question! . . . It's 'yes' or 'no'!" But at least in terms of perception, especially among more tech-savvy consumers, the representative's insistence on getting a simple answer to a complex question merely revealed his naïveté regarding the complexity of the technology on which he was depending.[25]

What these hearings illustrate is US society's utter dependence on technology and its reliance on technological progress. Even in our ignorance regarding their functioning, and even in the face of the possibility that our devices might deceive or destroy us, we would defend them and regulate them through hearings and legislation. Technology drives us; we do not drive it. The project of modernity is a project of control, to access more of the world so we can eventually wield power.[26] We have come to believe that everything is essentially controllable, so when something eludes our control, when we discover that the world is still in actuality uncontrollable, it scares us. According to Rosa, "Controllability in theory thus transforms uncontrollability in practice into a menacing 'monster,' the kind of threat that lurks around every corner but that we neither see nor control."[27] Indeed, we still must hand our iPhones over to the grandkids to figure out how to make them work.

Even while people depend on technologies like Facebook and Google to magically connect them and improve their efficiency, there is an air of ignorance, and subsequent fear, hovering over technological society. We have no choice, it seems, but to depend on these devices in this technological society, so anxiety over their regulation runs rampant. We love and trust our iPhones or Androids, but even the people we trust to run our government remain basically clueless as to how they work, and so even in our dependence on them, we are fearful of them: Is my phone spying on me? Our technology works like magic, whether it helps us or hurts us. We sorta hate technology, we don't even understand it, but we put our trust in it and we demand that it save us. I wonder if that's not too dissimilar from our relationship to some of our ministry programs. Anyone else think of Vacation Bible School?

THE MAGICAL POWER OF YOUTH MINISTRY

When the church encountered the problems of industrialization and its subsequent social construct of adolescence, it employed the technology of youth ministry to solve them. The "functional problem" that the church faced regarding this new social construction "was low religious commitment (kids didn't like church) and immoral behavior (kids were doing drugs, having sex, and not reading their Bibles)."[28] We placed our trust in this new technology without much choice, it seems, and without fully understanding how it would work. We assumed that, like magic, it would solve our problems by bringing us into the future and developing our young people into the mature Christians we believe they should be. As Root put it, "It is no surprise that the age of the technological, the age in which American society was gripped by a consumption-driven thirst for the new and better (that only a technological society could provide), was also the age of contemporary American youth ministry's beginnings."[29] Youth ministry became our means to an end, a teleological project of development, increasing capital, expanding influence, and producing the desired outcomes—most notably that of resolving adolescence through spiritual "growth" and "maturity." We care little about how it works as long as we make progress. Youth ministry is a technology.

Consequently, we assume youth ministry just cannot operate according to subjective standards of success. How could we even get along without the replicable and verifiable standards of attainable goals and measurable benchmarks? Objective knowledge, according to this mythology, *can* solve our problems and, quite literally, cure our diseases—even the "temporary brain damage" of adolescence[30]—through the magic of technology. The knowledge that can be controlled and managed can be wielded in our quest to actualize our potentiality. Developmentalism is a narrative that tells us all movement, moral or historical, is either improvement or decline, so everything, including knowledge itself, is reduced to an instrument for improvement. The horizons of mystery and ambiguity, even if they are true to our experience of reality, are sidelined as poor instruments in attaining measurable goals. When development is the horizon for rationality, empiricism is a foregone conclusion. On the other hand, theological epistemology is not about discovery but disclosure. When it comes to theological knowledge, "we desire to know in order to participate."[31] Theological knowledge embraces mystery and celebrates it as a location for divine encounter.

The field and practice of youth ministry has been caught up in the wrong narrative regarding its very identity. Since its conception, youth ministry has bought into the narrative of developmentalism, technologization, and instrumental rationality. It has been viewed as an object and robbed of its subjectivity instead of being grounded in theological knowledge. In light of secularization and the church's perceived loss of influence in society, youth ministry has too often been seen as how a young person can be influenced by the church. On an institutional level, it has been seen as how the church will be saved from staunch traditionalism and eventual death. The abstract strategy of "youthfulness" has supplanted the value of the lived experiences of young people,[32] and we have looked to the magic of youth ministry, like a fountain of youth, to rescue the church and give it its "true" identity. Ministry itself has been lost, subsumed by the anxieties of scarcity and decline, until youth ministry can hardly articulate what it means by *ministry* and has essentially been reduced to a technology for reviving and revitalizing the church. The starting point is not the joy of participating in the life and being of God through the lived experiences of human beings but anxiety. This is the anxiety of a church in the immanent frame that has narrowed its horizon and traded in the transcendence of ministry, the mystery of personal encounter, for the immanence of outcomes. Since everything exists on a scale of improvement and decline, ministry must be in the service of progress; otherwise, we have failed. As Craig Keen quite eloquently puts it, "The anxiety exuding from the pores of the leaders of established institutions is thick and acrid. A new ecclesial task force seems to be formed weekly to stem the tide of this recklessness. We no longer even know who we are, we say. And so, we huddle together, haul in bus-loads of experts, look at each other suspiciously in the eye, do market research, and ache to recover our identity."[33] Whether it be to disciple adolescents into mature Christian adults,[34] to help the church "grow young,"[35] to develop spiritual maturity,[36] or to "help develop long-term faith in teenagers,"[37] youth ministry is essentially a *teleological* project of modernity. Even the seemingly innocuous, if not more theological, rationale of "bringing kids into the presence of Jesus Christ"[38] is essentially about solving a problem, or as we put it in a previous chapter, it is about cure over care.

Some have hoped for a shift away from this technological anxiety. Some have optimistically claimed that youth ministry is moving away from its origins as a problem-solving tool of the institutional church. But anecdotal evidence notwithstanding,[39] developmentalism has proven far too strong a paradigm for youth ministry to break from it without a larger and more radical interpretive transition. Trying to engage in a more theological approach to youth ministry without replacing the epistemic and interpretive scaffolding on which it stands is like building a house on the sand. And Jesus told us what that leads to: "The rain fell, and the floods came, and the winds blew and beat against that house, and it fell—and great was its fall!" (Matt. 7:27, NRSV).

As youth ministry continues to be burdened with the anxieties of the institution, there remains a kind of scramble for survival: "How are we going to keep this sinking ship afloat?" The technological question haunts even those who are indeed inclined toward the theological. Whether from shrinking faculties at seminaries and divinity schools, congregants pressuring church leaders to miraculously produce young people, or senior pastors pressuring their youth staff to increase attendance at youth programs, there is still that functional and technological pressure, a desperation for results. Even those of us who are drawn toward the theological turn in youth ministry are swimming in the waters of instrumental rationality. The answer to the question is demanded from us: "What are you going to produce? Why does youth ministry matter?" In response, we reach for answers in expediency: "Look at all the good we are doing!"—and we work so hard to "do good."

MISSIONAL INNOVATION

Recently, a generation of young innovators has been working to discover the next best practice for youth ministry and to break out of the traditional forms of it that we have inherited in the United States, including the youth group model.[40] And this trend is growing. According to Dean, "Christian social innovation, redemptive entrepreneurship, missional innovation, spiritual entrepreneurship—pick your handle—is no longer niche. It's a full-blown, interfaith movement."[41] The trend, as it seems, is no mere fad or passing phase. The Lilly Endowment has poured millions of dollars into the project of innovation, offering grants to institutions of theological education and, by extension, to churches throughout the United States to fund new and innovative models of ministry.[42] As a result, organizations such as Ministry Incubators,[43] Entrepreneurial Youth Ministry,[44] and The Hatchery[45] are sprouting up nationwide. Hundreds of millions of dollars are going into ministry initiatives like Fuller Seminary's Ten X 10 collaboration, which gets its name from the premise that over ten years, ten million young people will likely leave the church—so if they can "reach" ten million young people over the next ten years, we might actually break even.[46]

These programs and projects are often drenched in theological language, which perhaps whets the appetite of those drawn to the theological turn in youth ministry. But while these calls for new and "innovative" approaches to ministry may indeed be innovative in a pragmatic sense and in regard to strategy and methodology, from a normative theological perspective, they remain quite traditional in their approach. The assumption is still that the church as an institution just needs better technology to be more effective. They are still grafted into the technological ethos of North American youth ministry of the 1950s: "Tied up in this technological ethos . . . ministry is always in search of the next big program, model, or idea. In other words, it's looking for the next big technological breakthrough."[47] The horizon of spiritual entrepreneurship, it would seem, is essential to solve a problem, to come up with results and solutions. Indeed, the very starting point of many of these endeavors is to find a problem and determine how the project will solve it.[48]

The Hatchery, a ministry innovation group in Los Angeles that offers a certificate in spiritual entrepreneurship, dedicates one of its modules to studying "technological horizons." "Technologies change the way we see the world," they write, "and technological shifts always herald new directions in human self-understanding and notions of the divine."[49] This approach is not actually innovative from the level of normative judgment. It is, rather, just another extension of the youth ministry we inherited from previous generations, the youth ministry that has struggled for far too long to articulate what it means outside of results and desired outcomes ("becoming") when it applies the term *ministry* to its practice. Youth ministry, when it is reduced to a means to an end, a means of survival, a purely teleological project, is much easier to discern as a project or a program than as a ministry in any theological sense. Innovation has great difficulty accounting for the divine imperative to stop and rest in God. Innovation, according to this technological definition, relies on the assumption that the new comes from *within* history—that history is moving from the past through the present and into the newer and the better; indeed, the newer *is* better. The present is just a bridge into the future, "a rung on the ladder leading to the goal."[50] Thus, innovation is simply the technology of developmentalism. The present reality is instrumentalized for the sake of future becoming. Being is reduced to a means by which the present *develops* into the future.

Not all creative thinking in current youth ministry is necessarily technological. While by and large, the organizations that are driving this missional innovation in the church, not least the Lilly Endowment, tend to begin with a crisis or problem and then try to articulate ministry as the implementation of a solution, there are those in the ranks of this movement who seem to operate from an alternative perspective, to participate in the work of God's creative spirit. To return to Dean, while her organization, Ministry Incubators, cofounded with Mark DeVries, sometimes defaults to a motivation of necessity, an alternative, profoundly theological motivation for creative work in youth ministry is hidden in the logic of Dean's theological work. For Dean, love is the best and only real reason to pursue missional entrepreneurship: "When you love someone, you will spin straw into gold to stop them from suffering. You will take a moon shot to restore joy for young people you love."[51]

Dean's earliest and perhaps most important academic contribution to youth ministry was her image of youth ministry as practicing passion. Drawing direct connections between the passion of young people in society and the passion of Jesus Christ in the gospel, she asks, "If adolescents and Christianity are both so full of passion, then why aren't young people flocking to church?"[52] The intent of the question, though it is packaged in the technological concern for "adolescent religious apathy,"[53] is actually to move away from technological approaches to youth ministry and toward theological approaches that seek to indwell the experience of youth and encounter God in and through it. Youth—"adolescence"—is not just a problem to be solved or a pathology to be cured but "the fingerprint of God" and a "symptom of being human":[54]

> We can no longer view youth as incomplete adults, people who are "missing something" that the institutional church must "supply." . . . If the church fails to offer a theological alternative to secular views of passion, Christian "youth programs" cannot significantly relieve young people who are in distress. . . . If the church's identity crisis is indicative of a larger crisis in American institutional life, youth ministry's potential lies not in reclaiming young people for the *church*, but in reclaiming young people *period*.[55]

Throughout her book *Practicing Passion* and her work in general, Dean invites youth ministry to search not for outcomes of achievement but encounters with the living God. The overall logic of Dean's work is an alternative to the technological rationale of youth ministry, and it invites an exodus, like that of the Israelites, out of the land of slavery that tells us we are what we can produce and into the freedom of relationship with God's Spirit. As she puts it, "Our identity in Christ depends not on our rituals, practices, or moral standards, but only on God's identification with us in the Incarnation."[56]

While Dean's motivations are deeply theological, she fails to sufficiently deconstruct her technological interpretive scaffolding. When the work still begins from a technological question of religious engagement, even if the question leads elsewhere, the search for *newer* and *better* is easily smuggled in. Ministry Incubators celebrates foremost not the inputs of the ministry or the depth of the encounter but the model and strategy of the program. We must learn to prioritize the blueprint for theological ministry in Dean's scholarship that can draw us away from outcomes and toward encounters.

For Dean, the antidote for the technological is joy. Instrumentalism leaves us operating out of anxiety over institutional survival, but joy invites us to encounter God in young people and participate in God's delight in them. Joy is the other side of the coin of passion, bearing the double meaning of looking at the pain of the world in the face without illusion and nevertheless inviting liberation from the anxiety of the technological. In ministry, joy invites us to listen to the right things. To listen to the Spirit instead of our anxieties. It invites us into encounters and liberates us from the tyranny of outcomes. It frees us from the magnetic force of the new and the innovative and draws us instead into the freedom of faithfulness, rest, and creativity.

The difference between innovation and creativity is that creativity, from a theological perspective, is a work of freedom in response to and participation with the creative God who liberates us from slavery and invites us to find rest for our souls (Matt. 11:28–30). It is not fundamentally a work of necessity or ambition. It is a work of love. The logic of creativity is the creative work of our Creator. God created the world because it delighted God to do so. In a way, this undermines the intent of the question "Why did God create the world?"—it demolishes the instrumental categories of goals and outcomes. God did not create the world to do or accomplish anything with it. God created the world for joy. Moving human ambition and anxiety out of the center of youth ministry enables us to fully practice passion and engage in the ministry of God. The church, unhindered by concerns about institutional survival, is free to go beyond itself and be for others—to be that one institution on the planet that exists precisely for those who do not yet belong to it. Youth ministry must not be done out of anxiety; it must instead be done for joy.

All this is not to say that ministry cannot begin from crisis. Recall again the double meaning of passion and joy. Ministry invites us into, not away from, the world's pain and crisis. Certainly, some of the greatest innovations in the church's history were the product of crisis and even desperation. As Dean eloquently put it, "This is the tremendous mystery of faith that Christians celebrate: that joy springs from anguish, that love abounds in passion, that life comes from death, that hope hallows despair."[57] The crisis of technology, however, is not a crisis of faith but rather a crisis of effectiveness—or, perhaps, a crisis of *relevance*. The church, in turning to innovation, has adopted this crisis of relevance as the key to understanding the mission of the church.[58]

As theologians and ministers, our crisis cannot be a crisis of effectiveness or relevance but rather a crisis of faith. Faithfulness is always a higher value than effectiveness. There are things that may work just fine but would not be faithful. And there are things that may have little impact or effectiveness, but we do them regardless as an act of faithfulness. If my only reason for praying is to get something out of it, I'm probably praying for the wrong reason. When our rationale for ministry is dominated by its effectiveness, we risk undermining our vocation as participants in the ministry of God.

LUTHER'S CRISIS

Martin Luther was born in Eisleben, Germany, in 1483.[59] His father, Hans Luther, was a prosperous copper miner of peasant origins who had lifted himself to prestige through work and marriage.[60] It seemed that Martin would continue this upward social trajectory. He excelled in his education, completing his MA degree at twenty-two, the earliest allowable age.[61] But Luther did not follow in his father's footsteps or even stay on a similar path. Not long after he entered the career of law, which his father had desired for him, he took a distinct vocational turn. According to Justo González, "Luther was led to the monastery by concern for his own salvation."[62] Throughout his education, he was "extremely sensitive to the problem of how one could become worthy to receive the grace of God rather than the damning consequences of [God's] righteousness."[63] He was haunted by this concern until it became overwhelming for him. Returning to Erfurt, where he was practicing law after visiting home one summer, he found himself in the midst of a violent thunderstorm.[64] In the storm, he cried out to God. Overwhelmed by his fear of damnation and his utter uncertainty regarding his worthiness of God's salvation, he vowed to become a monk.

This concern—indeed, this crisis—over the assurance of salvation was not only Luther's anxiety but the anxiety and crisis of the time. As Hall put it, "Luther's life absorbed, like a magnet, the spiritual crisis of his age."[65] Concern for eternal salvation was in the water, and Luther was well hydrated. To Luther, the present life was a waiting room, little more than preparation for the life to come. It seemed foolish to him to exert energy toward gaining wealth and status in the present through the practice of law if it meant risking his eternal salvation. Salvation was Luther's crisis. So as a "faithful child of the church," he entered the monastery with the "firm purpose of making use of the means of salvation offered by that church, of which the surest was the monastic life of renunciation."[66] But even as a monk, Luther could not free himself from the crisis. Reflecting on his time in the monastery, in his preface to his Latin writings, he wrote, "Though I lived as a monk without reproach, I felt that I was a sinner before God with an extremely disturbed conscience."[67] This crisis of salvation and damnation, the crisis of his day, became the birthplace of his innovation.

Luther's innovation,[68] a theological innovation that led to the social and ecclesial innovation of the Reformation itself, was the disclosure that it is

God who makes human beings worthy of grace, that we do not need nor can we hope to live up to the standards of righteousness, the standards of "the law" according to any measure of renunciation or holy living.[69] God's righteousness is revealed in the justification of sinners. Therefore, we are free to live in joy and freedom—not fear and anxiety—before God.[70] Works do not bring people closer to God. "Works," wrote Luther, "being inanimate things, cannot glorify God, although they can, if faith is present, be done to the glory of God."[71] We are dependent on God's coming to us, God's "identification with us,"[72] as Dean put it, and we are liberated to work as a response to God's grace, in freedom from striving, not as a prerequisite to our justification. "To fulfill the law," Luther suggests, is not to be more productive in following every rule: "We must meet its requirements gladly and lovingly; live virtuous and upright lives without the constraint of the law, and as if neither the law not its penalties existed. *But this joy, this unconstrained love, is put into our hearts by the Holy Spirit.*"[73] Luther's innovation was, in some sense, an exodus from the innovative. To really live "as if neither the law nor its penalties existed" is to live without the burden of having to move history forward toward progress or development. His was never a concern for the survival of the institutional church but a concern for the reality of God's grace.[74]

Like the youth ministry innovators of today, Luther engaged in his ministerial and theological project from a vantage point of crisis. It was a pervasive and profoundly personal crisis. Luther's, however, was not a crisis of *effectiveness* or *relevance* but of *faith*. It was not a crisis of survival, sustainability, or capital. It was the *spiritual* crisis of the world in which he lived. The crisis of effectiveness is a crisis of methodology, an institutional crisis that is fixated on creating better church programs and gaining back the church's relevance, which is often just code for getting our membership back up. The crisis of faith, on the other hand, is an existential crisis. What was at stake for Luther was not mere institutional survival or an experiment in methodology. It was not about finding a new way to reach the disaffiliated. For Luther, the stakes were as high as the gospel itself, and his innovation was not a task of merely striving in a new direction. It was more like the work of the Sabbath. Luther's innovation, his crisis, was an innovation of joy and freedom—freedom *from* striving. As he wrote in one of his sermons, "God wants to come down to us, God wants to come to us and we do not need to clamber up to [God], [God] wants to be with us to the end of the world."[75]

At issue here is whether we consider faith and the church to be sociological or theological realities: "How have we become a people who so often talk of faith as almost completely coated in a sociological shell, bound almost entirely in measured institutional participation, content to survey variables?"[76] Faith, after all, is a theological category. It must transcend sociological categories of religious participation. Church is a theological reality, not merely an institution to be preserved and expanded. Yes, the church has sociological and institutional qualities. But at its most fundamental level, a theology of the church cannot content itself with sociological analysis. Keen explains the point quite poignantly: "Insofar as the church is a faithful gift of the Holy Spirit it will have escaped sociological analysis, breaking exclusively through the bonds of institutional inertia, the way a fresh breath breaks from outside through pursed lips. It is a body gathered by the Spirit whose members differ from, even as they defer to, one another."[77]

The church's ministry cannot be reduced to an anxious crisis of effectiveness or institutional survival. The church's ministry, where its task is to address crisis, is to address the moment's crisis of faith, a theological crisis. The crisis of effectiveness is fundamentally grounded in anxiety and a lust for survival. The crisis of faith, even in its careful attention to the despair and suffering in the situation, can be grounded in joy and freedom. As Keen again puts it, "In Christ, the church moves out into the world, rejoicing in the opposition it meets there. It rejoices, because it remembers that the Father has already gifted the world with the Son."[78]

FROM OUTCOMES TO ENCOUNTERS

When it comes to missional innovation in the church, the impulse toward the technological has created a fork in the road, so to speak. One direction, the narrow path, leads to the theological—and down that path, innovation is not fundamentally about solving problems but participating in the life and being of God. This is the path of creativity. Surely we are free and invited through discipleship to try new and different ways of encountering young people, not out of a desperation for survival but out of the joyful imperative to rest in God. The other direction, the path that is trod by many practitioners as well as those providing their means through funding and training, leads right back to the technological. Without properly and thoroughly deconstructing the technological impulse in youth ministry, this path is inevitably the path most traveled. If we underestimate just how instinctive the pervasive drive toward progress and production is in youth ministry, if we fail to recognize the technological and diagnostic origins of youth ministry, then spiritual innovation or missional entrepreneurship can become just another technology, merely the instrumentalization of our empathy and theology in the service of development.

With the technological and the innovative, the *new* becomes normative, and encounters are replaced by outcomes. Our metrics for success and our moral horizon are overwhelmingly determined by the desire for something new. Our very sense of identity is co-opted by effectiveness. Far better to adopt Moltmann's view:

> Joy is the meaning of human life, joy in thanksgiving and thanksgiving as joy. In a way this answer abolishes the intent of such questions as: For what purpose [or outcome] has [humankind] been created? . . . For the answer does not indicate ethical goals and ideal purposes but justifies created existence as such. The important thing about this answer is precisely the awkward surprise it contains. When we ask, For what purpose do I exist?, the answer does not lie in demonstrable purposes establishing my usefulness but in the acceptance of my existence as such and in what the Dutch biologist and philosopher Buytendijk has called the 'demonstrative value of being.'[79]

When the new is normative, what we celebrate will not necessarily be that which is meaningful in the actuality of drawing people into encounter with the living God but that strategy, program, or innovation that has not yet been attempted. The technological invites us to scoff at the proposal that "there is nothing new under the sun" (Ecc. 1:9, NIV) and, in our anxious ambition, to respond, "Challenge accepted." Should we continue to wonder why so many youth workers experience fatigue and burnout in their work?

We cannot expect to escape the pitfalls of developmentalism merely with new methods and strategies without finding an alternative theory of ministry. This is what has led many to misunderstand Dean and Root's call to a theological turn in youth ministry. We want to have our cake and eat it too. We want to have theological motivations while still maintaining our penchant for outcomes and development. We want to have *theological* ministries without departing from our *teleological* and *technological* rationale for ministry. But we cannot overcome instrumentalism without departing from developmentalism. We cannot have a theological turn in youth ministry without abandoning the technological rationale that is so indigenous to its origins.

This is why it is also clear that the theological turn is not merely a championing of the importance of doctrine. Nor is it simply applied dogmatics (applying theology like applied sciences) for different outcomes. It is a much more radical paradigm shift. Per Root, "A youth ministry that turns to *theology* seeks to move young people into forms of formal knowledge (to assimilate to the doctrinal). A youth ministry bound in the *technological* seeks to increase numbers and behavior. A youth ministry that turns to the *theological* seeks to share in the concrete and lived experience of young people as the very place to share in the act and being of God."[80]

Developmentalism is the lifeblood of the technological and the *theology* approach to ministry through instrumental rationality. What it eventually forces us to do is interrogate our present experience for those parts of it that bear the greatest potential. But in the *theological*, we seek encounters with young people, not so that we can resolve their adolescence and develop them toward adulthood or even Christian spiritual maturity but because God encounters us in the eventfulness of their lived experience. Because God has come to us on the cross, in the broken body and shed blood, and has disclosed Godself not in potentiality but actuality, we are drawn to the one sheep and not merely to the ninety-nine. We are invited not just to minister in places where there might be a future but in places where development is simply not to be anticipated. We are invited to minister in every place to which God is coming, which is everywhere, including broken bodies and shed blood. If the paradigms for innovation and technology are effectiveness, revival, survival, restoration, and sustainability, the paradigm for the theological is creation *ex nihilo* (from nothing) and the resurrection of the dead.

MINISTRY FOR DEVELOPMENTAL REFUGEES

The theological turn in youth ministry is about encounters, not outcomes. When my brother, Jesse, first walked through the church doors, he encountered something. I believe that he encountered God. He was affirmed in his existence and embraced by a community. But as quickly as that affirmation came, it was undermined by the anxiety of the technological. The youth minister, with his standard of "spiritual maturity," reduced Jesse to his *potential*.

When it became clear that Jesse was not going to develop according to those standards, that he would not increase his religious engagement or change his behavior, the youth minister was stumped and forced to move to the next kid with potential—ironically, that kid happened to be me. Instead of seeing Jesse's experience as a place to encounter God, the youth pastor saw Jesse as a problem to be solved. And when it became clear to Jesse that he was never going to catch his youth minister's "spark" of spiritual maturity or meet the expectations of the youth ministry program—when it was clear that the youth ministry was not going to be satisfied in his being, in who he was already, in what he loved and what gave him joy—the youth pastor gave up.

The theological turn in youth ministry is about taking delight in young people—or more appropriately, enjoying God's delight in young people— just as they are. The theological turn is about changing the question from "How can I capitalize on your potential and influence you to be spiritually mature?" to "Where is God working in your experience, and how can I be a part of it? How can I encounter God with you and in you?" Whereas the technological approach to youth ministry is limited to its search for results, the theological turn invites the youth worker to freely delight in the experience of ministry without anxiety, even in the midst of crisis—to live in the newness of God, which brings a newness even to the old: "When [one] sees the meaning of life only in being useful and used, [one] necessarily gets caught in a crisis of living, when illness or sorrow makes everything including [oneself] seem useless."[81] The theological turn allows us to do ministry in illness and sorrow, in dying and death, in nothingness, because it embraces the horizon of being, the "depth of lived experience,"[82] and the "demonstrative value of being."[83]

The theological turn is youth ministry for developmental refugees. The technological tells us it is a bad investment, a poor use of time and energy, to go after the one lost sheep when there are ninety-nine perfectly good sheep that can be developed toward the success of our endeavors. Developmentalism forces us to prioritize those parts of the present that can be developed toward the future rather than looking with hope toward the hopeless. But this is precisely why ministry must turn to the theological and not to the technological. This is why we must engage and encounter God in God's eventful presence and activity and not simply seek extrinsic outcomes and results.

The theological turn in youth ministry is ministry not just for those who have the passion to innovate and move forward into the future but for those who are open to God's coming to us in the present. It is ministry for Jesse, and it is ministry for Neil Erikson—a ministry that encounters the person in the depth of lived experience, even if their experience will not lead toward some ideal vision of health and normalcy. In order to make this turn, however, we will need an alternative theoretical framework, a theological one grounded in God's action.

CHAPTER SEVEN

The *Locus Adventus*

An Eschatological Anthropology

Only a phantom man thinks that of himself he can know himself.[1]

—Karl Barth

Turning through the crucifixion toward the resurrection of Jesus is a turning to see and learn to see the world through the future that happens already— without ceasing to be future—in the Jesus who is the Christ who is precisely because the Spirit anoints him with the oil of resurrection.[2]

—Craig Keen

So if you have been raised with Christ, seek the things that are above, where Christ is, seated at the right hand of God. Set your minds on things that are above, not on things that are on earth, for you have died, and your life is hidden with Christ in God. When Christ who is your life is revealed, then you also will be revealed with him in glory.

—Colossians 3:2–4 (NRSV)

Often, what hinders us from being able to attend to the actuality of a young person's experience and to encounter God in that place is our expectation, our desire, and, relatedly, our underlying notion of what is "normal" and "healthy." Indeed, it is our very concept of what it means to be human that either opens us up or closes us off to others. We cannot have a broad enough horizon for ministry if we do not include in that horizon the theological anthropology of youth. If our conception of healthy humanity is that it should develop or change according to a particular itinerary, we will find ourselves closed to the experience of someone whose development transgresses our expectation, either by divergence or by omission. To move forward with a theological vision for youth ministry, one that sees all young people's experiences as a location for divine encounter and participation in divine action, we need a theological vision of what it means to be a young person. For that, we will need a theological vision of what it means to be a "normal" and "healthy" human being. We need a theological anthropology of youth. This chapter will seek to offer just that.

After a journey through the various anthropologies that have historically constituted the backdrop of normalcy by which we have judged human experience, and particularly the implicit anthropology of developmentalism, we will explore an alternative account of what it means to be human: an eschatological anthropology that is grounded in expectation without reducing human experience to expediency, futurity, or potentiality. Here I will draw from the insights of theologians generally situated within the reformed tradition. We must engage these sources critically, deductively, and without the illusion that they are divorced from their own contexts. However, for the purpose of this exploration, we will save a more inductive engagement for another space, engaging the ideas themselves as they relate to the problems and issues raised by empiricism and developmentalism in our current context.

THE SUBSTANTIVE FALLACY

One of the core challenges of theological anthropology is that it seeks to answer the question "What does it mean to be human?" (*anthropos*), by way of addressing questions about God (*theos*). In other words, theological anthropology answers the anthropological question theologically. Theologians have struggled over the years to hold *anthropos* and *theos* together in a theologically appropriate way. This is a logical challenge, especially in the epistemic ecosystem of empiricism, because the immanence of human experience often seems to contrast and contradict the transcendence of the divine. God, as Holy Other, cannot be contained in any description of the human being, and it can be difficult to faithfully attend to human experience in any abstract description of divinity. This has led theologians either to neglect the anthropological question altogether—to adopt a disembodied and arcane system for theological reflection that feigns or avoids accountability to the question of human being—or to neglect the *theological* element that should be at the heart of theological anthropology.

Practical theologians are especially prone to neglect the theological vantage point of theological anthropology. As we have outlined in previous chapters, our epistemic landscape tends to privilege nomothetic—generalizable—accounts of knowledge. The most "rational" form of knowledge is the most immanent one. Adequate knowledge must be verifiable, replicable, and falsifiable. The harder the science, the better. So our impulse has been to answer the anthropological question anthropologically, even in theological discourse.[3]

Philosophers, biologists, sociologists, and even legislators have suggested empirical solutions to the anthropological question: "Theological anthropology enters a sphere which was already fully occupied."[4] But theologians must resist the temptation to simply theologize an existing response. A truly theological anthropology will address both sides of the question without accepting a false dichotomy.[5] It will, however, address the anthropological from the vantage point and through the prism of the theological—that is, God's incursive self-disclosure through ministry. As Otto Weber put it, "We exclude the abstractly conceivable possibility that the Christian view of man [sic] is merely a reinterpretation of our self-understanding. The issue is not a change of our self-understanding but a transformation of our existence."[6] We have looked to the human to answer the question of what it means to be human, but an authentic theological anthropology calls us to look instead to God for our answer.

The reformed theologian Emil Brunner laid out an explicit guiding principle for theological anthropology: the "first article" of Christian anthropology is "that man [sic] cannot be known from himself [sic] but only from God."[7] God—not the human—is the criteria for being human. Otto Weber notes, "Man's [sic] very existence is solely who he [sic] is before God."[8] This is why theological anthropology has historically oriented itself around the doctrine of the *imago Dei*—the image of God. According to John Swinton, "The way in which one defines the *imago Dei* can have radical implications for the ways in which one conceptualizes God, and the nature of both the Divine and the human task."[9] Every human law, every practice of the church, every basic human encounter contains within it some implicit logic of what it means for humankind to be created in God's image—understanding that opens or closes the possibility of love and, thus, divine encounter. In short, theological anthropology that takes the *imago Dei* as its starting point can provide an interpretive horizon broad enough to embrace the mystery and diversity of young people.

In the Genesis 1 creation poem, on the sixth day of creation, when God turned to create human beings, God said, "Let us make humankind in our image" (Gen. 1:26). God created human beings, male and female,[10] in God's image. The word *image* in this passage is translated from the Hebrew word *tselem* (צֶלֶם), which also means "likeness" or "of resemblance."[11] In modern Hebrew, *tselem* can be translated as "photograph." So, in creating humankind, God created a living photograph of God: to see humankind is to see God or to see a true representation of who God is. The *imago Dei* bears within it and holds together all the tensions and challenges of theological anthropology. This, perhaps, accounts for the centrality of the *imago Dei* as a doctrine in the face of its relative scarcity, as a concept, in the biblical text.[12] Only the Genesis account mentions it specifically, and in the rest of the Bible, it is implicitly mentioned only a handful of times.[13] Because of its conceptual force in bearing the challenge of theological anthropology, however, it appropriately remains central to the task.

Stating that human beings are created in the image of God is simply a way of naming the problems of theological anthropology. It provides a theological starting point but does little, if anything, to solve those problems. As Barth observed, "We are nowhere told in Scripture what the image of God actually is."[14] The task of theological anthropology is the task of working out what *imago Dei* means and what it means to say that human beings are created as such. Simply employing the term *imago Dei* does not immediately rescue us from the theological fallacy of constituting the human according to the human, considering the human being as a "self-enclosed reality, or as having a purely general relation *ad extra*, to a part or the whole of the cosmos distinct from God."[15] For our purposes, we will refer to this theological fallacy as the *substantive* fallacy in anthropology.

As Oliver Crisp explains, "The substantive account of the image of God" is an account that "equates the image with something substantive about human beings, such as possession of an immaterial substance, or soul, or certain powers associated with the soul or the human person, such as ratio-nality."[16] In other words, substantive anthropology begins with something about the human—a structure or a function—and, from there, extrapolates a characterization or definition of the *imago Dei*. Theologians falling prey to this fallacy set out to discover that distinctive feature of the human being that sets them apart, specifically from animals and the rest of creation, as an image of the Creator. If they can find that unique quality that exists universally in human beings but does not exist in other created beings, they think, then they will have discovered and exposed the *imago Dei*. This is problematic because not only does it transgress the fundamental posture of theological epistemology outlined in chapter 4, prioritizing *discovery* over *disclosure*, but more importantly, it also breaks the rule of the first article of theological anthropology: the human being cannot be known *from* the human being but only from God. Rather than beginning with God—with the event of God's self-disclosure through ministry—the substantive account begins with the human.

Some theologians have critiqued the structural element of this substantive anthropology while trying to maintain a functional element. As Marc Cortez writes, "Any structural definition of the *imago* runs the risk of excluding certain categories of human beings from its definition of humanity."[17] Such an account cannot satisfy what it means to be human because, according to the biblical narrative—Genesis 1:26, in particular—and according to theological anthropology,[18] *all* people are created in God's image. "Male and female, God created them" (Genesis 1:27) not merely *one* aspect of *some* people. While Cortez rightly rejects the structural element of substantive anthropology, however, he does attempt to salvage a functional account by interlocking the concept with relational and covenantal elements. "First," Cortez writes, "the image of God is the task in which human persons serve as God's representatives by manifesting his [sic] presence in creation."[19] The human being is therefore the one who "performs" the *imago Dei*.[20] Cortez does helpfully self-correct: "It would actually be more proper to say that the *imago Dei* is something that God does (i.e., manifests himself [sic]) in and through human persons, a task in which human persons are called to participate."[21] While human beings are certainly called to participate in God's self-disclosure through ministry, it is not the function of the human that constitutes their humanity; otherwise, we run into the same problem we had with the structural element. Human action always comes second, as a response to God's action and God's orientation to human beings.[22]

The substantive fallacy is at play in both structural and functional accounts of the *imago Dei* because in either case we begin with human beings or with human agency. In doing so, we necessarily exclude some humans, either by virtue of their capacities or their behavior, from the primary theological starting point of the *imago Dei*. The *imago Dei* is not a function or a task but a reflection of God's very self, regardless of the human being's ability to emulate it—indeed, in spite of their *inability* to emulate it in their essence or in their action. The *imago Dei* is primarily something about God, not something about humans. The substantive fallacy reduces the theological constitution of human being and personhood to the human. Unfortunately, this fallacy is widely manifest in theological anthropology. The image of God is reduced to human faculties, including but not limited to reason, diversity, creativity, and morality.

The Image of God as Reason

The dominant perspective throughout the history of Western philosophy and theology is that what sets human beings apart from the rest of creation, and by implication constitutes the image of God, is the faculty of rationality or reason. For example, Thomas Aquinas wrote that "Man [*sic*] is said to be after the image of God . . . as regards that whereby he excels other animals. . . . Now man excels all animals by his reason and intelligence; hence it is according to his intelligence and reason, which are incorporeal, that man is said to be according to the image of God."[23] This perspective has become commonplace in the modern world, even in more "secular" accounts of anthropology. What scholars mean, of course, by "reason" is somewhat subjective, but in our Western context, we typically understand the reason as a power of cognition, an ability or capacity to perceive and analyze events, actions, and the reasons thereof with a degree of objectivity that will ensure verifiability, falsifiability, and replicability. In essence, the unique quality of human beings that sets them apart from the rest of the animal world is their ability to reflect on their existence. The "rational" human being can describe and ask questions of their experience using language. They can separate themselves to some degree of objectivity and wonder about meaning and cause. This, we suppose, is a uniquely human ability. Intellectual superiority to the animal world is distinct to human beings and therefore it is what makes us human. This rational account has become so commonplace that it is considered all but common sense, not only in science and philosophy but in theology as well. Gregory of Nyssa defined the human being as a "rational animal," univocally identifying rationality with the *imago Dei*.[24] While in modern theology this view has come under scrutiny, the perspective is alive and well in some circles of theological inquiry.[25]

But this account of human being has violent implications for those who are not perceived as possessing the powers of "reason" and language. In this view, as Swinton observes, "The more intellectually endowed a person is, the more human they become . . . the less intellectually endowed a person is, the less authentically they will image God."[26] With this rationalist anthropology, as with any substantive account of the *imago Dei*, a contingency is introduced: full humanity is made contingent upon that capacity or function that is considered to be the unique and defining quality of being human. Those who have yet to develop intellectual capacity, and those who have not and *will* not develop it, are implicitly proto-human or subhuman. Traditionally, the capacity of rationality has been defined primarily by men and has been viewed socially as a capacity belonging especially to masculinity (rugged male objectivity contra female subjectivity and emotionality). As a result, this view has not only reified hegemonic masculinity and misogyny in society but has aided in the historic subjection of women to social and systemic dehumanization. Though the implications may be slightly less documented, they are no less significant in the lives of children and young people who, in a gerontocentric society that equates rationality with adulthood, do not bear this apparently uniquely human quality. Hans Reinders, Swinton, Benjamin Conner, and others in the field of disability theology have also pointed out the implications for people who live with cognitive disabilities. They remind us that we cannot presuppose a narrow concept of intellectual rationality as a universal human capacity. As Reinders puts it, "If the point of our lives is what we are capable of doing, the implication must be that a human life lacking in the capacity for purposive action will be pointless."[27] This substantive account of the *imago Dei* as a capacity of reason will necessarily produce marginal cases, and, as Reinders again puts it, "there are no marginal cases of being human in the loving eyes of God the Father."[28] With the apostle Paul, "we are convinced that one has died for all" (2 Corinthians 5:14). Every person who draws breath in the world is a person that God loves, even enough to endure crucifixion. If there is a "marginal case" in any theology or anthropology, if there is any "refugee" of a system of thought or practice, we can rest assured that God goes with them as the shepherd who goes after the one lost sheep (Luke 15). God's stubborn insistence that each one matters precludes the possibility, from a theological perspective, of any "marginal case" regarding the status of being human. Everyone is created in God's image. A child or even an infant is no further from God, no less created in the image of God, than an adult. As Frederick Buechner put it, "When it comes to the forgiving and transforming love of God, one wonders if the six-week-old screecher knows all that much less than the Archbishop of Canterbury."[29]

The Image of God as Human Diversity

As Swinton has observed, a key mark of all substantive anthropology—of any attempt to define human beings "by something *within themselves*"—is that it leads "to the exclusion and alienation of the weakest members of society."[30] This structure or function of being human inevitably issues a backdrop of normalcy against which all variance is essentially pathologized. As we discussed in chapter 6, when a notion of adulthood or maturity is allowed to set the terms for what it means to be human, then youth is interpreted or "diagnosed" according to deficits. Anthropologically speaking, this constitutes a reduction of the humanity of those who occupy the social category of youth, even if adult society still fetishizes the fantasy of "youthfulness."[31] This problem has risen in history especially regarding gender and sexuality, at least in the West. Those who have proposed anthropologies have been male, identifying with a sort of masculinity that is stylized according to objectivity and rugged individualism. Thus, "the male sex [becomes] normative for humanity."[32] This is an implicit anthropology of biological determinism; there is a specific way of being human, a male way, and any deviation into female subjectivity, any variance from that norm constitutes sub-humanity. Elaine Graham summarizes,

> Feminists have argued that dominant views of human nature, self, knowledge, action and value are constructed *androcentrically*: that is, they assume that maleness and masculinity is the norm for adequate accounts of what it means to be human, how I achieve a sense of self, what counts as verifiable and reliable knowledge, the relationship between thought, will and action, and the sources and norms of ultimate value, truth and beauty.[33]

To correct this hegemonic form of substantive anthropology, some have adopted a more pluralist anthropology, one which embraces difference rather than attempting to reconcile it. From this kind of thinking they construct a kind of "two-nature anthropology, a vision of human being as divided into two distinct kinds, each with identifiable differences that become normative for the sex."[34] Another option is a kind of apophatic anthropology wherein what it means to be human is only articulated through the rejection of any universal or totalizing account of humanity. David Auten writes, "Eccentricity is one of the most fundamental features of your life. You are by virtue of your *difference* from everything else around you."[35] In other words, there is not one thing that makes one a human being; indeed, that which makes one individual human may differ from that which makes another human. "You stand out in *some* way from the myriad other things that stand out in their own ways."[36] Our difference is all we really have in common. "God is different as different can be. It is in *that* likeness that we are created and called into participation with existence."[37] This participation with existence, however, implies that we must not allow eccentricity to be reduced to individualism. Because of our difference, humankind is expressed more creatively and authentically in community. The God who is revealed in difference, even in the triune difference of Father, Son, and Holy Spirit, is a God who is love (1 John 4:8). There is a unity to be realized in difference. Thus, an anthropology of difference that embraces the uniqueness of humankind might thus embrace youth not as pathology, but as a difference in which we are invited to delight.[38]

There is still, however, a theological risk in embracing such an apophatic anthropology. Feminist and disability theologians have pointed to the problem of associating the image of God with one specific aspect of humanity, but if we seek to associate God's image with the plurality of difference in humanity, then even our diversity becomes substantive insofar as it constitutes another aspect of our humanity to be associated with God's image. God's own personhood may become subsumed into an aspect of humanity, this time into the plurality of human expression. We may have solved the anthropological question anthropologically by creating a theological problem. Humanity casts God in its image rather than the other way around. This eccentric or pluralist anthropology still constitutes a substantive anthropology insofar as it sets out to know the human being from the human being, even if it does so without falling into abstraction and totalization. The self is the "inescapable starting place" and the initiating subject of this anthropology, not God.[39] An anthropology begins with self will always smuggle in a certain standard. Auten, for example, notes "There are many forms of difference. What really matters, however, is the very personal discernment of the difference that God calls *you* to be, in the totality of your life."[40] Not all human beings, however, may bear the powers of "personal discernment."

You Are What You Love?

In his groundbreaking work *Desiring the Kingdom* James K. A. Smith lays out a philosophical anthropology to undergird his project of reorienting Christian education toward "*formation* of hearts and desires."[41] In order to do so he offers a pointed critique of two claims in society regarding what it means to be human, two "options in philosophical anthropology."[42] These options are to see the human person fundamentally as a "thinking thing" or "as believer."[43] Smith critiques both of these models of anthropology as too abstract and "reductionistic."[44] His former critique in some parallels our earlier critique of rationalist substantive anthropology. His concern, however, is not that we will produce refugees or marginal cases and reduce some human persons to a subhuman status. Rather, he fears that Christian education will be too narrowly focused on ideas. "The result is a talking-head version of Christianity that is fixed on doctrines and ideas . . . because the church buys into a cognitivist anthropology, it adopts a stunted pedagogy that is fixated on the mind."[45] As welcome as this critique may be for our purposes, his concerns are less about a distortion of theology and more about a limitation in pedagogy.

Regarding the latter—the human-as-believer anthropology—again, Smith is less concerned about theology than pedagogy. In this perspective, a human being is not just a "talking-head" but a person with commitments and orientations that run deeper than mere cognitive assent to ideas. "What defines us is not what we think—not the set of ideas we assent to—but rather what we *believe*, the commitments and trusts that orient our being-in-the-world."[46] Smith attributes this perspective to the Reformed tradition of Christianity, "developed precisely as a critique of more rationalistic construals of Christianity."[47] But Smith is not satisfied with this perspective, either. "The person-as-believer model still gives us a somewhat reductionist account of the human person—one that is still a tad bit heady and quasi-cognitive. And that is significant because of the pedagogy it yields."[48] In Christian education, a "believing" pedagogy still essentially focuses on *in*formation rather than formation. It may be less interested in discrete ideas, but it is still interested in orienting the person to the correct set of commitments that underlie their cognitive conclusions.

Smith recognizes the substantive fallacy in these anthropologies. "They take the slice to be the whole and thus absolutize just one aspect of the human person."[49] Smith's alternative to these ideas, a shift he seems to see as radical in regards to anthropology, is to suggest that human beings are not thinking things or believing animals but "essentially and ultimately desiring animals."[50] Smith summarizes, "To be human is to love, and it is what we love that defines who we are."[51] He goes on to describe this anthropology as essentially teleological. It is not our ideas but our *ends* that should be our primary concern. Human beings are always being formed toward certain ends and goals. This provides a fine scaffolding for the kind of work Smith is interested in doing pedagogically. His shift from "you are what you think" or "you are what you do" to "you are what you love" is interesting and helpful in many ways, but does it suffice as a *theo*logical anthropology?

It is certainly helpful for philosophers to engage in the conversation regarding Christian education, but from a theological standpoint, Smith's philosophical anthropology falls short of providing a theological anthropology for ministry. While Smith seems to regard his "shifting the centre of gravity . . . down from the heady regions of mind closer to the central regions of our bodies . . ."[52] as a radical shift, he has not yet, in doing so, shifted the center of gravity to the theological. To say, "you are what you love" is not actually radically different from saying "you are what you think" or "you are what you do." In fact, this is implied in the title of Smith's chapter "*Homo Liturgicus*"—a Latin phrase that can be understood to mean, "the human as a liturgical being" or "the human as determined or shaped by their work or service." Perhaps the title is somewhat unfortunate, because his primary intention is to see the human as a "lover" or "worshiper," but the difference is not so radical. Nor is the difference between the human as a "lover" so radical from the human as a "thinker" or a "believer." These claims all share the quality of emanating from within the person, within the self. The two claims—you are what you do and you are what you love—were, after all, side by side in the mind of Sigmund Freud, the architect of the ego and the super ego in psychological thought, and Erik Erikson's teacher. When he was asked, "what must a 'normal' person be able to do well?" Freud answered, "*lieben und arbeiten*" ("to love and to work").[53]

The really dramatic shift, therefore, would not be for us to move from "you are what you do" to "you are what you love," but instead to insist, "you are a child of God" and to answer the question posed to Freud; "a person must *be* loved." The *theological* shift would be to insist on an anthropology that emanates not from the self but from God. We are not determined by what *we* love but, as Swinton has put it, "a person's humanity is defined and maintained by God's gracious movement towards them in love."[54]

To be human is not to love, as Smith suggests. Rather, to be human is to *be* loved. In this way human beings reflect God's image perfectly and always, regardless of their actions, thoughts, or even their desires! I anticipate that this claim will be perceived as quite bold. One might well ask how someone can be said to reflect God's image if they are committing sin or perpetuating great injustice? How can one reflect God's image if they are fundamentally oriented *away* from God? But herein lies the real radical shift of theological anthropology. God's image is not determined by human beings or their behavior—whether it is evil or good. It is not just one aspect of the human, nor is it *every* aspect of the human, nor is it the diversity of human subjects before God that reflects God's image and reveals true humanity. God's image is reflected in the love God shows toward every human being. And at no point in all human sin and injustice does God's love for the human being ever waver or diminish. Thus, it is always perfect for every human person.

Only God, only Christ, reveals the *imago Dei*. We can make this audacious claim because the image of God in human beings is not revealed by some substantive correspondence between how people act and how God acts. The image of God is revealed only in how God loves human beings. And God loves human beings perfectly and always, despite their actions. In fact, God's love, and thus God's image, is revealed most fully and exhaustively in Christ's passion, death, burial, and descent into hell—when God met us at our very worst. We are united to God, then, not in our strength and glory, but in the cross itself, when God loved us completely and perfectly. To claim that one is created in God's image is not to elevate them to a certain standard or demand that they love rightly, but to acknowledge God's condescension to us in coming to be with us in Christ. To claim that one is created in God's image is to simply say, "God loves you!"

HUMAN BECOMING: THE ANTHROPOLOGY OF DEVELOPMENTALISM

Developmentalism bears within it its own implicit substantive anthropology. As a pervasive ideological framework in Western society, with corresponding economic and social implications, developmentalism has provided perhaps the dominant interpretation of the meaning of human life and, by extension, what makes us human. It has been fertile soil for the kind of rationalist and hypercognitive anthropologies mentioned above, as well as other anthropologies that take their starting point in the human being rather than in the theological. Most particularly central to developmentalism's account of what it means to be human, however, is the quality of growth or *becoming.* By becoming I do not simply mean movement and encounter. Indeed, such concepts are not necessarily developmental in essence or form. But *becoming,* under the auspices of developmentalism, refers specifically to the actualization of one's potential—in the case of youth, the potential to achieve the social status of "the adult." Developmentalism reduces being (*ontos*) to becoming (*telos*); the human being isn't so much a human being as a "human becoming."[55] What determines an adequate account of what it means to be human in developmentalism is the actualization of potentiality, not the actuality of lived experience. The abstract and static, yet unattainable, status of adulthood provides the target toward which the human being must always be moving, becoming, to properly be understood as fully human. The meaning of human life is contingent upon its movement toward this *telos.*

This is the basic orienting principle of Erik Erikson's work. His "eight ages of man [*sic*]," his "schedule of virtues," and his "stages in the ritualization of human experience" all represent a kind of universal ideal for "healthy personality" development that provides a backdrop for interpreting all human experience.[56] The picture that these stages paint—figuratively insofar as they offer an image of the meaning of human life, and literally insofar as Erikson himself characterized human growth in charts resembling an ascending staircase—are of human life as an ascent toward maturity. This ascension metaphor relegates every stage to a deficit position until it has reached its peak: "generativity." According to James Fowler,

> *Generativity,* for Erikson, means creativity and productiveness, to be sure, but is also means much more. It means, deriving from the same root as *generation,* the adult person having found ways, through love and work, creativity and care, to contribute to the conditions that will provide the possibility for members of the oncoming generations to develop their personal strengths at each stage.[57]

The *telos* of human life, in this view, is essentially *telos* itself. The point of development is development for development's sake. Human life is a constant transition from deficit to resolution through crisis.

"Healthy things grow." So goes the adage of church growth and innovation specialists. One might say that to be human is to grow. Developmentalism supposes that to be human is to *become*, moving toward maturity, and it even goes as far as to imply that adulthood (whatever that may be) is, in fact, the truest form of humanity. Developmentalism sets all accounts of what it means to be human on a scale of improvement and decline. There is really no such thing, in this imaginary, as simple movement. Everything is mechanism, everything contributes or detracts. Nothing simply changes; it develops. The anthropology of developmentalism emanates from the human being. It is human being's "good or optimal development"[58] toward "ideal personhood"[59] through maturity that sets them apart, distinguishes them from nonhuman animals, and determines the *imago Dei*. This cuts out, or at least diminishes the humanity of, those who are not yet mature, those who are maturing *improperly*, those who are in *decline*, and those who simply *will not* mature. The child is still becoming human. The young are still on their way to "full human status"[60] by virtue of their youth and are thus reduced to a pathology or a subhuman status.[61]

We see the pervasiveness of this implicit anthropology represented in the dominance of socialization theory. We have tended to make sense of "the child as a potential and inevitable supplicant at the altar of the corporate rationality implicit within the social system."[62] In his work on childhood, Jenks addresses this perspective. He offers the example of Oscar W. Ritchie and M. R. Kollar, who, "writing solidly in their tradition, state: . . .' Children are not to be viewed as individuals fully equipped to participate in a complex adult world, but as beings who have the potential for being slowly brought into contact with human beings.'"[63] Jenks goes on to say that "as a consequence of the adult member being regarded within theory as mature, rational and competent (all as natural dispositions), the child is viewed, in juxtaposition, as less than fully human, unfinished or incomplete."[64] When youth is seen from the vantage point of developmentalism, it carries within it a distinct, though implicit, dehumanizing quality.[65]

For MacIntyre, "In early childhood . . . human beings have not yet made the transition from being only potentially rational animals to being actually rational animals."[66] In MacIntyre's scheme, the human must be directed in some way toward the good, always oriented toward and moving in the direction of that good, discerning along the way appropriate actions to contribute to the acquisition of the highest good. "The first step in this transition," that is, the transition from potentially rational to actually rational existence, "takes place when the child becomes able to consider the suggestion that the good to the achievement of which it is presently directed by its animal nature is inferior to some other alternative good and that this latter good therefore provides a better reason for action than does the good at which the child has been aiming."[67] By centralizing this transition, equating the fullness of humanity with practical reason,[68] not only does MacIntyre fall into the cognitive trap he is trying to avoid[69] but, like Smith, the shift he is trying to make—from humans as independent and higher than animals to humans as dependent practical reasoners—turns out to be similar in form to that from which he is trying to depart. Dependent or independent, human beings are still understood as essentially prototypical and transitional. *Ontos*, "being," is conflated with and consumed by *telos* in such a way that there can hardly be such a thing as "being" at all. Can the child be understood as human if humanity is the movement from childhood to adulthood?

There are certainly ways to apply developmental categories of interpretation without falling into *developmentalism,* perhaps as it is possible to talk about biology without falling into biological determinism. But as soon as these developmental observations are taken up into abstract schemes and universal itineraries, they become hegemonic; development becomes developmentalism.

Unfortunately, in practical theology, more has been done to baptize this developmentalist anthropology than to replace it. As we mentioned above, James Fowler and others not only adopted a kind of developmentalist perspective but used it to help legitimize practical theology as a form of knowledge in an empiricist regime of epistemology. "The goal of terrestrial life is thus to pass through the stage of existence in such a way as to actualise and preserve, so far as possible, one's spiritual essence and so to enhance the prospect of membership in the communion of saints."[70] Practical theology has done little theological work to correct this anthropological perspective.

From a theological perspective, however, human *ontos* (being) is not merely an empty shell awaiting actualization through *telos*. The Christian tradition holds that the only intrinsic of humankind is, in fact, death.[71] The pinnacle of maturity, too, is death. Whatever qualitative distinctions we have attached to maturity through social construction, they are neither natural nor intrinsic. "Because in some human beings there are no intrinsic qualities to build on, any anthropology and ethics that proceeds from such qualities cannot be truly universal for that very reason."[72] Human *telos*, even at its best, is but filthy rags (Isa. 64:6). If we are to rely on human potentiality for the value and constitution of humanity, we are without much hope. But the Christian tradition also holds that being is not dependent upon *potentiality* for its value.[73] The possibility for human value comes from without. It is not something within the human, waiting to be expressed or realized, that gives meaning to her life. That meaning and value is ascribed to the person extrinsically, by God. "Being human is never without meaning, because it always means something to God: because there is God, there is purpose."[74]

There is no value to being except by virtue of its relation to God. "'Worth' is received rather than earned."[75] *Ontos* is, therefore, relational. The variances of human diversity and the disorder of human desire notwithstanding, it is by God's action in relating to us as our creator, and doing so in the way in which God has, through freedom and love, that human beings are determined to be human—and thus, valuable. We must talk about God if we wish to speak of what it means to be human. It is not through the actualization of *ontos* through *telos*, but in the affirmation of *ontos* through *adventus* (coming or arrival) that being finds its meaning and its quality.

The paradigm for theological anthropology, then, is not *becoming*, nor is it mere being, but it is God's *coming*—the advent of God-with-us so that we are, essentially and fundamentally, being-with-God, and consequently human being-with one another.[76] Horizontal relationships are an extension of our vertical relationships. Our being-with-God precedes our being-with one another. The "reciprocating self" is only a response to that which makes us human; reciprocity is not determinative of human *ontos*, but rather symptomatic of it.[77] It is not, foremost, our relationships with other humans that constitute a reflection of God's image. Rather, it is our being-with-God, our humanity before God as the object of God's love and friendship that reflects God's image and thus constitutes our humanity. Humans are not fundamentally *teleological* but *eschatological* beings.[78] If the theological rationale for anthropology is not *telos* but *eschaton*, then we must address the eschatological error implicit in developmentalism. By conflating the qualities of growth and progress with maturity and development, making development not only an arbitrary and natural process but a social and ethical goal toward which human beings are meant to strive, developmentalism lays claim to how we are to view history and its ends.[79] Developmentalism's basic claim about history is that it is a linear progression of the past moving through the present and into the future. This claim about history reduces the present to *transitionality* and determines the human according to the human's *orientation* to the future by way of the pursuit of goods.

The human's orientation toward a prescribed goal or *telos*, then, becomes the determinative quality of the *imago Dei*.

Reflecting on Erikson's work, Donald Capps writes,

> Erikson asks: How does the individual acquire and maintain a sense of orientation in this ongoing process of change? Orientation language abounds in Erikson's writings . . . he stresses the importance of having a clear sense of orientation in life, a steady image of where we have been and where we are going. He rejects the romantic notion that disorientation and disorder are more 'natural' to the human species and therefore more desirable or worthwhile.[80]

Erikson was troubled by disorder and disorientation, perhaps because of how much of it he had endured himself in his childhood. Indeed, it was the disorientation of fathering Neil, a child with Down syndrome—a child who, by Erikson's understanding, was from birth improperly oriented—that propelled Erikson to return to positivist psychological reflection.

So, when Erikson's orientation language is taken up into abstract formulas of developmentalism, it prescribes a particular orientation. This orientation toward the future as potentiality is fundamental to developmentalism's anthropology. When developmentalism, then, co-opts theology in practical theology, it does so by a distortion, an error in eschatology that confuses and conflates development with the coming of God. In developmentalism *the* future is *our* future—the future that proceeds out of the potential inherent in the present. But in eschatology, *our* future is *God's* future, and our identity is hidden in and held by Christ. In what way is God oriented toward us? God's orientation toward us is such that God's future determines history, and not the other way around. "God reveals himself [sic] in the form of promise and in the history that is marked by promise."[81] It is *eschaton*, not *telos*, that determines the world and its history.

When we talk about God's future, we may think of apocalyptic images of Christ's coming reign in glory from the books of Revelation or Daniel. But we are also permitted to think of the incarnation and of the actual birth of Jesus in Bethlehem. Jesus, even at birth, is incarnation in actuality and not merely potentiality. It is not *telos* that makes his birth significant, it is that through him, even his infant body, God is with us. Even then, even now. The eschatological reality of the renewal and restoration that comes in God's arrival, *from* nothing in us, *to* the nothing that we are, is what makes the actuality of the incarnation and of human *ontos* and dignity the truest thing about every living person. It is love that makes us human. "In this is love, not that we loved God but that he loved us and sent his Son to be the atoning sacrifice for our sins" (1 John 4:10, NRSV). This is not some ethereal or abstract concept, but the flesh and blood particularity of the man from Nazareth. The present is made worthy not by virtue of its orientation toward the future but by God's orientation, as the God of promise, toward the present.

There are, of course, passages in Scripture that remain perplexing. While it is clear throughout the gospels that Jesus does not prioritize adulthood over childhood—indeed, Jesus said, "unless you change and become like little children, you will never enter the kingdom of heaven" (Matt. 18:3, NIV)—we are yet challenged by Paul. It is a bit jarring, for example, to read 1 Corinthians 3 in light of Jesus' perspective on childhood. Paul writes to the church in Corinth, "Brothers and sisters, I could not address you as people who live by the Spirit but as people who are still worldly—mere infants in Christ. I gave you milk, not solid food, for you were not yet ready for it. Indeed, you are still not ready. You are still worldly. For since there is jealousy and quarreling among you, are you not worldly? Are you not acting like mere humans?" (1 Cor. 3:1–3, NIV). There is an apparent condescension in Paul's understanding of the child and an apparent developmentalism in Paul's understanding of spiritual formation. However, even here, we must not miss the subversiveness of Paul's explanation of maturity. While it seems as though Paul is teaching a kind of developmental hierarchy of the adult over the child, he goes on to say, "Do not deceive yourselves. If any of you think you are wise by the standards of this age, you should become 'fools' so that you may become wise" (1 Cor. 3:18, NIV). Even within his apparently teleological explication of spiritual "growth," the traditional standards of the wisdom of age are upended. Paul still clearly locates wisdom not in the "growth" of the individual, but in the coming of Jesus Christ. In this sense, even Paul's understanding of what it means to be human is eschatological and not teleological.

ADVENTUS VS. FUTURUM

If eschatology and not teleology is to provide the logic of theological anthropology, then we must be clear in distinguishing eschatology from development. Where development prioritizes an itinerary of growth and qualifies everything according to the standards of progress, eschatology prioritizes actuality. This may seem somewhat counterintuitive at first notice. Is not eschatology characterized by a preferential option for the future? However, if we understand that our future comes to us extrinsically as God's future and does not issue from the "history of the old,"[82] we can look to everyone, regardless of whether they are developing "optimally" or not, as that in which the saving presence of God is to arrive. As Kathryn Tanner puts it,

> The consummation of the world is not brought about by the world. A gap exists between the results of world processes and the world's consummation, a gap to be bridged by a God with the power to reverse those results, the power to bring what is otherwise absolutely unexpected into existence.[83]

Therefore, we need not mine the present for signs of its potentiality or seek to invest our energies where we might have the greatest influence upon the present for its development into the future. Instead, we can look to every present as the location to which the future of God is coming. We can hope in actuality and not merely in potentiality.

The fundamental grounding for this eschatology is the theology of the cross. Hope is not born from the notion that there is necessarily something in the present bearing qualities that correspond to a prescribed future. Indeed, we can hardly say any intrinsic potential exists within the mangled corpse of a Galilean man hanging from a Roman cross. Under the theology of the cross, eschatology depends not on any expectation that something should have the potential to progress according to a standard of maturity. Hope does not expect development, it expects resurrection.

The cross, therefore, represents an indispensable element of Christian eschatology. The hope for the future represented in the resurrection of Jesus is hope for the crucified Jesus. Only by recognizing the "god-forsakenness of all things" can we hope for the redemption of all things, for "the whole of reality."[84] In this way, eschatology allows our energies as youth workers to be directed toward developmental refugees, young people who do not otherwise measure up to the standards of potentiality—things that are worthless according to developmentalism. Hope does not refuse to see the god-forsakenness of the present, so it does not optimistically search for those parts of the present that have the potential to be developed into the future. Rather, it insists on the belovedness of all creation. Hope looks not to potentiality, but marches straight into actuality and impossibility awaiting God's self-disclosure through the resurrection of Christ.

The paradigm of hope is Advent—*adventus* as opposed to *futurum*. As Moltmann explains it, "*Futurum* means what will be; *adventus* means what is coming."[85] Hope, in the paradigm of *adventus*, is hope for the radically new creation, a hope for what is coming into our impossibility. According to Hall, "Christian hope, which is first of all hope in God and not in human institutions, system, ideologies, and 'dreams,' does not have to lie to itself about what is really there in the world."[86] It is shaped by the story of "one who was 'crucified, dead and buried.'"[87] Looking at the cross, there is no way to see life as a potential for the crucified. But resurrection can be expected insofar as it is coming, as opposed to becoming. "The *novum ultimum* – the ultimate new thing – does not issue from the history of the old."[88] The coming of God provides the real basis for eschatological hope. *Adventus* depends on nothing from the present but meets it with grace and hope. *Futurum* judges the present according to its standards and demands its conformity. Therefore, it does not have a horizon broad enough to include the present that stands in its very face. *Adventus* is the coming of God by grace alone and, as such, it is the coming of God into the *nihilo*.

LOCUS ADVENTUS

According to the doctrine of *creatio ex nihilo*, the work of creation is essentially an act of grace, for it is an act performed completely in the freedom of love. There is nothing outside of God that compels God to create the world, and so there is nothing outside of God that compels God to come into the world to offer redemption. God will save the world with the same freedom in which God created the world.[89] Creation, resurrection, and consummation are all the work of God, by the grace of God, from nothing–*ex nihilo*. In the *creatio ex nihilo*, the human being, as the *imago Dei*, is understood at the most fundamental level in theological anthropology as the *locus adventus*: the location of divine arrival.

To be human is to be the location in which we expect God to arrive in history. And since God's future determines history, the God of promise is already present according to promise. Every *nihilo* becomes *locus adventus*, a location for holy expectancy. Every encounter is sanctified and made holy, not because of itself but because of the God who arrives in its place. The useless human being, the *nihilo*, is the *imago Dei*, because in waiting with that which has no potential for development God might be revealed to us as Christ breathes the Holy Spirit into the lungs of those who wait.

In *adventus,* as opposed to *futurum,* our expectation does not proceed from the situation itself. That for which we hope does not proceed from the potentiality of the present. What we hope for is a radically new thing—the *novum ultimum*[90]—so radically new that it bears no analogy to the present. According to Keen, "The hope of a future in Christ is a hope that does not lean on present and available ability, some power-pack of recovery."[91] Hope is not latent in the present, but comes to it from outside, from God through God's arrival. "Truly being human is not constituted by intrinsic features that mark the domain of the self, nor is it a developmental stage of potentialities entailed in human nature."[92] Potentiality—as with its analogues in development and innovation—does not bear within it a broad enough horizon to reach the kind of radical hope that is born in Christian eschatology. As Keen puts it, "An act of the properly potential may restore, satisfy, and complete, but will never break the chain that keeps it tethered to the essentially old. It may be relatively, but it isn't absolutely new."[93] The paradigm for this *novum ultimum* is the resurrection of Jesus Christ. "The hope of the world comes as the resurrection of the Crucified comes . . . by the Spirit of life and redemption."[94]

The resurrection of Jesus Christ—the resurrection of a dead body which contains within it no generative potential for a life of its own, outside of decomposition and perhaps fertilization for other lives—permits us to look upon every human experience, even those which do not have potential, as a location for this expectation and an occasion for hope. We are permitted to look upon every human being as a person with and to whom God is arriving, and to minister to them by waiting with them for God's arrival, even in the most hopeless of situations. It is only from the perspective of the God of promise, the God who has resurrection, not development, as God's future, that we can look upon broken bodies and shed blood as the location of God's coming. "Only in the perspective of this God can there possibly be a love that is more than *philia,* love to the existence and the like—namely, *agape,* love to the non-existent, love to the unlike, the unworthy, the worthless, to the lost, the transient and the dead; a love that can take upon it the annihilating effects of pain and renunciation because it received its power from hope of a *creatio ex nihilo.*"[95]

Since that which we anticipate in *adventus* does not emerge from present possibilities within the person—since our anticipation is not for some potentiality latent within them—even while we wait in anticipation, the person's existence is not reduced to some pedestrian transition in a process of development. Their actuality, their being, is sanctified according to the future that is coming *to* it. Hope does not negate the past or present or try to look past actuality. Hope does not forget.[96] It remembers the past and attends to the present as the very location to which God is coming. The future for which we wait in that place is not a future that can be conjured through the investment of energy or the application of some innovative strategy. It is, after all, God's future for which we wait, and it is only by virtue of it being God's that we can, by grace, hope for it to come to us in the present and as our future as well. "For if we have been united with him in a death like his, we will certainly also be united with him in a resurrection like his" (Romans 6:5).

MINISTRY IN THE *LOCUS ADVENTUS*

Because of God's unity with human beings in the cross of Jesus Christ and the hope we have in the coming of God, what constitutes human being is not the actualization of potentiality or the development into maturity (or generativity), but the eschatological anticipation of God's arrival and God's ministerial communion with human beings. The truth and reality of human life, according to the apostle Paul, "is hidden with Christ in God. When Christ who is your life is revealed, then you also will be revealed with him in glory" (Col. 3:2–4, NRSV). Human life, human being, is *locus adventus*—a location for hopeful anticipation of divine presence. Ministry, then, is not determined through the paradigm of "investment" or "innovation" but through waiting.

Moltmann writes that "patience is the greatest art of those who hope. Hope accepts the 'cross of the present' in the 'power of the resurrection.' It takes upon itself the real unredeemed state of the present as it is, the torture and the pain of the negative, without resignation and without illusion."[97] Ministry takes place in the sharing of personhood as we share in the anticipation of God in the "cross of the present." Faith in Christ "transports one into the heart of the world's darkness. It does not function to insulate one from what is wrong; rather, it brings with it a greater courage to confront the world's wrongness."[98] We are permitted to look upon the cross, a symbol of impossibility and death, as a location to which God is coming and, therefore, as a location of hope. Ministry takes place in the sharing of personhood as we share in the anticipation of God. This eschatological anticipation has a proleptic quality insofar as, like Mary's song in Luke 2, it takes the future of God as a present reality without ceasing to see it as future reality. To embrace humankind as the *locus adventus* is to already, now and not yet, expect God to be present and active in one's life. According to Abigail Visco Rusert, "Encountering young people with the expectation that God is *already* at work in their lives removes the pressure that we must somehow conjure God up for them—or worse, attempt to play God for them ourselves."[99] Ministry itself, God's ministry through the Spirit, reveals the person in their humanity and allows us to see Christ in them. We do not bring to the person an essential definition that precedes actuality. We do not operate in abstraction. We wait for them to be disclosed to us in relationship.

The human being as the *locus adventus* is revealed only in relationship through the particularity of God's action in the concrete lived experience of the human being; humanity is disclosed theologically through God's ministry. It is for human beings, as ministers, to wait in expectation for that action and to seek ways of participating in it. This is the human side of ministry, which belongs primarily and definitively to God.

I invite those working with youth to attend to the lived experience of young people, to share their place,[100] not for the purpose of influence or "formation," but to wait with them for the coming of God. Our task in ministry, then, is no longer a process of spiritual formation or development, and we are no longer agents of formation or development. We are, as ministers, those who wait on God's agency and God's self-disclosure through ministry; whatever formation may come in ministry will come from and through God's arrival into the person and, by extension, their present situation. As ministers, we wait on and tend to God's arrival, prayerfully naming it and witnessing to it along the way. Our task is essentially the reception of God's ministry. There is a primal passivity to this reception, but in that passivity our agency is restored to us. Waiting bears within it its own intensity—indeed, according to W. H. Vanstone, "waiting can be the most intense and poignant of all human experiences"[101]—and in this way it bears its own kind of agency. "*Any* kind of waiting presupposes some degree of *caring*."[102] Even agency is a gift we receive passively as those who could not, without God's grace, attain it through our action. As those who, in encountering God, receive God's action, ministers are agents insofar as they perceive that action in the life of another. Only God, however, can disclose Godself to us. The ultimate agent of ministry is always the God revealed in Jesus Christ.

There is an implicit imperative to action in this passivity. Philip Jacob Spener, the theologian and leader of the pietist movement that brought reformation to the Lutheran church,[103] had a keen awareness of the importance of God's action and its priority in relation to human action. He was deeply invested in human participation in ministry. We might suspect that Spener and those in subsequent spiritual awakening movements, including August Hermann Francke and John Wesley, would take issue with seeing ministry fundamentally as waiting on God. Is this not an excuse to do nothing? Is this not just a lazy spirituality? But Spener might surprise us. He did write, "Let us not abandon all hope before we have set our hands to the task. Let us not lay down our rod and staff if we do not have the desired success at once."[104] All this is quite characteristic of the fervent hope that motivated Spener to spiritual action and piety. But he doesn't end there: "What is impossible for men remains possible for God. Eventually God's hour must come, if only we wait for it."[105] In our modern world, where transcendence is reduced to a commodity and immanence sets the terms for what constitutes truth and rationality, it is difficult for us to connect waiting with action. Passivity, for us, is often synonymous with inaction. But the passivity of receiving God's grace is galvanizing. It awakens us to God's transcendence in immanence and calls us to participate. We set our hands to the task precisely because it is God who will accomplish it. We set our hands to the task because for God all things are possible, even in our impossibility. We actively wait on God. We do not work only in those locations where our action can be effective, but we work in every location where God can arrive—which is everywhere.

The anthropology of the *locus adventus* opens up a new and liberating vision for ministry—not only for young people but for youth workers and youth ministers as well. If youth ministers perceive young people as objects of ministry and themselves as the primary agents of ministry, they burden themselves with the work that only the Holy Spirit can do. They will inevitably pressure young people with the weight of that burden even as they crumble beneath it themselves.

CHAPTER EIGHT

Good Fruit

He who loves his dream of a community more than the Christian community itself becomes a destroyer of the latter, even though his personal intentions may be ever so honest and earnest and sacrificial. God hates visionary dreaming.[1]

—Dietrich Bonhoeffer

The fruit of the Spirit is love, joy, peace, patience, kindness, generosity, faithfulness, gentleness, and self-control. There is no law against such things. And those who belong to Christ Jesus have crucified the flesh with its passions and desires. If we live by the Spirit, let us also be guided by the Spirit.

—Galatians 5:22–25 (NRSV)

I was the director of youth ministry for the church of which I am now the pastor, a United Church of Christ congregation in Ramona, California. As a young and ambitious youth worker, fresh out of undergraduate studies, I had dreams of creating the most effective youth ministry in town. I also took networking with other youth ministers in the area very seriously. Having cultivated relationships with several youth workers at other churches, I occasionally got invited to speak or lead discussions with young people at other churches and at the Bible club at the local high school. When I visited these other ministries, I could not help but compare them with my own. I noted the quality of their facilities, their resources, and especially the number of young people they had in attendance at their gatherings. By all the metrics I was taught to use, these ministries all seemed to be very effective. There were lots of young people, and they all seemed to know a lot about the Bible. I was often impressed by the spiritual maturity of the young people at these other churches, and I began to notice a trend. Many of them seemed to really take their spiritual formation seriously. They read their Bibles on their own at home, they evangelized to their peers at school, and they even prayed with their families. Despite my concerns about the theological differences I held with these other ministries, I could not deny they were having a noticeable impact on the lives of the young people who attended them. Meanwhile, it seemed the young people at my own church were not nearly as mature in their faith. Few of the young people we had at our gatherings actually read their Bibles much at home. They were not leading the Christian clubs on their high school campuses. To my knowledge, they were not evangelizing or praying with regularity. If I mentioned the apostle Paul or Moses, I had to give plenty of background before anyone had a clue who I was talking about. "This Moses . . . was he friends with Jesus?" We even had a few young people in our group who did not consider themselves Christians. They came anyway, and we loved them. It did not really matter that they were not Christians. They were part of our group, and they belonged.

But I began to wonder if I was failing. Was it not my job, after all, to cultivate spiritual maturity in these young people, to help them discover Christ, accept the gospel, and grow in their faith? I mean, what did it say about me that we had atheists in our group and they were not converting? I was reading the Bible and praying with these young people. I was preaching the gospel of Jesus Christ as best as I knew how. Why was I failing to make "super Christians" out of them? I tried to increase the pressure, to intensify my expectations of them and even introduce ultimatums—"Five people need to pray out loud, or we cannot play any games tonight!" "If you don't bring a friend to the movie night, you cannot come"—but none of that felt right, and none of it lasted very long. In increasing the pressure on the young people in my ministry, I was also increasing the pressure I placed on myself. I began to question my calling and started to feel myself burning out. I felt alienated from my own vocation, my own identity, my calling. Maybe I should have done something else with my life. I was exhausted, and it all felt wrong.

But then something in me began to change.

When I was buried deep in my feelings of failure, burnout, and alienation, I found myself sitting in the wilderness at a camp and conference center in the beautiful San Bernardino mountains of Southern California. As their ministry leader, I was there with the college-aged young people from my little Ramona church at a retreat event called Briefing.[2] The keynote speaker at the event was Bart Campolo, whose main message was that we, as Christians and especially as ministers, should not try to *change* anyone but simply *love* everyone, trusting that love changes things. Though this message was supposed to be for my college students, it ended up being transformative for me. It was a simple message but profound, seemingly taken right out of Mother Theresa's playbook.[3] "If your goal is to change people," Campolo said, "you're not gonna make it! . . . You're gonna burn out fast."[4] These words cut to the very core of my frustration and confusion. I may not have been achieving the outcomes toward which I had been trained to orient my programs and resources. But what if I was asking the wrong question? What if rather than asking whether I was producing mature Christian adults, I should have been asking whether I was actually loving these young people well? What if I was measuring the outcomes when I should have been measuring the orientation of my input and particularly my own openness to God's action in these young people's lives?

As I pondered that simple but profound message from Campolo, as well as the reading I had recently taken up in the works of Henri Nouwen and Andrew Root, I began to realize I was looking at these young people in the wrong way, and by extension, I was looking at ministry itself in the wrong way. I was only seeing and measuring the ways young people could be *changed* and *influenced*—how they could be developed by my ministry. You see, all the things I was desiring—spiritual maturity, acceptance of the gospel, enthusiastic participation in evangelism and religious activity—were outcomes born of a developmental rationale for ministry. I sought the spiritual development of the young people in my care, so development was the thing I measured as I weighed the value of what I was doing against the expectation of getting young people to reach my idea of what mature Christian faith was supposed to look like. I saw my own vision of what spiritual maturity was, and I made it my mission to develop young people toward that end. I was so obsessed with *telos*, with outcomes and potential, that I was missing out on the actual people I had before me (*ontos*). The value of the lives of these young people, their being, was limited by my expectations for them and reduced to mere becoming—to the possible future that I thought issued out of their innate potentiality. I had been grasped by the anthropology of developmentalism, and I was burning out under its pressure.

What I needed was a new approach to assessment born of an alternative theological anthropology, a new vision for what it meant to be human. Then I would be able to adopt new criteria, theological criteria, for what it meant to be faithful and "successful" in youth ministry. In this chapter, I intend to outline just such an approach to youth ministry assessment.

Throughout this project, I have been implicitly deconstructing many of the traditional metrics for youth ministry assessment, even as I hope to have offered some constructive theological rationale for the practice of youth ministry. If developmentalism—*telos* and pure potentiality—no longer provide the rationality for our ministry, we can no longer measure success and failure against our ability to get young people through their *adolescence* and into adulthood with faith intact.

The church must learn to measure its faithfulness, and thus its success, in ways other than the outcomes it produces regarding the faithfulness of young people, especially when that faithfulness is conflated with adherence to doctrine and/or affiliation with religious programs. We must instead assess the success of our participation in ministry according to the *processes* by which it is conducted, the inputs of "love, joy, peace, patience, kindness, goodness, faithfulness, gentleness and self-control" (Gal. 5:22). These come not by our work of discovery but by the spirit of God through our openness to God's incursive self-disclosure through the act of ministry itself. There is a division of labor when it comes to ministry, and youth ministry is no exception. God is the primary actor, and God is responsible for outcomes. Our job is to follow Jesus and to participate in God's ministry, trusting God with the outcomes.

GIVE ME RESULTS!

In his famous book *Life Together,* Dietrich Bonhoeffer made the somewhat notorious claim that "God hates visionary dreaming."[5] Of course, anxious that his pronouncement might have been a bit too harsh, many have sought to explain his meaning into oblivion. He could not have meant that theologians and ministers should stop dreaming for the church, could he? This certainly does not sit well within our ecclesial culture of achievement, with our infatuation with the new, our penchant for innovation, and our apparent desperation for better models and strategies for ensuring the survival of the church. But perhaps we should allow Bonhoeffer's meaning to be as sharp as the words he used to convey it. Bonhoeffer goes on to write, "The man who fashions a visionary ideal of community demands that it be realized by God, by others, and by himself. He enters the community of Christians with his demands, sets up his own law, and judges the brethren and God Himself [*sic*] accordingly."[6] The magnetic force of modernity, the acceleration of the immanent frame,[7] pulls us toward measurable expectations, dreams of vitality and innovation, thereby pulling us away, if Bonhoeffer is right, from the very people with whom we have been called to minister.

The innovation trend, grafted into instrumental rationality, is fundamentally invested in outcomes. Indeed, it is blinded to much else. These outcomes construct the criteria by which we judge the church and indeed "ministry" itself. It asks us to measure our ministry so that we can replicate it in other contexts. But if we do away with instrumental rationality and technological approaches to youth ministry, how are we to measure our success? In other words, in the theological turn in youth ministry, how do we know if we are doing well?

In our current epistemic ecosystem—call it the *immanent frame* or the *empiricist regime*—we have come to trust in nomothetic forms of knowledge over idiographic knowledge. This is perhaps most pronounced among youth workers and theologians because their very field of practice, the practice of ministry, is itself contested under the immanent frame. Ministry has felt pressure to constitute its necessity according to its efficacy and expediency rather than its faithfulness to Christ. Thus, the center of gravity in ministry has shifted from the more subjective, yet profound, experience of divine encounter to the magnetic and mythical abstraction of objectivity. In theology, as in any practical reasoning, this is unsustainable. Youth ministry does not need to substantiate itself according to the metrics of this empiricist assumption of the "absolute." It can return to its native epistemology, a theological epistemology such as the one outlined in chapter 4. We can abandon the substantive anthropology of developmentalism and embrace the fact that "[we] are not beings whose only authentic evaluations are non-qualitative as the utilitarian tradition suggests."[8] We can learn to allow the more subjective, yet more profound, criteria of divine encounter to be our metric for assessment.

Adults have placed a premium on outcomes in our relationships with young people. Even outcomes of holy living that are expected from many visions of spiritual "maturity"—praying with consistency, leading Bible studies, quoting Bible verses, and evangelizing—are empiricist. We love them because we can measure them. Since its origins, as Root observes, youth ministry has been understood as a technology for solving the crises of religious affiliation and participation. "As a technology created to functionally solve these problems," Root writes, "youth ministry could only be judged by its increased capital; if *more* kids were coming to church or youth group on Sunday and Wednesday, and if more kids were sober and sexually pure, youth ministry was successful— it was meeting the functional end it was created for."[9] In a society that is as possessed by the desire for productivity and achievement as ours is, youth ministry has felt the pressure to compete.

In my own ministry in Toms River, New Jersey, it was a constant concern among older generations that there are so many other activities for young people to engage in that they no longer have time for church. "They never used to play sports on Sundays," they will say. "If only they could just cancel all sports on Sunday mornings, young people would come back to the church." When I heard this, I tried to remind them that our Jewish friends in the United States have been dealing with this reality for a long time. Sports on Saturdays have never been taboo, yet the Jewish faith persists. These other activities that young people are apparently choosing over religious activity are activities that provide some sort of capital—social or otherwise. So in the pressure to compete, youth ministry tries to measure itself according to the kind of capital it can provide—a sort of "spiritual" capital. We seek, through the technology of youth ministry, to provide young people with the "seeds and tools"[10] they need to allow the faith to continue into the future—not only so they will have what they need to navigate life but so they eventually return to the church, perhaps after they have children of their own.[11]

Even youth ministry theologians and educators who do allow for the possibility of focusing on inputs rather than outcomes in assessing the success of ministry have an underlying teleological bias for human accomplishment and improvement. Youth ministry educator Dave Rahn offers an evenhanded approach to youth ministry assessment. He outlines both outcomes and processes as potential focuses for assessment and looks as well at the underlying "reasons for doing assessment," both internal and external motivators.[12] While he allows for external motivations for doing assessment (i.e., a denominational leader, a senior pastor, a Christian education committee, etc.) and for outcomes to be a focus of assessment,[13] Rahn cautions his readers to balance such an approach with a preference for the internal motivation of faithfulness and a focus on processes of ministry (inputs) rather than a program's outcomes. "Here's the lie in a nutshell," writes Rahn: "If we can count on the fact that our right efforts will bring about the desired results, it should be fair to target outcomes as the focus of our ministry assessment."[14] In referring to this as a "lie," Rahn qualifies his allowance of attention to outcomes. He goes on to say, "Our partnership with God in ministry means that we do as we are told and leave the results up to [God]."[15] Rahn ultimately encourages youth workers and theologians to assess youth ministry not according to the results one can measure but according to the faithfulness we bring to the task. However welcome as this shift may be in a society that is otherwise consumed by marketing and institutional results, the shift is not radical enough to shake us from our obsession with improvement and development. The assumption remains, even in Rahn's work, that what is measured is ultimately human action, even if that action is more about process than outcome, and what accounts for ministry is ultimately a structured program that must grow and "continuously improve," even if it is God who is responsible for the growth.[16] The radical shift we require is one that shifts assessment out of the developmental rationale of improvement and decline and into the theological rationale of God's action in lived experience.

WHAT IS MINISTRY?

Because of the empiricist impulse of the immanent frame, we tend to think of ministry in terms of human action that corresponds to goals. Ministry is a practical reality, and we tend to reduce it to practices. But as Andrew Root has boldly put it, "Ministry itself can only be conceived as a practical reality because it is first a theological one," and he elaborates that "it is the practical (concrete and lived) theological conception of God's being as the becoming of ministering subject to human subjects called to respond to God's action of ministry by becoming ministers themselves."[17] The human action of ministry is distinct from and yet dependent on God's action as minister. To reduce ministry to human action is to succumb to synergism, which is to claim human action as divine action itself; that is to say, when something is done well by human beings, we can embrace it as a divine act, stripping divine action of any transcendent cause of its own.[18] When we measure our success in ministry according to replicable outcomes and verifiable metrics of development, we foreclose on the freedom of God to act as a subject. In other words, because God is ontologically a minister, to reduce ministry to an object is to alienate God from God's very being.

The third chapter of Exodus tells a story of Moses's encounter with the mysterious subjectivity of God. Moses, who had been raised by royalty in Egypt, presumably interpreted his world and his experience through the lens of Egyptian pantheistic and animistic epistemology. The divine and human worlds were interconnected through a reciprocal-relational matrix of necessity and responsibility. Everything on which the Egyptians relied for their survival and flourishing was controlled by a deity. Every season of life, every catastrophic rhythm of destruction and death, was upheld and maintained by a god. There were gods of sun and moon, of air and the river. Everything had a god, and every need of human beings depended on their being in good enough standing with the gods to be afforded the means of their flourishing. Moses's relationship with the divine was an objective and a transactional relationship, determined by necessity and appeasement, command and obedience, supply and demand.

When Moses, who had fled from Egypt and was now keeping sheep for his father-in-law, came on a mysterious flaming bush that was burned but not consumed, his intuitive impulse was to name it. After God tells Moses to remove his sandals and listen, after God tells Moses the story of his people's suffering and the promise of their coming liberation, Moses asks the question, "If I come to the Israelites and say to them, 'The God of your ancestors has sent me to you,' and they ask me, 'What is his name?' what shall I say to them?" (Exod. 3:13). In other words, Moses wants to know the nature of this transaction. Which god is this? Is it Ra, the god of the sun; or Horus, the avenger? Is it Set, the god of storm and desert; or Tawaret, the goddess of hippos? "Who are you, and what are you the god of?"

But this God is not determined by a function or duty. This God is not to be reduced to mere *doing*, to a mode or a utility.[19] This God is *being*, subject and mystery. God's answer to Moses is, "I am who I am" or "I am who I will be," which is, under the circumstances, a way of saying, "You have to *know* me to know *about* me, so just watch." God tells Moses, "You shall say to the Israelites, 'I am has sent me to you'" (Exod. 3:14). And then this subject, this I Am, lays out a plan to liberate the Israelites from their suffering, a plan that includes Moses but belongs in principle to God alone. This work is God's, but this work will also be gifted to Moses. For Moses, this work is not to be reduced to the solving of a problem. How presumptuous a reduction that would be! It is not as though Moses, through great strategy and innovation, could liberate these people. His work is about participation and faithfulness, not effectiveness. As such, Moses's action will be *ministry*, and it is in this action that he will know this I Am, this mysterious subject who burns before him as a minister and not as an object.

Human action in ministry is connected to God's action in ministry through the personhood of human beings as subjects created in God's image and called to reflect that image through action of their own. It is through a differentiated unity of divine action and human action that we can begin to conceive of ministry and therefore of what qualifies as its success. Moses's work was never the same as God's work, even as God worked through Moses. It was God who liberated the people from slavery in Egypt. But Moses's act of ministry was gifted to him as his own because it first belonged to God's very being. Moses became a genuine participant in ministry by the grace of God. Ministry is, in essence, a category of grace, just as sanctification is a category of justification. The human act of ministry is different from God's, but in the person of Jesus Christ, through the Spirit's work of bringing something from nothing (of *creatio ex nihilo*), ministry is gifted to us as authentically our own. The fruit of the Spirit becomes evident even in human beings' experience and in their participation in the liberating and life-giving movement of the Spirit amid human situations and experiences.

ENDEAVOR TO TELL STORIES

When we speak of ministry, we are speaking in theological terms. This, in fact, is one of the key issues we face in youth ministry—we have too often tried to speak of ministry in corporate, psychological, sociological, or purely pragmatic terms. "Ministry" has been reduced to the models and programs we implement, and as such it is measured by its innovation, its resources, and the outcomes it produces.

"Are more young people attending the church or fewer?" When we have reduced ministry to human action, this is the question from which we in the United States cannot seem to escape. If the answer is "more" or "better" or "faster," we think we must be doing a good job. But if ministry is fundamentally about God and God's action, then the questions become more about love, joy, and kindness and less about more, better, and faster.

What if we asked not "How many are there?" but "Are they experiencing God? And how?"

When we are dominated by questions of functionality and outcome, we skip past naming the mystery of divine encounter and allow our understanding of youth ministry to stay limited to what we can quantify and replicate. At most youth-ministry conferences where youth workers gather to network and continue their education, you will find a plethora of seminars and presentations that will give you "tools" for "growing" your ministry, "connecting" with young people, solving the problems of the nones and the dones. You will find a whirlwind of anxiety regarding the effectiveness of youth ministry. Even conferences that do attempt to privilege the theological will sometimes inadvertently centralize the technological.[20] Organizations such as the Princeton Institute for Youth Ministry that have a strong and storied history of centering themselves around the theological turn in youth ministry have at times themselves succumbed to the anxieties of institutional decline and have engaged in projects that center on the pragmatic technology of innovation.[21]

We have thought like power brokers and CEOs when we should think like theologians. Because ministry is theological, when we speak of ministry, we cannot really speak in terms of measurable outcomes or replicable models and strategies. This is not to say there can be no discussion regarding such things. It is only to say that when we talk about these things, we have ceased talking about ministry *as* ministry. Talking about programs of social structures is not inherently problematic, but when this talk becomes a de facto placeholder for the ministerial, we have abandoned the theological task of recognizing the mystery of our encounter with God. To speak theologically about ministry, which is the only way we can speak of ministry *as* ministry, we must speak in terms of God's *being* as a minister. We must speak of God's eschatological and sanctifying interruption of human experience and action, and to do so we must learn to tell stories.[22]

According to Jüngel, "If thinking wants to think God, then it must endeavor to tell stories."[23] As we discussed in chapter 4, theological knowledge or ministerial epistemology is determined not by the discovery of facts but by the disclosure of persons—and particularly, the person of Jesus Christ: "No one, not even a believer or a Church, can boast of possessing truth, just as no one can boast of possessing love."[24] Theological knowledge is relational, and as such, it is ministerial. Only by encountering God as minister through the experience of ministry does one come to know God. God is revealed in

Jesus Christ. The theologian is only a theologian by encountering this God who comes to us in resonance—more on resonance below—by participating in God's self-disclosure through ministry that we receive from the person of God. We can't quantify or measure this experience. We can only describe and participate. In short, theology is mystery.[25] A mystery, as opposed to a puzzle, cannot be solved. A mystery is without resolution.[26] We only engage mystery by encountering it anew. We cannot control the mystery, nor can we control the conditions by which we engage it.

Jüngel does note, "Although it cannot be resolved, it desires to be grasped."[27] What he means by this is that just because mystery isn't a puzzle to be solved doesn't mean we can't try to understand it. We may not comprehend it fully, but we are invited to apprehend it. Indeed, mystery compels us to give an account of it, to name it and narrate it.[28] That is the work of theology, including practical and ministerial theology. Doctrine, appropriately understood, is the art of understanding and naming a mystery that cannot be contained in any defined space. To resolve the mystery, as the most rigid dogmaticians have attempted to do, would be to step outside of the mystery, to step outside of the theological, and to abandon the doctrine of God for a sham certainty.

However, the appropriate response to the realization that ministry cannot be quantified and measured is not resignation. Some may wrongly infer that if we cannot employ our traditional developmental metrics for the success of our ministry with young people, then we must simply refrain from assessment, withdrawing from the question of whether we are doing ministry well. Not only would such resignation threaten to perpetuate some deeply problematic practices in ministry; it would also represent a failure of ministry itself. "This mystery," writes Gustavo Gutiérrez, "must be communicated and not kept for oneself; it is not the possession of any individual or group."[29] We must stop seeing assessment as something we do *after* the work of ministry is done, something we do in an incubator or a laboratory, involving flow charts and graphs in a static space separate from the work of ministry itself. We must begin to see that assessment is integral to ministry, simultaneous with participation, and it happens through the narration of experience through story. We must see that narration itself is an assessment.

To adequately describe ministry requires improvisation. We must place our attention not on the action itself but on the God revealed in and through that action. This is what the innovation trend in the church tends to miss. The focus is not on God but on performance, on solving problems, on *getting it right*, even through failure and adversity. "The community of disciples that has been formed in the habits of the Christian story," however, "has all its attention on the surprises God will bring. It is not racked with anxiety about what inspired thing it must now do."[30] What will determine the success of our ministry is not the outcome it brings or the problem it solves; nor will it be the number of people we recruit into our fold: "The business of the Christian community is not to organize God's work for him [sic], but to participate in it wherever it finds that work in progress."[31] What will determine the success of our ministry is whether the stories we tell to describe it resonate with the story of God.

WHAT ARE WE ASSESSING?

Assessment in ministry is more like the assessment that takes place in ethics and anthropology than that which occurs in the laboratories of the hard sciences. According to Samuel Wells, "The retreat into the indulgently cerebral is a denial of the incarnation; theological reflection must always be a spiraling dialogue with embodied community."[32] We need to be in the business of description, of storytelling, because the hard science of numbers—How many young people are attending our meetings and events? How much information about Scripture and theology do they know? How often are they praying or engaging in religious activity?—simply does not have a horizon wide enough to hold the mystery of divine action.

Assessment is always an act of description. A church or a program becomes what it measures. The data we use determines what we are actually describing, and the adequacy of our description depends on our ability to interpret that data. Wherever data is implemented, it must always remain in the service of telling the story of a situation, giving a clear understanding of what is actually happening so that we can make interpretive judgments about whether that situation resonates with particular criteria. The challenge of assessment is to locate the appropriate criteria that do not foreclose or limit the story. Ministry finds its criteria not in abstract standards but in resonance; it allows the criteria for judgment to emerge *from* the situation. To impose criteria onto the situation from the outset, prior to description, would be to pull the rug out from under ourselves and to make an essentialist reduction. So we need to put the horse before the cart and determine what we are measuring and describing before we determine the criteria for our assessment.

We must reject the instrumental rationale that reduces youth ministry to a technology and measures success according to the meeting of outcomes and instead assess our success through describing the frame of incursive disclosure, telling the story of divine and human encounter in the experiences of young people. We cannot simply say whether a church or youth worker has met certain standards. Whether certain goals were accomplished is a secondary question. We should describe how, through their work, God has been encountered and disclosed. Otherwise, in measuring *our* development, we may miss out on *God's* action.

Thankfully, there has been a recent call in youth ministry to amplify young people's voices in ministry, to allow platforms for young people to speak for themselves, to testify to their experience of God. In *Saying Is Believing*, Amanda Hontz Drury calls youth ministers and theologians to centralize the importance of allowing and helping young people to articulate their experience— to testify. According to Drury, "Engaging in the practice of testimony develops and deepens authentic Christian faith for adolescents."[33] But even while Drury does well to give voice to young people in this way, her concern is still developmental, preoccupied with outcomes. Not enough attention is given to the listener's posture or to how the listener might be "disrupted" by the experience of youth.[34] The reader is not explicitly challenged to reconsider their assumptions. This is the promise of what Erin Raffety and I have called an ethnographic turn in youth ministry, inspired by the ethnographic turn in childhood studies. Alison James writes, "Although the need to listen to children's voices is . . . often paid lip service outside the academy, all too often those voices are silenced by images of childhood that cling to the more traditional, developmental discourse of children's incompetence, rather than competence, as social actors."[35]

In other words, giving voice to young people is not enough. If, in giving voice, our assumption as listeners is that we are encountering one who is definitively and fundamentally in need of development, then we risk undermining the task itself. We must be at least as concerned with the "ethical symmetry" of our engagement as we are with our effectiveness in amplifying their testimony. Young people must be "given central and autonomous conceptual status."[36] "For too long," writes Amy Jacober, "narratives that do not conform to the standards of the dominant culture were taken as an outlier or aberration—as something to be explained away as an anomaly or pathology, declared outside the bounds of what was intended."[37] When we impose criteria prior to the performance of description, we marginalize the very object of our assessment and foreclose on the mystery of divine and human encounter.

Think back to the example of my brother, Jesse. My brother's youth pastor was so inclined toward a specific vision of maturity, a specific outcome to determine the success and effectiveness of his ministry, that he neglected to give an account of what God was doing in my brother's life. His performance of assessment never led him to explore the questions of why my brother was there or what he was feeling and experiencing in the space he was given in the church. The youth pastor instead persisted in his attempts to get my brother "on the right track." His criteria amounted to a foreclosure; it did not have the horizon to hold the mystery of God's self-disclosure in Jesse's life. His assessment was focused on the outcome, the expectation of my brother, not on the actuality of his lived experience. He was engaged in "visionary dreaming" and missed out on God's presence.

VISIONAL ASSESSMENT

So if we need an account of assessment that is more similar to ethics than to the hard sciences, what does such assessment look like? Craig Dykstra has made an important distinction between what he calls *juridical* and *visional* ethics. In a juridical model, the criteria are already set before a situation is encountered. A standard is imposed, and the task of ethical assessment is to determine whether the situation lines up with that standard. The presumption of this approach is that because analysis is essentially problem-solving, everything is a problem with a solution. When you are a hammer, everything looks like nails. When we operate according to this rationality in ministry, we are always at risk of reducing ministry to a technology of the church.

There is a risk in practical theology of operating according to this juridical hermeneutic. In Richard Osmer's descriptive account of the four tasks of practical theology, for example, the normative task involves asking the question "What ought to happen?"[38] The implication of the *ought* is that what is being described and interpreted *ought* to be something that it is not.

According to Dykstra, the "roots" of the differences between this perspective and the visional approach he wants to outline is the "quite distinct pictures they have of the world and the human person."[39] "The juridical picture," writes Dykstra, "conceives of the world as intrinsically knowable through rational powers potentially available to all of us as free persons in control of ourselves and our environment. The visional picture is one of a world shot through with mystery that is hidden from us as frightened and self-deceived persons, and that only a strenuous effort of moral imagination and deep discernment can begin to plumb."[40] The juridical picture is the default picture of the immanent frame—a picture of the world as ever before us and of the self as buffered and self-determined. The visional picture opens us to the possibility of immanence by holding a broad enough horizon to allow for transcendence and for reality to spill over epistemology. The "frightened" self of visional ethics is the self that is subject before the mystery of life and death—even, perhaps, the subject before God. The assessor, the ethicist, the one making interpretive judgments regarding the success of ministry is one who is *in* a situation—not only standing above it—conditioned by that experience even as they describe or listen to and interpret the experience of others. According to Douglas John Hall, "The ethics of the cross presuppose vulnerability and the risk of engagement. They know neither the question nor the answers *in advance.*"[41] As such, we must approach the tasks of assessment not with hubris that presumes to impose a set of expectations without attending first to the description itself—an essentialist and empiricist epistemology, searching to discover a solution—but as people with the epistemic humility to wait on God's incursive disclosure within the mystery of the *locus adventus.*

WHAT IS STORY FOR?

What is essential in assessment, then, if it is to hold the mystery of divine encounter in human experience is the practice of storytelling and story listening—the actual hearing and interpreting of young people's experiences of God.[42] But if we are going to take a visional approach to assessment, we need to be clear about what we mean and do not mean by storytelling. In visional assessment, there is no script. Some approaches to narrative theology have run the risk of treating the relationship of divine and human agency in a deterministic way. We simply lay an interpretation of God's story upon our own, constructing a dualism of God's story and our story, and set up a prototypical narrative as a diagnostic backdrop for the stories of others.

In a way, this is what happened with my brother's story. The youth pastor who worked with Jesse presumably *thought* he was listening to my brother's experience—what youth pastor would actually admit they do not care to listen to what young people are experiencing?—but he was really only listening for a specific story. When my brother's story did not align with his understanding of God's story, there was nothing left to do but keep trying to force a round peg into a square hole.

In a broader way, this is what happened in Neil Erikson's story. Erik Erikson may not have been thinking specifically of God or God's story or the narrative of Scripture, but Neil certainly did not fit the script of what a healthy person, in Erikson's view, should look like. Erikson's recourse, it seems, was to resolve the problem of Neil by dispensing with Neil's story, doubling down and writing a clearer narrative, a more authoritative script, of development—the eight stages of development in his monumental work *Childhood and Society*. In our empiricist epistemic ecosystem, we are ever at risk of reducing experience to a script and listening only for that script, with clear plot lines and climaxes, when we hear the stories that young people tell us.

We also need to be clear that when we use terms such as *story* and *narration*, we run the risk of reductionism—we risk reducing the meaning and significance of human life to discrete events, ordered by beginning, middle, and end. There is no final and "correct" narration that can account for the mystery of human life or its meaning. Every narrative that helps us access the mystery of the person and their encounter with God is fundamentally provisional, and human identity always overspills the stories we can tell to name it. Story is a vehicle that can transport us to a destination, namely, the actuality of lived experience and the persons themselves. We must never mistake the vehicle for the destination. It is important to make this point, especially in the context of a theology of youth ministry that aspires to attend to developmental refugees like Neil Erikson.

Further, while I am convinced of the importance of storytelling for the purpose of accessing and participating in the experiences and personhood of others, I remain unconvinced that one needs to have the ability to narrate one's experience to have an identity in the first place. For example, I worry that Root overstates his point when he writes, "To have an identity I need a story about myself. My identity is the story of events I live through. But to have a story about myself I must hear and share the stories of others."[43] He is right that "there is no way to be human outside of a history and a culture,"[44] but while "even young people with cognitive challenges who cannot repeat and retell a narrative are bound within stories,"[45] we need not have the cognitive powers of self-representation—or even the ability to hear others' stories—in order to have an identity. Otherwise, we confine ourselves to a relatively meaningless and limited definition of identity. Indeed, one need not have even a "*sense* of story"[46] to have a firm identity. Story can take us to identity, but story cannot contain identity. Therefore, while I believe that storytelling and story listening are fundamental to the task of assessment, I am suspicious of their role in identity construction. Thus, we now need to be more specific about what kind of stories we are actually telling and listening for in the task of assessment.

IS THIS A MOVIE OR A SITCOM?

I love movies. Sometimes I fear that I might love movies more than real life. What I love about movies is that I understand them. They are far tidier than real life. There is really no such thing as coincidence in a movie, down to the time on a prop clock and even the products the characters use. All these things hint toward keys in the plot. In a good movie, nothing is wasted. Everything is a clue, a tip, about what is coming. One of my favorite movies is Rian Johnson's masterpiece *Knives Out*, starring Ana de Armas, Daniel Craig, Jamie Lee Curtis, and Chris Evans. In a *Vanity Fair* video published on YouTube, Rian Johnson reveals a clue that might ruin every mystery movie you will see in the next few years. "Apple," as in the American multinational technology company headquartered in Cupertino, California, says Johnson, "will let you use iPhones in movies but . . . bad guys cannot have iPhones on camera."[47] So when you see a character in a movie holding an iPhone, you can rest assured—at least until the policy changes, which, I imagine, could be any moment—that they are not the villain. Nothing is wasted in a movie, and in fact, if something *is* wasted in a movie—if there is a plot point that never gets resolved, a character that never gets developed—you can judge the movie accordingly. Every detail is a punctuation mark in a story that moves from its beginning to its end. And as viewers, we are trained to watch accordingly.

The sitcom television show, however, is a little different. While I am a movie person, my wife, Amanda, is definitely a TV person. When we sit down in our living room after the kids have gone to sleep, I will always suggest we watch a movie—maybe *Star Wars* or *Dead Men Don't Wear Plaid* (if you had not heard of that one before, you can thank me later)—and Amanda will always suggest a TV show like *The Unbreakable Kimmy Schmidt* or *Schitt's Creek*. Perhaps a reason for this is that I enjoy a clear timeline and a more definite climax. I love the story itself more than I love the characters in it. Amanda is the opposite. She wants to enjoy the characters and see how they handle various challenges and situations in each new episode of their experience. And therein lies the most substantial distinction between movies and television shows.

Movies are about plot and character arc, and a sitcom is about character consistency. In a movie, we expect—indeed, we need—the character to change, to be transformed through a decisive plot line to reach either their demise or their redemption. The movie depends on the character's development from point A to point B, perhaps on and on to point Z. We need them to change, to *mature*, to be resolved—one way or another. But television shows, specifically sitcoms, depend on the character's consistency. What would we have done if Jerry Seinfeld moved to Florida? Jake Peralta can never *really* leave the nine-nine, can he? The show would be over! We need them to stay home, to stay the same. If the character changes too much from one episode to another, it is disorienting and can even become incoherent—"Is this even the same show? Grace would never do that to Will!"

In a sitcom, the story comes second to the characters themselves. What we are watching is not just one story but characters facing a series of stories, dealing with various situations that challenge who they are and put their consistency at risk. The resolution of a story is not the tidy development of a plot but the character's ability to keep their integrity.

So when we talk about storytelling and story listening, we have to ask ourselves, "What sort of story is this? Am I watching a movie or a show? Am I in love with the story—with the clear plot line punctuated by discrete details—or am I actually paying attention to the character, the person themselves? Am I dependent on their ability to mature, to change, to develop, or am I attending to who they really are here and now?" In youth ministry, the task of assessment must become less about a plot line and a script and more about people themselves.

DRAMA OF RELATIONSHIP

I have implied some hesitation with the term *narrative* when it comes to assessment. My hesitation is that in assessment, as in human life more generally, we cannot be driven by essentialist and juridical standards that stand like a script before us, telling us what to do. As Samuel Wells puts it in his discussion regarding Christian ethics, "Christian ethics cannot, like *King Lear*, be read off the page of the text: Christians do not have 'parts' in the drama, with 'lines' pre-prepared and learned by heart."[48] Above, we compared characterizations of viewing movies and television shows to illustrate this point; after all, though life and its assessment are not determined by plot and script, it is still a drama—the drama of God's coming to us, ministering to us, and drawing us to eternal life. We attend to this drama not by attending to its particular plot points and props—we are certainly not on the lookout for villains with Android phones—but by attending to characters.

If youth ministry is about attending to "characters"—actual people—and not just a particular script to which we compel young people to conform, then the characterization of the television show still brings us one stop short of illustrating how we are to hear the stories of young people's experience. It is not enough to simply say that youth workers should attend to the lived experiences of young people and dispense with the script and plot expectations that are characteristic of watching movies. There is one more important element of story listening that we need to grasp to position ourselves to actually interpret storytelling and discern what young people are experiencing in ministry—and thus whether we are faithfully participating with God in that experience. That element is the element of *relationality*. You see, as Erin Raffety and I have argued elsewhere, what distinguishes a youth worker from, for example, an ethnographer in the task of assessment is that "while the ethnographer is fundamentally concerned with people's experiences, the minister is fundamentally concerned with *the God whom people are experiencing*."[49] What we are listening to, therefore, is not just young people but young people who are fundamentally *in relationship* with God. Indeed, youth workers and theologians, on account of the eschatological anthropology we outlined in the previous chapter, should operate on the theological claim that human beings' relationship with God is not secondary but primary to their very ontology. God's coming to them as *locus adventus* determines their very being. We *are* our relationships.[50] Therefore, story is not determined by a narrative per se—we are not to assess ministry against the backdrop of a script or a plot. Nor, however, is it simply determined by discrete characters. The drama of human experience is a drama conditioned by relationships. To illustrate relationality in youth ministry, we actually should turn to one more genre of storytelling—improvisation.

IMPROVISATION

In improv, there is a story, and there is definitely drama. But this story is not determined by a plot. The characters do not read a script. Indeed, the story is determined by the relationship between characters. In other words, the relationship is what sets and determines the narrative. The actor is guided not by prescribed lines but by their character and their character's relationship with the other characters in the drama.[51] Often, the characters discover who they are in reference to others as the other characters reveal things about *them* they may not have known. Their character's identity can change as their relationships with other characters open them to new possibilities. Indeed, we could go as far as to say that the relationship determines the characters themselves. Identity and story emerge from a person's interaction in relationship and their openness to the relationships of others. When we watch an improvisation, we expect to be surprised. And the surprise is genuine precisely because the characters themselves are surprised as well.

What we are listening for in the stories of young people, then, is not a script provided by developmental models that play out in "stages" or acts. We are listening to relationships. We are watching as human beings are being encountered by God in unexpected ways, and we are waiting to discover how we might be able to join that drama by saying yes to God. This kind of approach to assessment "creates space for a variety of stories in all their particularities instead of requiring every story to fit a prototype."[52] It also opens us up to God's action in the lives of young people without reducing the object of assessment to mere numbers and rules of religious affiliation. It allows us to listen not merely for stories that fit our desired plot line but for stories that resonate with God's work in the world. We measure what matters to us, and we become what we measure. Youth ministries that adopt a visional and improvisational approach to assessment, opening our ears to the ways in which every young person is being encountered by God, regardless of whether they conform to our preconceived notions of spiritual maturity, will be able to measure what matters and become ministries that resonate with God's life-giving presence.

Most importantly, what this opens us to is participation itself. The key turn that improvisation makes is that it almost never allows for passivity from its spectators. Indeed, in improv, there really are no pure spectators. Everyone, including the audience, is a potential actor in the drama. If you have ever attended an improv show, you probably witnessed an audience member getting pulled on stage and invited—or forced—to participate. It may have been you. There are all sorts of games actors will play in improv—some require audience members to call out and help change the setting or conditions of the drama. As youth workers, we must embrace our role as audience members—when we encounter young people, we always begin in the audience—but to be good audience members, we cannot remain passive; we need to be on the lookout for invitations to join in. And when we receive that invitation, we must be reverent with the drama and faithful to its characters. A minister is successful when they are open and able to faithfully receive the invitation to participate in the drama that is determined by God's relationship with the young people in our midst. And a ministry is successful when it creates conditions for the audience to contribute to the drama in life-giving ways.

According to one of our greatest authorities on the subject, Tina Fey, "The first rule of improvisation is AGREE. Always agree and SAY YES. When you're improvising, this means you are required to agree with whatever your partner has created."[53] The negative way of stating this rule is "don't deny": "Denial is the number one reason most scenes go bad. Any time you refuse an Offer made by your partner your scene will almost instantly come to a grinding halt. Example: Player A) 'Hi, my name is Jim. Welcome to my store.' Player B) 'This isn't a store, it's an airplane. And you're not Jim, you're an antelope.'"[54] Samuel Wells refers to this kind of denial as "blocking."[55] What this rule tells us is that the drama of improvisation is an open drama that requires its actors to be open to receiving what is offered to them. Therefore, as good participants in the drama, we are to be open to what is offered to us. A story that's determined by a script is definitively closed. If someone offers something that is not in the script, the director says, "Cut," and you start over.

Too often, youth workers and theologians think they are watching a movie when they are actually watching improv. They assess what they see according to scripts of developmental psychology and sociological accounts of "faith formation" that essentially boil down to measurements of religious affiliation.[56] And when something is offered that does not fit, they simply try to cut the scene and start over, maybe even bring in the understudy. This is basically what happened in my brother's experience. Our youth pastor was intent on getting Jesse and me to read a script. I obliged him, which worked out fine for me. I am deeply grateful that the particular script I was offered happened to resonate profoundly with my experience of God. But when my brother did not oblige, when he declined the script, our youth pastor had no recourse. He was not open to what my brother was offering, and he essentially denied, blocked, whatever God may have actually been doing in my brother's life.

If my youth pastor had been a good audience member, he would have known that his job was not to redirect the story but to accept it and then participate in it. This participation is what Tina Fey refers to as the "yes, and" rule:

> The second rule of improvisation is not only to say yes, but YES, AND. You are supposed to agree and then add something of your own. If I start a scene with "I can't believe it's so hot in here," and you just say, "Yeah . . ." we're kind of at a standstill. But if I say, "I can't believe it's so hot in here," and you say, "What did you expect? We're in hell." Or if I say, "I can't believe it's so hot in here," and you say, "Yes, this can't be good for the wax figures." Or if I say, "I can't believe it's so hot in here," and you say, "I told you we shouldn't have crawled into this dog's mouth," now we're getting somewhere.[57]

Our job is to agree and then join the drama ourselves.

Of course, improvisation is merely an illustration to provide us with principles for storytelling and story listening. Where it breaks down, as all illustrations do, is that unlike in improv, where every character has equal agency in changing the story, in ministry and life the story is always the story of God's coming. It is open to the future, as improv is, but it is open in particular to *God's* future, not merely to *any* future.[58] Thus, as actors in this drama, we are dependent on God's coming. Our primary role is to wait and to receive, and when we participate, we are participating in what is fundamentally and genuinely *God's* action before ever it is our own.

What improv helps us understand is that the most important thing we can measure in youth ministry is not outcomes but inputs. It is our ability to say "yes, and" that marks our success. It is, in other words, our *faithfulness.* Youth workers and youth ministries should be assessed in their openness to what is being offered in relationship and their ability to contribute, to join with young people in the drama of waiting on God's coming to them.

JUICY RESONANCE

In these pages, I have offered an account of assessment that is both visional and improvisational—one that is grounded in phenomenology rather than essentialism, in relationship rather than measurable outcomes. In other words, I have offered a way of thinking about assessment in relational youth ministry. I have suggested that what we are to measure in youth ministry are not programmatic outcomes but faithfulness, and the only way to measure the mystery of faithfulness is to listen to stories—stories that are driven by persons in relationship. But what are the actual questions we should ask of our ministries? In other words, what is our criteria for assessment? How do we know we are faithfully listening to the stories of God's action in young people's lives and participating in that action?

When I was sitting in the wilderness, questioning my adequacy as a youth worker and as a disciple of Jesus, I was struggling with deep feelings of alienation precisely because I was assessing my action as a script I needed to "get right" so that I could "transform" the world. The reason this was alienating from my actual calling to be a minister and to participate in God's ministry is because ministry itself is about *being* and not *doing*. It comes as a gift, *ex nihilo*, from God to us in our barrenness.[59] It is not *telos* but *eschaton*. It is thus driven by relationships—chiefly, God's relation to us as a minister—not by an external plot or script or third thing to which human beings must anxiously direct themselves: "We can speak of discipleship arising only from our communion with Christ, the head who directs the body, the vine who supplies life to the branches."[60] So when we measure action as merely *doing*, which is the only account of action that is offered to us by the instrumental rationality of developmentalism, we are alienated from our being.

Ministry is a different kind of action altogether. It is the kind of action that does not sit well with the epistemology of the immanent frame or the instrumental rationality of developmentalism. It is action that is not reduced to mere *doing* but is "bound deeply in the welcoming mystery of relationship itself."[61] Drawing on the work of Hartmut Rosa, Root calls this kind of action "resonance." In Rosa's work, resonance is contrasted with "aggression" and "alienation."[62] Resonance is what happens in our concrete experience of the world when we let go of the need to measure, control, and manipulate everything. When the world ceases to be relationless, cold, and detached—when life ceases to be about winning and losing and instead becomes about relating and connecting. According to Root, "Resonance is the only thing that can be the antidote to alienation":[63] "Reading that poem, watching that movie, looking over that mountain vista, laughing and playing with that four-year-old. Such experiences are full. . . . In these moments of resonance you experience your own life teeming with meaning. But it's meaning that seems to be *coming to you*."[64]

We do not control resonance. It is the concrete form of ministerial transversal rationality's concept of incursive disclosure in theological knowledge. It must find us. We can put ourselves in a position to receive it, but like falling asleep, sometimes the harder we *try* to make resonance happen, the more elusive it becomes. It is the lived experience of God through ministry that penetrates the immanent frame with the transcendence of God's love and grace. It is the "fruit of the Spirit." We cannot control it, but we can—we must—participate in it.

In his letter to the Galatians, the apostle Paul wrote, "The fruit of the Spirit is love, joy, peace, patience, kindness, generosity, faithfulness, gentleness, and self-control. . . . If we live by the Spirit, let us also be guided by the Spirit" (Gal. 5:22–25, NRSV). The criterion for ministry is not the *doing* of certain programmatic performances that will produce developmental outcomes. The criterion for ministry is the resonance of love, joy, peace, patience, kindness, generosity, faithfulness, gentleness, and self-control. These are actions that come to us in our being, not actions that are produced by us through programs of *doing* and offering resources. In this way, our alienation is overcome: "The fullness of busyness is frantic and stretching. The fullness of resonance a delight in being."[65] Rather than being overwhelmed by failure and burnout, we can recover the experience of joy in ministry, both as receivers of God's ministry and as participants in it.

When a young person finds their way into an encounter with your church—when they enter the doors of your ministry, so to speak—the questions a minister asks are questions of anticipation and hope: "Where is the fruit of God's Spirit?" and "How can this young person's encounter here participate in that resonance?"

How is this young person experiencing God's love? What in their life delights God and brings them joy? Where is their peace? What allows them to sit still, be patient, and not rush their life? Where are they experiencing kindness from others, and how are they demonstrating it to others? What are they offering of themselves to the world, and what are they receiving? How can we offer them our faithfulness, our friendship, and where are they already experiencing friendship? What compels them to reverence and gentleness, and what in them requires gentleness from us? Where are we at risk of manipulating and instrumentalizing our friendship, and how can we receive self-control and remain fully open to God's action?

CONCLUSION

Ministry is not about control, and it's not something we can figure out on a spreadsheet. It is not a simple pattern or cause and effect, and it is not displayed in an itinerary of growth or maturity. Just because someone is deeply entrenched in church activities and programs doesn't mean they are going to display "spiritual maturity," and none of our ministry programs will ensure this. Conversely, the most "spiritually *immature*" person may at times disclose a deep and *mature* spiritual encounter. Ministry is God's work; we only participate in it. And as God's work, it can neither be forced nor be prevented with absolute certainty. The wheat will grow right alongside the weeds. So the church's obsession with human activity and the exertion of energy toward development and maturity turns out to be a scam. Our job is not to make mature Christians. Our job is to look for God even in unlikely places such as the experience of developmental refugees, nones, and youth group dropouts.

What has been called for here is a shift from *doing* to *being*, from measuring outcomes through numbers and capabilities to measuring fidelity through storytelling and story listening, from measuring effectiveness to narrating faithfulness. This is a need that has been expressed by the lives of people like my brother, Jesse—young people for whom the standard metrics of the church never allowed his youth pastor to see or participate in what God was doing in his life in *actuality*. It is a need that has been expressed by the lives of people like Neil Erikson, whose life could never have measured up to the standards and logics of "growth." Our metrics of assessment, grounded in the concerns of institutional affiliation and rules of verifiability and replicability, have themselves been far too abstract to attend to the concrete stories of these young people.

What we need to be sure of is that our assessment allows us to attend to God's action in lived experience. We need to attend to our actual community, and we need to heed Dietrich Bonhoeffer's warning: "He who loves his dream of a community more than the Christian community itself becomes a destroyer of the latter, even though his personal intentions may be ever so honest and earnest and sacrificial. God hates visionary dreaming."[66] Assessment in ministry is the task of seeing and hearing what God is doing. And as such, it is the task of loving the Christian community of young people in our midst more than we love our dream of that community.

I will always wonder what may have been different had my youth pastor been able to apply the criteria of resonance to his ministry with Jesse. I certainly do not expect that my brother would have gone on to be a pastor like his little brother, Wes. In fact, to be preoccupied with such an expectation would be to succumb to the same old teleological impulse of developmentalism. But I do wonder, had that youth pastor asked different questions of his ministry, if my brother may have found resonance, if he might have encountered the animating presence of God's Spirit—if he would have been captivated by that delight in being that fills life with meaning—even in that little church in Ramona, California. I am left to wonder, but I cannot help but hope that this way of assessing ministry might actually draw youth workers into participation in God's ministry, even in the lives of those developmental refugees who simply will not read the script that we may try to hand to them. I wonder if we would, ourselves, as youth workers and theologians, begin to encounter the spirit of the living God in ways that were previously foreclosed to us. I wonder if God would disclose God's self to us in the Jesses and the Neils and the "collateral damage" of what we used to celebrate as the success stories of developmental youth ministry.

The key proposal of this book has been that God is present and active in the depth of lived experience, the *actuality*, and not merely the potentiality of human achievement. Adults' preoccupation with development and the church's reduction of ministry to "improvement" has obstructed us from encountering the spirit of God in the lives of developmental refugees—those young people who do not conform to our best-laid plans for spiritual maturation. Under the auspices of our empiricist epistemic impulses, we have foreclosed on mystery and contented ourselves with puzzles. Indeed, the lives of young people have been diagnostically interpreted as problems to be solved rather than mysteries in which we as ministers might participate. When ministry is seen as development—developing mature Christian adults—and when youth is reduced to "potential adulthood," we are hindered from encountering God in the concrete and lived experiences of young people. In this book, I have tried to construct a broader theological horizon. I hoped to have provided adults with a path toward the embrace of mystery and the conviction that God is here and that we are invited, with an extravagant welcome, into the life and being of God through the awesome, joyous, and overwhelming work of ministry in the lives of young people.

Notes

CHAPTER ONE

1 Ken Wilber, *No Boundary: Eastern and Western Approaches to Personal Growth* (Boulder, CO: Shambhala, 2001), 21.

2 See You at the Pole is a national event supported by a plethora of organizations including Young Life, the Salvation Army, Group Publishing, and Christianity Today. It's a nice thought since it empowers young people to be public about their faith, but it's definitely taken on a sort of Christian Nationalist flair in a lot of contexts. See www.syatp.com.

3 "Concrete and lived experience" is a phrase I am drawing from the work and theology of Andrew Root. While the term may have varied and complex, if not ambiguous, definitions in the fields of sociology and anthropology, in this work, it will simply be employed as a way of differentiating experience as something particular and peculiar (concrete) as opposed to something merely theoretical or abstract. To deal with concrete and lived experience is not to deal primarily with a theory of experience or an abstraction from real people's existence but to encounter—quite personally—how one encounters reality and is encountered by it.

4 American youth ministry has a somewhat complex history. According to Andrew Root, "The dominant form of age-specific youth ministry between 1900 and 1940 actually had its start on February 2, 1881, when young pastor Francis Clark from Maine inaugurated the first 'Young People's Society for Christian Endeavor.' The idea came about after Clark's frustration that in his growing church young people were not going on to become vital members of the congregational life after initial conversion experiences. . . . In committing to Christian progress through Bible study and witness, adolescents were able to grab hold of a distinct tradition and claim it for themselves." Andrew Root, *Revisiting Relational Youth Ministry: From a Strategy of Influence to a Theology of Incarnation* (Downers Grove, IL: IVP Books, 2007), 38. These youth societies—which themselves were preceded by Robert Raikes's "Sunday school" (see Root, *Revisiting Relational Youth Ministry*, 30)—eventually gave way to Jim Rayburn's Young Life organization (see Root, *Revisiting Relational Youth Ministry*, 51) and the creation of what we would now recognize as the "youth group" in congregational youth ministry across denominations in the United States (see Root, *Revisiting Relational Youth Ministry*, 59–61).

5 See Kenda Creasy Dean, ed., *OMG: A Youth Ministry Handbook* (Nashville: Abingdon Press, 2010), 22–23.

6 Rob Nixon, *Slow Violence and the Environmentalism of the Poor* (Cambridge, MA: Harvard University Press, 2011), 166.

7 Nixon, *Slow Violence*, 166.

8 Nixon, *Slow Violence*, 156.

9 Nixon, *Slow Violence*, 152.

10 Nixon, *Slow Violence*, 152, 168.

11 Nixon, *Slow Violence*, 152.

12 Nixon, *Slow Violence*, 150.

13 Nixon, *Slow Violence*, 150–151.

14 Wayne Rice, *Junior High Ministry: A Guide to Early Adolescence for Youth Workers*, updated and expanded (Grand Rapids, MI: Zondervan, 1998), 19.

15 This framework is built on a particularly modern concept of time, helpfully outlined in three dimensions by the philosopher Jean Baudrillard—the chronocentric, linear, and historic dimensions. According to Calvin Schrag, "The chronocentric dimension provides the matrix for a quantitative measurement of time. The linear dimension fixes time as an irreversible succession of instants moving across a continuum of past, present, and future. The historic dimension, which Baudrillard sees as providing the dominant expression of the modern concept of time particularly since Hegel, portrays time as a dialectical becoming that actualizes the potentialities of a beginning in a consummatory end." Calvin O. Schrag, *The Resources of Rationality: A Response to the Postmodern Challenge* (Indianapolis: Indiana University Press, 1992), 43.

16 See Erica Burman, *Deconstructing Developmental Psychology*, 2nd ed. (New York: Routledge, 2007), 32.

17 Dawn DeVries, "Toward a Theology of Childhood," *Interpretation* 55, no. 2. (2001): 161–173, at 162.

18 William Kessen, *The Child* (New York: Wiley, 1965), 75.

19 James W. Fowler, *Becoming Adult, Becoming Christian: Adult Development and Christian Faith* (New York: Harper & Row, 1984), 20.

20 See Thomas E. Bergler, *From Here to Maturity: Overcoming the Juvenilization of American Christianity* (Grand Rapids, MI: Eerdmans, 2014).

21 Allison James and Alan Prout, eds., *Constructing and Reconstructing Childhood*, 2nd ed. (New York: Routledge, 1997), 239.

22 Chris Jenks, *Childhood*, 2nd ed. (New York: Routledge, 2005), 11.

23 Hartmut Rosa, *The Uncontrollability of the World* (Medford, MA: Polity, 2020), 9.

24 I highly recommend Mark DeVries, *Sustainable Youth Ministry: Why Most Youth Ministry Doesn't Last and What Your Church Can Do about It* (Downers Grove, IL: IVP Books, 2008).

25 Mark DeVries, *Family-Based Youth Ministry*, 2nd ed. (Downers Grove, IL: InterVarsity Press, 2004), 26.

26 See Thomas E. Bergler, *The Juvenilization of American Christianity* (Grand Rapids, MI: Eerdmans, 2013).

27 For an example of biological determinism in popular youth ministry literature, see Crystal Kirgis, *In Search of Adolescence: A New Look at an Old Idea* (San Diego, CA: The Youth Cartel, 2015). What's unsettling about this particular book is not so much that it is a popular argument in favor of a deterministic and deeply positivistic approach but that it has received enthusiastic endorsements from many of the most

influential youth ministry educators and researchers in the United States, including Duffy Robbins, Chap Clark, and Kenda Creasy Dean.

28 Jim Burns and Mike DeVries, *The Youth Builder* (Ventura, CA: Gospel Light, 2001), 23.

29 Lawrence O. Richards, *Youth Ministry: Its Renewal in the Local Church* (Grand Rapids, MI: Zondervan, 1991), 24.

30 Amy E. Jacober, *The Adolescent Journey: An Interdisciplinary Approach to Practical Youth Ministry* (Downers Grove, IL: InterVarsity Press, 2011), 50.

31 Jacober, *The Adolescent Journey*, 72.

32 Kelly D. Schwartz, "Adolescent Brain Development: An Oxymoron No Longer," *Journal of Youth Ministry* 6, no. 2 (2008): 85–93, at 90–91.

33 Dean, *OMG: A Youth Ministry Handbook*, 23.

34 Notable exceptions might include Andrew Zirschky's *Beyond the Screen* (Nashville: Abingdon Press, 2015) and Mike King's *Presence-Centered Youth Ministry* (Downers Grove, IL: InterVarsity Press, 2006). But it is important to note that virtually every exception to this rule is only an exception by virtue of the fact that it does not include large sections or chapters on adolescence or the constitution of "youth." By leaving *youth* largely undefined and uninterpreted, some authors avoid a clearly detectable dependence on developmentalism.

35 Morgan Schmidt, *Woo: Awakening Teenagers' Desire to Follow in the Way of Jesus* (San Diego, CA: The Youth Cartel, 2014), 91.

36 Craig S. Keener, *The IVP Bible Background Commentary: New Testament* (Downers Grove, IL: IVP Academic, 1993), 162.

37 Jesus's initial response is, "Why do you call me good? No one is good but God alone" (Mark 10:18, NRSV).

38 The point is made even more sharply in contrast to developmentalism in a similar story from John's gospel, wherein Jesus tells an eager Pharisee with a similar question that "unless one is born again, he cannot see the kingdom of God" (John 3:3, NASB). The return to infancy is hardly compatible with developmentalism's fetish for maturity.

39 See Jürgen Moltmann, "The Disarming Child," in *The Power of the Powerless: The Word of Liberation for Today* (San Francisco: Harper & Row, 1983), 28–37.

CHAPTER TWO

1 John Swinton, *Spirituality and Mental Health Care: Rediscovering a 'Forgotten' Dimension* (Philadelphia: Jessica Kingsley Publishers, 2001), 47.

2 See Andrew Root and Kenda Creasy Dean, *The Theological Turn in Youth Ministry* (Downers Grove, IL: IVP Books, 2011).

3 See Charles Taylor, *A Secular Age* (Cambridge, MA: The Belknap Press, 2007), 542.

4 Rosa, *The Uncontrollability of the World*, 11.

5 Jürgen Moltmann, *God for a Secular Society: The Public Relevance of Theology* (Minneapolis: Fortress Press, 1999), 5.

6 Andrew Root, "Being a Pastor within the Secular Frame Means Teaching People How to Pray," *Christian Century*, July 3, 2019, https://www.christiancentury.org/article

/critical-essay/being-pastor-within-secular-frame-means-teaching-people-how-pray, accessed June 23, 2023.

7   Charles Taylor, *Sources of the Self* (Cambridge, MA: Harvard University Press, 1989), 80.

8   For more on the distinction between idiographic and nomothetic forms of knowledge, see John Swinton and Harriet Mowat, *Practical Theology and Qualitative Research* (London: SCM Press, 2006), 40–44.

9   See Andrew Root, *Christopraxis: A Practical Theology of the Cross* (Minneapolis: Fortress Press, 2014), 194–197.

10 As J. Wentzel van Huyssteen aptly put it, "The often stellar performance of the sciences in our time have again managed to elevate this mode of human knowledge to a status so special and superior that it just had to emerge as the paradigmatic example of what human rationality should be about." J. Wentzel van Huyssteen, *The Shaping of Rationality: Toward Interdisciplinarity in Theology and Science* (Grand Rapids, MI: Eerdmans, 1999), 2.

11 See Root, *Christopraxis*, 201. See also T. M. Luhrmann, *When God Talks Back: Understanding the American Evangelical Relationship with God* (New York: Vintage, 2012).

12 Douglas John Hall, *Thinking the Faith: Christian Theology in a North American Context* (Minneapolis: Fortress Press, 1991), 137.

13 According to John B. Watson, "Psychology as the behaviorist views it is a purely objective experimental branch of natural science." Cited in Kessen, *The Child*, 229.

14 According to Charles Taylor, "The criterion for belonging to the data language for any term is that it can be used to make statements which describe observed events without any further interpretations or operational definitions." Taylor, *The Explanation of Behavior* (New York: The Humanities Press, 1964), 88.

15 Fowler, *Becoming Adult, Becoming Christian*, 15.

16 Taylor, *A Secular Age*, 360.

17 See James K. A. Smith, *How (Not) to Be Secular: Reading Charles Taylor* (Grand Rapids, MI: Eerdmans, 2014), 1–10.

18 According to Calvin Schrag, "Pretty much in concert, we are advised to have done with classical and modernist overarching metaphysical designs and unifying epistemological principles that purport to tell the whole truth and nothing but the truth about our insertion in the world. The question that remains is whether after such a radical overhaul of our traditional philosophical habits of thought there is indeed any truth left to tell." Schrag, *The Resources of Rationality*, 23.

19 See Karl Barth, *Church Dogmatics I.1* (New York: T&T Clark, 1936), 3–11.

20 Tillich describes his own experience as being "on the boundary." See Paul Tillich, *On the Boundary: An Autobiographical Sketch* (Eugene, OR: Wipf and Stock, 1966).

21 Mark Kline Taylor, *Paul Tillich: Theologian of the Boundaries* (Minneapolis: Fortress Press, 1991), 23.

22 See Wolfhart Pannenberg, *Theology and the Philosophy of Science* (Philadelphia: Westminster, 1976). A generation after Barth and Tillich, Pannenberg broke ground with his work *Theology and the Philosophy of Science*. In it, he argues for a broader understanding of knowledge itself, one that is not limited to "deductive-nomological" and empirical forms of knowledge. "Knowledge of reality," writes Pannenberg, "cannot be limited to knowledge of general rules." For Pannenberg, the problem of "science" is not just the problem of explanation but of the understanding of meaning

itself: "The reduction of understanding to the pattern of deductive-nomological explanation thus turns out to be impossible. . . . A better way of thinking about the relation of explanation and understanding is to say that the former always presupposes the latter" (68). Therefore, according to his argument, theology must be considered "scientific" in this broader account of knowledge insofar as it interrogates reality, as such, and seeks meaning beyond mere explanation. In this sense, for Pannenberg, one might say theology becomes a model for all sciences and a corrective of the more reductive forms of knowledge represented in behaviorism and empiricism. Representing a more phenomenological epistemology, defending views of the likes of Gadamer and Habermas, he proposed that "description by means of natural laws cannot deal with a particular but essential aspect of the human world, that of the perception of meaning" (137). Empiricistic impulses may direct sciences in offering thin descriptions of what lies before us at the molecular, chemical, and even behavioral levels, but their horizon is too narrow to hold the mystery of meaning itself, which is intrinsic to reality as such. Reality is not merely a question of what is. The question of reality, for Pannenberg, must include the question of *why* things are as they are. Thin description is incomplete, for Pannenberg, because science is the investigation of reality itself, which includes the question of meaning.

23 For example, Andrew Root makes the case that many youth ministry theologians who are concerned with "faith formation" have outsourced their definition of faith—a distinctly theological term—to sociology. The categories of interpretation, centering on moralistic therapeutic deism and "nones," who opt out of participation and affiliation with the church, are "helpful ideas but nevertheless entirely sociological descriptors." Rather than define *faith* theologically and shape the conversation around a concern for divine action and transcendence, which are the marks of practical theological rationality, we are essentially "discussing faith as if it were only a natural and social reality." Andrew Root, *Faith Formation in a Secular Age: Responding to the Church's Obsession with Youthfulness* (Grand Rapids, MI: Baker Academic, 2017), xvii.

24 This sort of objectification of spirituality is closely related to what Charles Taylor refers to as "instrumental rationality" or "instrumental reason": "Objectification of the world gives a sense of power . . . which is intensified by every victory of instrumental reason." Taylor, *A Secular Age*, 548.

25 See David Hay and Rebecca Nye, *The Spirit of the Child* (Philadelphia: Jessica Kingsley Publishers, 2006), 19.

26 "The shift uprooted theological education as it moved from places of formation and repotted it in the soil of empirical science." Root, *Christopraxis*, 20.

27 "Historical Theology, accordingly, forms the proper *Body* of the theological study; and is connected with *Science*, strictly so called, by means of Philosophical, and with the active Christian *Life* by means of Practical Theology." Friedrich Schleiermacher, *Brief Outline of the Study of Theology* (Eugene, OR: Wipf and Stock, 2007), 102.

28 See Root, *Christopraxis*, 21 n5.

29 For example, Joyce Ann Mercer writes, "Some persons easily mistake the assertion of practical theology as a 'useful' theology to mean that it entails the mere application of some biblical or theological proposition to a problem posed in human experience to generate a supposed theological solution to the problem. Such a distorted perspective on the practical aspect within practical theology confuses usefulness with simplicity. Paradoxically, this distortion originates in the idea that certain foundational ideas

exist that come prior to actions and practices. Actions and practices in this view serve as the ideas' (secondary) application, after which the theory may be dispensed with as irrelevant to everyday life. . . . Practical theology is not hostile to theoretical complexity. Rather, it is a way of doing theology that takes seriously local contexts and practices and the everyday lives of persons in those contexts as they seek to walk in the way of Jesus." Joyce Ann Mercer, *Welcoming Children: A Practical Theology of Childhood* (St. Louis: Chalice Press, 2005), 12–13.

30 Tillich is persistent in distinguishing the paradox and mystery of the Christian message from the "grotesque consequences" of "absurdities." See Paul Tillich, *Systematic Theology, Volume 2* (Chicago: University of Chicago Press, 1957), 91.

31 Ray S. Anderson, *Historical Transcendence and the Reality of God* (Grand Rapids, MI: Eerdmans, 1975), 46.

32 Paul Tillich, *Systematic Theology, Volume 1* (Chicago: University of Chicago Press, 1951), 61.

33 Tillich, *Systematic Theology, Volume 1*, 60.

34 Tillich, *Systematic Theology, Volume 1*, 62.

35 Root, *Christopraxis*, 276.

36 While Tillich was indeed committed to transcendence as a reference to a reality beyond epistemology, beyond the access of human experience, his characterization of this reference as the symbolization of that to which humanity's question about ultimate reality points certainly exposed him to more immanental revision. According to Ray Anderson, "Without the regulative function of the symbol, Tillich's language of transcendence collapses into immanent transcendence" (i.e., conceiving "no fixed point external to the contingent world"). Anderson, *Historical Transcendence*, 24–25, 29.

37 Pete Ward, *Introducing Practical Theology: Mission, Ministry, and the Life of the Church* (Grand Rapids, MI: Baker Academic, 2017), 78.

38 Root, *Christopraxis*, 274.

39 It is worth noting again that even though practical theology definitively seeks God's action as located within human experience and the practices of the church, including youth ministry, practical theology's primary focus is still divine action. It is only insofar as its focus is God that practical theology investigates human practice and experience.

40 Root, *Christopraxis*, 194 n10. This note in Root's *Christopraxis* foreshadows his thesis in *Faith Formation in a Secular Age*, wherein he is concerned that theologians and faith leaders who are interested in "faith formation" have essentially outsourced definitions of "faith" to the social sciences. He writes, "How have we become a people who so often talk of faith as almost completely coated in a sociological shell, bound almost entirely in measured institutional participation, content to survey variables?" Root, *Faith Formation in a Secular Age*, xviii.

41 See Root, *Faith Formation in a Secular Age*, 194.

42 James W. Fowler, "Practical Theology and the Social Sciences," in Friedrich Schweitzer and Johannes A. van der Ven, eds., *Practical Theology—International Perspectives* (New York: Peter Lang, 1999), 291–292.

43 James W. Fowler, *Stages of Faith: The Psychology of Human Development and the Quest for Meaning* (New York: Harper Collins, 1981), xiii.

44 According to James Hunter, writing specifically about moral education, "When it comes to the moral life of children," and we might add *youths* to that, "the vocabulary

of the psychologist frames virtually all public discussions." James Davidson Hunter, *The Death of Character: Moral Education in an Age without Good or Evil* (New York: Basic Books, 2000), 81.

CHAPTER THREE

1   This quote is attributed to Kierkegaard in several publications, including Robert A. Hipkiss, *Jack Kerouac: Prophet of the New Romanticism* (Lawrence: Regents Press of Kansas, 1976), 83. But the phrase may be more Kierkegaard-esque than actually Kierkegaardian. In any case, it conveys an idea that Kierkegaard would have endorsed.

2   Kenda Creasy Dean has noted that Erikson's thought "has influenced Protestant theology, practical theology in particular, more than any other developmental theorist." Kenda Creasy Dean, *Practicing Passion: Youth and the Quest for a Passionate Church* (Grand Rapids, MI: Eerdmans, 2004), 12.

3   Nancy Going, "The Way of Jesus: Adolescent Development as Theological Process," *Journal of Youth Ministry* 9, no. 2 (2011): 49–66, at 50.

4   Kara Powell, Jake Mulder, and Brad Griffin, *Growing Young: 6 Essential Strategies to Help Young People Discover and Love Your Church* (Grand Rapids, MI: Baker Academic, 2016), 94–95, 116.

5   The influence of psychology is explicit since references to the *Journal of Adolescent Research*, the American Psychological Association, and the work of Jeffrey Arnett abound.

6   Erikson considered identity formation to be the key task of the adolescent stage of the life cycle. "Identity vs. role confusion" marks the key crisis of adolescence. This concept emerges in Erik H. Erikson, *Childhood and Society* (New York: W. W. Norton, 1963), 261–263. And it is developed more thoroughly in Erikson, *Identity: Youth and Crisis* (New York: W. W. Norton, 1968).

7   Erikson, *Identity*, 87.

8   Erikson, *Identity*, 129. Also, according to Lawrence Friedman, Erikson's interest was always in a "view of development characterized by a telos or goal." Lawrence J. Friedman, *Identity's Architect: A Biography of Erik H. Erikson* (Cambridge, MA: Harvard University Press, 1999), 52.

9   See Root and Dean, *The Theological Turn in Youth Ministry*.

10 See Richard S. Osmer, *Practical Theology: An Introduction* (Grand Rapids, MI: Eerdmans, 2008), 4.

11 Dean, *Practicing Passion*, 6.

12 Dean, *Practicing Passion*, 100–102.

13 Most youth ministry scholars, since Dean began her work, have rejected, or attempted to reject, the pathographic view of youth. One notable exception, however, is Thomas Bergler, in whose work adolescence is consistently viewed as a pathology. See Bergler, *The Juvenilization of American Christianity* (Grand Rapids, MI: Eerdmans, 2013). Also see Bergler, *From Here to Maturity*.

14 Dean, *Practicing Passion*, 10.

15 Dean, *Practicing Passion*, 24.

16 Dean, *Practicing Passion*, 13.

17 In Dean's later work, she has become more self-aware of this criticism. In a moving confession and with courageous vulnerability, reflecting on her early work as a minister and as a theologian, she writes, "But the truth is . . . I have not done ministry with youth who would be likely to refuse what I was offering. I've picked my horses carefully; I've chosen winners. I've trained leaders, worked with 'alpha' kids, served on camp staffs for self-selected, spiritually interested teenagers. I've bet on safe horses. As a result—after thirty years of youth ministry—I am confronting the fact that my ministry has likely missed the young people who needed me, and Jesus, the most. I didn't just fail them. *I didn't even see them.*" Kenda Creasy Dean, Wesley W. Ellis, Justin Forbes, and Abigail Visco Rusert, *Delighted: What Teenagers Are Teaching the Church about Joy* (Grand Rapids, MI: Eerdmans, 2020), 87.

18 Dean, *Practicing Passion*, 84.

19 Friedman, *Identity's Architect*, 42.

20 Robert Coles, *Erik H. Erikson: The Growth of His Work* (Boston: Atlantic Monthly Press, 1970), 138.

21 Friedman, *Identity's Architect*, 221–222.

22 Coles, *Erik H. Erikson*, 75.

23 Coles writes, "Certainly, like Kierkegaard, he saw life as far more than the sum of any or all descriptions." Coles, *Erik H. Erikson*, 138.

24 Friedman, *Identity's Architect*, 29.

25 Friedman, *Identity's Architect*, 28.

26 When Erik was four months old, Karla received news, and evidence, that Valdemar had passed away. See Friedman, *Identity's Architect*, 30.

27 Erikson's biographers seem to agree that it was not Valdemar.

28 Erik H. Erikson, "Autobiographic Notes on the Identity Crisis," *Daedalus* 99, no. 4 (1970): 730–759, at 742.

29 Friedman, *Identity's Architect*, 36.

30 See Coles, *Erik H. Erikson*, 14.

31 See Marshall Berman, "Erik Erikson, the Man Who Invented Himself," *New York Times*, March 30, 1975, https://archive.nytimes.com/www.nytimes.com/books/99/08/22/specials/erikson-history.html, accessed May 26, 2021.

32 Coles, *Erik H. Erikson*, 24.

33 See Friedman, *Identity's Architect*, 81.

34 See Friedman, *Identity's Architect*, 96–97.

35 See Coles, *Erik H. Erikson*, 32.

36 Coles, *Erik H. Erikson*, 33.

37 Coles, *Erik H. Erikson*, 36, 43.

38 See Erikson, *Identity*, 73.

39 Erikson, *Identity*, 45.

40 Erikson, *Identity*, 45.

41 Burman, *Deconstructing Developmental Psychology*, 69.

42 Erikson, *Identity*, 87.

43 Friedman, *Identity's Architect*, 208.

44 See Ananya Mandal, "Down Syndrome History," *News Medical Life Sciences*, https://www.news-medical.net/health/Down-Syndrome-History.aspx, accessed December, 23, 2020.

45 See Friedman, *Identity's Architect*, 209.

46 Friedman, *Identity's Architect*, 210.
47 Friedman, *Identity's Architect*, 209.
48 Friedman, *Identity's Architect*, 210.
49 Friedman, *Identity's Architect*, 215.
50 As Erik's daughter, Sue Erikson Bloland, would later document, her father dealt with "lifelong feelings of personal inadequacy." Robert Leiter, "The Corrosive Nature of Fame," *Jewish World Review*, http://www.jewishworldreview.com/on/media112999. asp, accessed December 24, 2020.
51 Craig Dykstra, *Vision and Character: A Christian Educator's Alternative to Kohlberg* (Eugene, OR: Wipf and Stock, 1981), 59.
52 Friedman, *Identity's Architect*, 219.
53 See John Swinton, "The Body of Christ Has Down Syndrome," *Journal of Pastoral Theology* 13, no. 2 (2003): 66–78.
54 Swinton, "The Body of Christ," 71.
55 Martin E. Marty, *The Mystery of the Child* (Grand Rapids, MI: Eerdmans, 2007), 16.
56 Quoted in Marty, *The Mystery of the Child*, 17.
57 Marty, *The Mystery of the Child*, 18.

CHAPTER FOUR

1 van Huyssteen, *The Shaping of Rationality*, 2–3.
2 Hall, *Thinking the Faith*, 370.
3 Hall, channeling Martin Buber, goes on to say that "this *first principle of our knowing* sets us at once in conflict with a society which has made it less and less possible for human beings even to say 'thou' to one another, let alone to address an 'Eternal Thou.'" Hall, *Thinking the Faith*, 371.
4 Hall, *Thinking the Faith*, 403. Hall goes on to say that "in the relation between reason and revelation in Christian epistemology, revelation has noetic priority," 420.
5 Hall, *Thinking the Faith*, 399–400.
6 According to Hall, "The sciences do not provide theology with the fullness of perspective that it needs. They present aspects of the world to which only they have access; but these remain aspects." Hall, *Thinking the Faith*, 313.
7 John Swinton, *From Bedlam to Shalom: Towards a Practical Theology of Human Nature, Interpersonal Relationships, and Mental Health Care* (New York: Peter Lang, 2000), 9.
8 Root, *Christopraxis*, 295.
9 There is a correlation here between *interpretation*, as we are understanding it, and *apologetics*, as Hall understands it. For Hall, apologetics is not just to answer the questions that the situation is asking but "to create a climate in which the real scandal of the *kerygma* can be encountered." Hall, *Thinking the Faith*, 342.
10 Root, *Christopraxis*, 294.
11 The notion of agency, as far as it can be applied, must contain nuance that is particular to the individual person from whom it is expected. Agency is a moving target and a post-reflective concept. It does not define the personhood of the disciple, but rather the disciple defines the nature of agency.
12 Hall, *Thinking the Faith*, 79.

13 Hall, *Thinking the Faith*, 109.

14 See Hall, *Thinking the Faith*, 110–112.

15 Hall, *Thinking the Faith*, 94.

16 Hall, *Thinking the Faith*, 73.

17 Hall, *Thinking the Faith*, 99.

18 For more on "bracketing," see Swinton, *Spirituality and Mental Health Care*, 102.

19 Erin Raffety and Wesley W. Ellis, "Disruptive Youth: Toward an Ethnographic Turn in Youth Ministry," *Ecclesial Practices* 4, no.1 (2017): 5–24, at 18.

20 Dean, *Practicing Passion*, 14.

21 The Chalcedonian method of interdisciplinarity takes its shape according to a Barthian understanding of the Chalcedonian pattern for explaining the hypostatic union—namely, that the divine (theology) and human (social sciences) are related to one another in an asymmetrical and differentiated unity. This approach was introduced as a method for interdisciplinarity by Deborah Van Deusen Hunsinger and has been affirmed by various other practical theologians, including John Swinton. See Deborah Van Deusen Hunsinger, *Theology and Pastoral Counseling: A New Interdisciplinary Approach* (Grand Rapids, MI: Eerdmans, 1995). The concept of transversal rationality can be attributed to the philosopher Calvin O. Schrag. It was later taken up and introduced to the theological enterprise, specifically in interdisciplinary reflection on faith and science, by J. Wentzel van Huyssteen of Princeton Theological Seminary. The conversation was not taken up in practical theology per se until it was further introduced by Richard Osmer and, later, by Andrew Root.

22 van Huyssteen writes, "A postfoundationalist rationality should be developed beyond the extremes of modernist universalism and postmodern, historicist relativism, and as such will imply a refiguring of the dynamics of critique as we assess and discern how our discourses and networks of belief are intellectually shaped by our social contexts." Van Deusen Hunsinger, *Theology and Pastoral Counseling*, 120.

23 Swinton and Mowat, *Practical Theology*, 84.

24 Swinton and Mowat, *Practical Theology*, 87.

25 Schrag, *The Resources of Rationality*, 54.

26 van Huyssteen, *The Shaping of Rationality*, 121.

27 Schrag, *The Resources of Rationality*, 43.

28 Schrag, *The Resources of Rationality*, 43.

29 van Huyssteen, *The Shaping of Rationality*, 64.

30 Except, of course, if they concern the ontological status of pluralism itself—and even this normative claim is best left implicit.

31 Andrew Root refers to this as "the epistemic fallacy." See Root, *Christopraxis*, 194–200.

32 As Schrag puts it, "This will provide an alternative to the concept of the universal logos that remained the bane of both premodern cosmological/metaphysical speculation and modern subject-centered epistemological reflection. It will also . . . rescue the resources of reason from a postmodern diaspora in which reason succumbs to a rhapsodic play of *différance* and a rampant pluralism. Situated between the Scylla of a hegemonic and ahistorical universalism and the Charybdis of a lawless, self-effacing particularism and enervated historicism, transversal reason charts the course of comprehending the configurative practices and forms of life that comprise our socio-historical inherence." Schrag, *The Resources of Rationality*, 9.

33 Root, *Christopraxis*, 283.

34 van Huyssteen, *The Shaping of Rationality*, 136

35 Richard Osmer, *The Teaching Ministry of Congregations* (Louisville, KY: Westminster John Knox Press, 2005), 312.

36 According to Douglas John Hall, "reliance on what it *professed* [i.e., theology]—on *what* is professed!—must be exchanged for a newly realized, naked reliance on the One *whom* faith professes." Douglas John Hall, *Confessing the Faith: Christian Theology in a North American Context* (Minneapolis: Fortress Press, 1996), 173.

37 Schrag, *Resources of Rationality*, 9.

38 Hall, *Thinking the Faith*, 21.

39 Schrag, *Resources of Rationality*, 62.

40 Jürgen Moltmann, *God in Creation: A New Theology of Creation and the Spirit of God* (Minneapolis: Fortress Press, 1993), 11.

41 Schrag, *Resources of Rationality*, 57.

42 Osmer, *The Teaching Ministry of Congregations*, 312.

43 "Knowledge and truth are the effects of the practices engaged in by a community of investigators and interpreters, and they become part of the text discourse only through the dynamics of consent and disavowal, agreement and disagreement, acceptance and rejection, that textures the forces of communicative praxis." Osmer, *The Teaching Ministry of Congregations*, 136.

44 Osmer, *The Teaching Ministry of Congregations*, 2.

45 Osmer, *The Teaching Ministry of Congregations*, 312.

46 "The reality of God is problematical to human knowledge apart from the concretion of Spirit in historical form." Anderson, *Historical Transcendence and the Reality of God*, 71.

47 Dietrich Bonhoeffer, *Christ the Center* (New York: Harper & Row, 1978), 32.

48 Anderson, *Historical Transcendence and the Reality of God*, 70.

49 Ray S. Anderson, *The Soul of Ministry* (Louisville, KY: Westminster John Knox Press, 1997), 3.

50 Anderson, *The Soul of Ministry*, 3.

51 I am again indebted to Andrew Root for his understanding of God as a minister. This is apparent throughout Root's works. He makes the claim that "God is ontologically a minister" in *Christopraxis*, but it is perhaps best explained in the second part of *The Pastor in a Secular Age*, where he discusses God's arrival in human experience in history. See Root, *Christopraxis*, 178. See also Root, *The Pastor in a Secular Age* (Grand Rapids, MI: Baker Academic, 2019), 173–247.

52 Anderson, *The Soul of Ministry*, 7.

53 John Swinton, "Who Is the God We Worship? Theologies of Disability; Challenges and New Possibilities," *International Journal of Practical Theology* 14, no. 2 (February 2011): 301.

54 John Wesley quoted in Frank Whaling, ed., *John and Charles Wesley: Selected Prayers, Hymns, Journal Notes, Sermons, Letters and Treatises* (New York: Paulist Press, 1981), 20.

55 Hall, *Thinking the Faith*, 404.

56 We will see later how this kind of relational—or ministerial—epistemology becomes the foundation for our eschatology. For it is not in the *becoming* or the development of the world that we discover God's future but through God's coming to us that God's future invades present experience.

57 John Calvin, *Institutes of the Christian Religion*, vol.1 (Louisville, KY: Westminster John Knox Press, 1960), ch. 5.9, 62.

58 Stanley J. Grenz, *Theology for the Community of God* (Grand Rapids, MI: Eerdmans, 2000), 49.

59 Hall, *Thinking the Faith*, 408.

60 Hall, *Thinking the Faith*, 407.

CHAPTER FIVE

1 Henri J. M. Nouwen, "Care, the Source of All Cure," Henri Nouwen Society, https://henrinouwen.org/meditation/care-the-source-of-all-cure/, accessed June 14, 2021.

2 Chap Clark, "The Changing Face of Adolescence: A Theological View of Human Development," in Kenda Creasy Dean, Chap Clark, and Dave Rahn, eds., *Starting Right: Thinking Theologically about Youth Ministry* (Grand Rapids, MI: Zondervan, 2001), 44.

3 In 2015, Clark endorsed a popular publication that sought to refute the social construction of adolescence using some historical references from the literature. In that endorsement, Clark stated that adolescence has "always been a contextual struggle" and that it is a "historically 'normal' stage of life." Given the claims of the book, this endorsement implies Clark may have changed his mind in regard to the historical novelty of the adolescent paradigm. See Crystal Kirgiss, *In Search of Adolescence* (San Diego, CA: The Youth Cartel, 2015).

4 To name just a few examples that represent this consensus, see Root, *Revisiting Relational Youth Ministry*; Jacober, *The Adolescent Journey*; Dean, *OMG: A Youth Ministry Handbook*; Jack O. Balswick, Pamela Ebstyne King, and Kevin S. Reimer, *The Reciprocating Self: Human Development in Theological Perspective* (Downers Grove, IL: InterVarsity, 2005); and Jeremy Paul Myers, *Liberating Youth from Adolescence* (Minneapolis: Fortress Press, 2018).

5 Cynthia Lightfoot, *The Culture of Adolescent Risk-Taking* (New York: The Guilford Press, 1997), 15.

6 Lightfoot, *The Culture of Adolescent Risk-Taking*, 15.

7 Lightfoot, *The Culture of Adolescent Risk-Taking*, 16.

8 Allison James and Alan Prout, *Constructing and Reconstructing Childhood: Contemporary Issues in the Sociological Study of Childhood* (New York: The Falmer Press, 1990), 7.

9 Clark, "The Changing Face of Adolescence," 44.

10 Arthur Kleinman, *Rethinking Psychiatry: From Cultural Category to Personal Experience* (New York: The Free Press, 1988), 7.

11 John Swinton, *Finding Jesus in the Storm: The Spiritual Lives of Christians with Mental Health Challenges* (Grand Rapids, MI: Eerdmans, 2020), 25.

12 Jacober, *The Adolescent Journey*, 51.

13 See Root, *Revisiting Relational Youth Ministry*, 25.

14 John Swinton, *Becoming Friends of Time: Disability, Timefullness, and Gentle Discipleship* (Waco, TX: Baylor University Press, 2018), 35–53.

15 Daniel Siegel, *The Developing Mind: How Relationships and the Brain Interact to Shape Who We Are* (New York: The Guilford Press, 2012).

16 Erikson, *Childhood and Society*, 261.

17 Erikson, *Childhood and Society*, 262–263.

18 Peter Blos, *The Adolescent Passage: Developmental Issues* (New York: International Universities Press, 1979), 148.

19 According to Dean Borgman, "God alone is—ultimately and beyond comprehension—*mature.* . . . Ultimately all growth is progress toward God and all lack of growth, a process of death and decay." Dean Borgman, *Foundations for Youth Ministry* (Grand Rapids, MI: Baker Academic, 2013), 86.

20 Raffety and Ellis, "Disruptive Youth."

21 James and Prout, *Constructing and Reconstructing Childhood.*

22 Jenks, *Childhood.*

23 Myers, *Liberating Youth from Adolescence*, 22

24 Julie Passanante Elman, *Chronic Youth: Disability, Sexuality, and US Media Cultures of Rehabilitation* (New York: NYU Press, 2014), 11.

25 Myers, *Liberating Youth from Adolescence*, 24.

26 Elman writes, "A rational stable subject position that is established in contrast to the unstable and irrational teen." Elman, *Chronic Youth*, 3.

27 According to Chris Jenks, "Childhood is to be understood as a social construct; it makes reference to a social status delineated by boundaries that vary through time and from society to society but which are incorporated within the social structure and thus manifested through and formative of certain typical forms of conduct. Childhood always relates to a particular cultural setting." Jenks, *Childhood*, 6–7.

28 Jenks, *Childhood*, 11. Italics mine.

29 Jens Qvortrup, "Childhood as a Structural Form," in Jens Qvortrup, William A. Corsaro, and Michael-Sebastian Honig, eds., *The Palgrave Handbook of Childhood Studies* (New York: Palgrave, 2009), 4.

30 Elman, *Chronic Youth*, 3.

31 Allison James, "Life Times: Children's Perspectives on Age, Agency and Memory across the Life Course," in Jens Qvortrup, ed., *Studies in Modern Childhood: Society, Agency, Culture* (New York: Palgrave, 2005), 249.

32 Jenny Hockey and Allison James, *Social Identities across the Life Course* (New York: Palgrave, 2003), 66.

33 Gender roles are also constructed through industrialization in this way. See Burman, *Deconstructing Developmental Psychology*, 16.

34 Erik H. Erikson, *Identity and the Life Cycle* (New York: W. W. Norton, 1980), 104–105.

35 Donald Capps, *Life Cycle Theory and Pastoral Care* (Eugene, OR: Wipf and Stock, 1983), 19.

36 Capps, *Life Cycle Theory*, 19.

37 Michael J. Nakkula and Eric Toshalis, *Understanding Youth: Adolescent Development for Educators: Adolescent Development for Educators* (Cambridge, MA: Harvard Education Press, 2006), 19.

38 Jens Qvortrup, ed., *Studies in Modern Childhood: Society, Agency, Culture* (New York: Palgrave, 2005), 5.

39 Qvortrup, *Studies in Modern Childhood*, 5.

40 Burman, *Deconstructing Developmental Psychology*, 67

41 Martin Woodhead, "Child Development and the Development of Childhood," in Qvortrup, Corsaro, and Honig, *The Palgrave Handbook of Childhood Studies*, 53.

NOTES

42 Quoted in Bonnie J. Miller-McLemore, "Childhood Studies and Pastoral Counseling," *Sacred Spaces: e-Journal of the American Association of Pastoral Counselors* 6 (2014): 29–30.

43 Charlotte Hardman, quoted by Michael-Sebastian Honig, "How Is the Child Constituted in Childhood Studies?" in Qvortrup, Corsaro, and Honig, *The Palgrave Handbook of Childhood Studies*, 63.

44 Allison James, "Agency," in Qvortrup, Corsaro, and Honig, *The Palgrave Handbook of Childhood Studies*, 35–36.

45 Woodhead, "Child Development and the Development of Childhood," 52–53.

46 We might list Erica Burman and William Kessen as two of them.

47 William Kessen, "The American Child and Other Cultural Inventions," *American Psychologist* 34, no. 10 (1979): 815–820, at 815.

48 See Wesley W. Ellis, "Human Beings and Human Becomings," *Journal of Youth & Theology* 14, no. 2 (2015): 119–137; and Raffety and Ellis, "Disruptive Youth."

49 Honig, "How Is the Child Constituted in Childhood Studies?," 62.

50 Jürgen Moltmann, *The Crucified God: The Cross of Christ as the Foundation and Criticism of Christian Theology* (Minneapolis: Fortress Press, 1993), 40.

51 It is notable that in Matthew's Gospel, this passage is part of the ecclesial discourse, shortly after Jesus presents children as "the community's ideal members." See note in Carol A Newsom, Shaon H. Ringe, and Jacqueline E. Lapsley, eds., *Women's Bible Commentary*, 3rd ed. (Louisville, KY: Westminster John Knox Press, 2012), 474.

52 "By contrast," as R. Alan Culpepper points out, "God is never called a shepherd in the [New Testament], and the image is limited to Jesus's parables." R. Allan Culpepper, "The Gospel of Luke," in *The New Interpreter's Bible: A Commentary in Twelve Volumes*, vol. 9 (Nashville: Abingdon Press, 1995), 296.

53 Moltmann, *The Crucified God*, 249.

54 Benjamin T. Conner, "Disabled Adolescents, Enabling Youth Ministry," *Journal of Disability and Religion* (2018), https://doi.org/10.1080/23312521.2018.1521765.

55 Michael D. Langford, "Abusing Youth: Theologically Understanding Youth through Misunderstanding Disability," in Wesley W. Ellis and Michael D. Langford, eds., *Embodying Youth* (New York: Routledge, 2020), 75.

56 Friedrich Gogarten, *Christ the Crisis* (Richmond, VA: John Knox Press, 1970), 1.

57 See Jürgen Moltmann, *The Trinity and the Kingdom* (Minneapolis: Fortress Press, 1993), 105–108.

58 According to Moltmann, "Any functional and merely soteriological christology is manifestly on the wrong track. . . . The incarnation of the Son is more than merely a means to an end. Christology is more than the presupposition for soteriology." Moltmann, *The Trinity and the Kingdom*, 115.

59 Wolfhart Pannenberg, *Jesus—God and Man* (Philadelphia: Westminster, 1975), 38.

60 Pannenberg, *Jesus—God and Man*, 48.

61 Anderson, *Historical Transcendence*, 127.

62 As Gogarten put it, "Christ in his humanity or more precisely in the strange double action, in itself so curiously contradictory, which God carried out in him, in this man, is the direct revelation of God." Gogarten, *Christ the Crisis*, 5.

63 Jürgen Moltmann, *The Church in the Power of the Spirit* (Minneapolis: Fortress Press, 1993), 56–60.

64 Elaine A. Heath, *The Mystic Way of Evangelism* (Grand Rapids, MI: Baker Academic, 2017), 94.

65 Heath, *The Mystic Way of Evangelism*. Heath here is drawing on insights from Zachary Hayes. See Zachary Hayes, "Incarnation and Creation in the Theology of St. Bonaventure," in Romano Stephen Almagno and Conrad L. Harkins, eds., *Studies Honoring Ignatius Charles Brady, Friar Minor* (St. Bonaventure, NY: Franciscan Institute, 1976), 328.

66 Moltmann writes, "Since . . . each individual event, taken as an act of God, only partially illumines the nature of God, revelation in the sense of the full self-revelation of God in his glory can be possible only where the whole of history is understood as revelation . . . 'Since it is not yet finished, it is only in light of its end that it is recognizable as revelation.'" Jürgen Moltmann, *Theology of Hope* (Minneapolis: Fortress Press, 1993), 77.

67 According to Kathryn Tanner, "Nature, rather than sin, is the primary reference point for understanding grace." Kathryn Tanner, *Christ the Key* (Cambridge, UK: Cambridge University Press, 2010), 58.

68 Moltmann, *The Trinity and the Kingdom*, 33.

69 According to Paul Tillich, "We are known in a depth of darkness through which we ourselves do not even dare to look. And at the same time, we are seen in a height of a fullness which surpasses our highest vision." Paul Tillich, *The Shaking of the Foundations* (Eugene, OR: Wipf and Stock, 1948), 50.

70 Root, *Revisiting Relational Youth Ministry*, 89.

71 Clarence Edwin Rolt, *The World's Redemption* (New York: Longmans, Green, 1913), 227.

72 Moltmann, *The Trinity and the Kingdom*, 115.

73 Craig Keen, *After Crucifixion: The Promise of Theology* (Eugene, OR: Cascade, 2013), 63.

74 Philip G. Ziegler, *Militant Grace* (Grand Rapids, MI: Baker Academic, 2018), 51.

75 Ziegler, *Militant Grace*, 49.

76 Of course, it bears mentioning that *friendship* here must have a deeper theological definition than the "Buddy Christ" image from *Dogma*. Kevin Smith, *Dogma* (Culver City, CA: Columbia TriStar Home Video, 2000).

77 Paul Tillich, *The Protestant Era*, trans. James Luther Adams (Chicago: University of Chicago Press, 1948), 170.

78 Swinton, *Spirituality and Mental Health Care*, 57.

79 Andrew Root, *Bonhoeffer as Youth Worker* (Grand Rapids, MI: Baker Academic, 2014), 7.

80 Swinton, *Becoming Friends of Time*, 175.

81 Andrew Root, *Exploding Stars, Dead Dinosaurs, and Zombies: Youth Ministry in the Age of Science* (Minneapolis: Fortress Press, 2018), 102.

82 Root, *Exploding Stars*, 102.

CHAPTER SIX

1 Jürgen Moltmann, *Theology of Play* (London: Harper & Row, 1972), 61.

2 iSpot.tv, "2019 Audi A7 TV Spot, 'Night Watchman Part 1' [T1]," accessed June 10, 2021, https://www.ispot.tv/ad/dyEw/2019-audi-a7-night-watchman.

3 Moltmann, *Theology of Play*, 32.

4 Religious education and secular education were not two distinct categories as they are now. Here, for example, how closely they are tied together in Thomas Martin's

account: "[Children] have claims . . . to be *instructed* in the great truths and duties of religion . . . which are to produce all that public and social virtue, all that private and personal worth, and all that assurance of future and eternal bliss, which are the glory and happiness of man [sic]." Thomas Martin, "The Characters of Childhood," in Kessen, *The Child*, 40.

5 Thomas Martin, "The Characters of Childhood," in Kessen, *The Child*, 37–38.

6 Root and Dean, *The Theological Turn in Youth Ministry*, 14.

7 Root and Dean, *The Theological Turn in Youth Ministry*, 15.

8 Root and Dean, *The Theological Turn in Youth Ministry*, 15.

9 I am thinking particularly of the work of people like Andrew Zirschky, Amanda Hontz Drury, Nathan Stucky, Christy Lang Hearlson, Katherine M. Douglass, and Andrew Root.

10 According to Jürgen Moltmann, "Israelite faith in God is determined by the Exodus experience." Jürgen Moltmann, *The Coming of God: Christian Eschatology* (Minneapolis: Fortress Press, 1996), 67.

11 According to Abraham Joshua Heschel, "The Sabbath day of rest, as a day of abstaining from toil, is not for the purpose of recovering one's lost strength and becoming fit for the forthcoming labor. . . . The Sabbath is not for the weekdays; the weekdays are for the sake of the Sabbath. It is not an interlude but the climax of life." Heschel, *The Sabbath* (New York: Farrar, Straus and Giroux, 1951), 14.

12 Andrew Root, "Youth Ministry as a Magical Technology: Moving toward the Theological," *Catalyst* 40, no. 1, (2013): 1–3, http://www.catalystresources.org/youth-ministry-as-a-magical-technology-moving-toward-the-theological/, accessed June 6, 2023. Jürgen Moltmann also said essentially the same thing: "Technologies are nothing but applied sciences." Moltmann, *God in Creation*, 23.

13 Swinton, *Becoming Friends of Time*, 43.

14 Swinton, *Becoming Friends of Time*, 43.

15 Myers, *Liberating Youth from Adolescence*, 22.

16 Root, "Youth Ministry as a Magical Technology."

17 According to Root, "During the world wars the scientific worldview of western societies turned headlong into the pursuit of efficiency; how could science help create the most efficient guns and bombs? Science operationalized for efficiency was bound to technology. After World War II the battlefield moved from the fronts of Europe and the Pacific to the consumer marketplace. The technology that provided the weapons to defeat Germany and Japan would now provide the refrigerators and televisions that would shape the capitalism that would win the Cold War. If technology provided the magic to win the war, then technology could solve all our problems, whether those problems be medical, engineering, or even the decline in religious involvement." Root, "Youth Ministry as a Magical Technology."

18 Root, "Youth Ministry as a Magical Technology."

19 Richard Stivers, *Technology as Magic: The Triumph of the Irrational* (New York: Continuum, 2001).

20 Root, "Youth Ministry as a Magical Technology."

21 For example, one video entitled "Zuckerberg Explains the Internet to Congress" set some of the more humorous questions to a comedic score and received over two million views on YouTube, https://www.youtube.com/watch?v=ncbb5B85sd0, accessed June 6, 2023.

22 *Washington Post*, "Transcript of Mark Zuckerberg's Senate Hearing," https://www
.washingtonpost.com/news/the-switch/wp/2018/04/10/transcript-of-mark-zuckerbergs
-senate-hearing/?utm_term=.d4a3c312f47b, accessed June 6, 2023.

23 *Washington Post*, "Transcript of Zuckerberg's Appearance before House Committee," https://www.washingtonpost.com/news/the-switch/wp/2018/04/11/transcript-of
-zuckerbergs-appearance-before-house-committee/?utm_term=.1dc38558d106,
accessed June 6, 2023.

24 YouTube, "Google's Congressional Hearing Highlights in 11 Minutes," https://www
.youtube.com/watch?v=-nSHiHO6QJI, accessed May 27, 2021.

25 See Slate, "Google's Web of Confusion," https://slate.com/technology/2018/12/google
-congress-hearing-sundar-pichai-confusion-regulation.html, accessed February 14,
2019; and Mashable, "At the Google Hearing, Congress Proves They Still Have No
Idea How the Internet Works," https://mashable.com/article/google-hearing-congress
-no-idea-about-internet-search/#VM1T1fmsCSqg, accessed February 14, 2019.

26 For this point, I am once again indebted to Hartmut Rosa.

27 Rosa, *The Uncontrollability of the World*, 112.

28 Root, *Bonhoeffer as Youth Worker*, 5.

29 Root, "Youth Ministry as a Magical Technology."

30 Conner, "Disabled Adolescents, Enabling Youth Ministry," 84.

31 Moltmann, *God in Creation*, 32.

32 "Thanks to the convergence of the counterculture and admen, youthfulness became
a strategy disconnected from the concrete persons of the young." Root, *Faith Formation in a Secular Age*, 73.

33 Keen, *After Crucifixion*, 38.

34 DeVries, *Family-Based Youth Ministry*.

35 Powell, Mulder, and Griffin, *Growing Young*.

36 See Bergler, *From Here to Maturity*.

37 Kara E. Powell and Chap Clark, *Sticky Faith* (Grand Rapids, MI: Zondervan, 2011).

38 Mike Yaconelli, quoted in Mark Cannister, *Teenagers Matter: Making Student Ministry
a Priority in the Church* (Grand Rapids, MI: Baker Academic, 2013), xx.

39 For example, Root shares a story about giving a lecture on Dietrich Bonhoeffer, which
promised no "practical" points for application, at a youth ministry conference and
being surprised by the turnout, saying, "This technological ethos has begun to feel like
a noose around the neck of any youth workers." Root, *Bonhoeffer as Youth Worker* 5.

40 Perhaps a once-innovative concept, the youth group—the weekly gathering of young
people hosted by the church, including games, pizza, and the occasional Bible study—
has become somewhat synonymous with youth ministry. But these innovators are
rightly parsing youth ministry and youth group and suggesting things can be done
differently, outside the walls of the youth group model.

41 Kenda Creasy Dean, "Spiritual Entrepreneurship: It's a Full-Blown Movement Now,"
Ministry Incubators, https://ministryincubators.com/spiritual-entrepreneurship-its
-a-full-blown-movement-now/, accessed May 27, 2021.

42 See, for example, the Zoe Project (https://zoeproject.ptsem.edu/, accessed May
24, 2023), the Log College Project (http://iym.ptsem.edu/the-log-college-project/,
accessed May 24, 2023), the CYMT Innovation Laboratory (https://www.youthmin-
istrylaboratory.com/, accessed May 24, 2023), and the Missing Voices Project (https://
missingvoices.flagler.edu/, accessed May 24, 2023).

43 https://ministryincubators.com, accessed March 3, 2019.

44 http://www.youthministryinnovators.com/, accessed March 3, 2019.

45 https://www.hatcheryla.com/, accessed March 3, 2019.

46 See https://www.tenx10.org/, accessed February 2, 2023.

47 Root, *Bonhoeffer as Youth Worker*, 5.

48 I am hesitant to cite the Zoe Project, a project funded by the Lilly Endowment for young adult ministry in which I am involved. This project took as its interpretive framework a design-thinking strategy that starts with problems and searches for solutions, a kind of instrumentalization of ethnography.

49 "What Will I Learn?," The Hatchery, https://www.hatcheryla.com/cse-12-week-course -AP, accessed January 25, 2019.

50 Moltmann, *The Coming of God*, 44.

51 Kenda Creasy Dean, "Why Churches Should Be Talking More about Social Entrepreneurship," *Caring*, August 31, 2017, http://caringmagazine.org/churches-talking -social-entrepreneurship/, accessed December 24, 2020.

52 Dean, *Practicing Passion*, 4.

53 Root, "Youth Ministry as Magical Technology."

54 Dean, *Practicing Passion*, 10.

55 Dean, *Practicing Passion*, 13–14.

56 Dean, *Practicing Passion*, 16–17.

57 Dean, *Practicing Passion*, 198.

58 Andrew Root, *Churches and the Crisis of Decline* (Grand Rapids, MI: Baker Academic, 2022), 96.

59 Justo L. González, *The Story of Christianity, Volume 2: The Reformation to the Present Day* (New York: HarperOne, 1985), 15.

60 John Dillenberger, ed., *Martin Luther: Selections from His Writings* (New York: Anchor Books, 1962), xiv.

61 Dillenberger, *Martin Luther*, xiv.

62 González, *The Story of Christianity*, 16.

63 Dillenberger, *Martin Luther*, xiv–xv.

64 Dillenberger, *Martin Luther*, xiv.

65 Hall, *Professing the Faith: Christian Theology in a North American Context* (Minneapolis: Fortress Press, 1993), 465.

66 González, *The Story of Christianity*, 16.

67 Dillenberger, *Martin Luther*, 11.

68 Here I would qualify the use of the term *innovation* as something entirely distinct from developmentalism's definition of the term. *Innovation* in this sense is Luther's openness to the newness that comes through God's grace, living *in* the *new* (*in* the *novum* of God's arrival).

69 There is certainly some irony in referring to this as an innovation since, after all, Luther was not the first to encounter such revelation. But its bearing on society at the time constitutes a true innovation insofar as the recovery of this theological disclosure produced unprecedented social and ecclesial change—indeed, reformation.

70 Martin Luther, "Preface to Romans," in Dillenberger, *Martin Luther*, 21.

71 Martin Luther, *Three Treatises from the American Edition of Luther's Works* (Minneapolis: Fortress Press, 1970), 288.

72 Dean, *Practicing Passion*, 16.

73 Luther, "Preface to Romans," 17. Italics mine.
74 "The righteousness of God is that by which the righteous lives by a gift of God, namely by faith ... [it] is revealed by the gospel, namely, the passive righteousness with which merciful God justifies us by faith." Dillenberger, *Martin Luther*, 11
75 Dillenberger, *Martin Luther*, 242.
76 Root, *Faith Formation in a Secular Age*, xviii.
77 Keen, *After Crucifixion*, 55.
78 Keen, *After Crucifixion*, 63.
79 Jürgen Moltmann, *Theology and Joy* (London: Hymns Ancient and Modern, 2013), 42.
80 Root, *Bonhoeffer as Youth Worker*, 7.
81 Moltmann, *Theology and Joy*, 43.
82 Jürgen Moltmann, *In the End—the Beginning* (Minneapolis: Fortress Press, 2004), 7.
83 Moltmann, *Theology and Joy*, 42.

CHAPTER SEVEN

1 Karl Barth, *Church Dogmatics III.2* (Edinburgh: T&T Clark, 1960), 75.
2 Keen, *After Crucifixion*, 44.
3 In chapters 2 and 4 we talked about the limitation of practical theology's favorite interdisciplinary methodology—the critical correlational model—as accepting and theologizing answers given by the social sciences, rather than actually offering theological answers to theological questions. Theological anthropology is a case study for this limitation. We have an history of answering the anthropological question anthropologically and then baptizing that answer with theological language. This is not truly theological anthropology but theologized anthropology.
4 Otto Weber, *Foundations of Dogmatics, Vol. 1* (Grand Rapids, MI: Eerdmans, 1981), 532.
5 "... the human self-understanding is not erased by revelation." Weber, *Foundations of Dogmatics, Vol. 1*, 538.
6 Weber, *Foundations of Dogmatics, Vol. 1*, 541.
7 Emil Brunner, *Man in Revolt* (Philadelphia: Westminster, 1939) 64.
8 Weber, *Foundations of Dogmatics, Vol. 1*, 532.
9 Swinton, *From Bedlam to Shalom*, 18.
10 This includes, of course, alternative and non-binary gender identities. The point is that all human beings, regardless of difference, are created in the image of God, not only one gender or another.
11 See Francis Brown, Emil Roediger, S. R. Driver, Charles A. Briggs, Edward Robinson, and Wilhelm Gesenius, *The Brown-Driver-Briggs Hebrew and English Lexicon* (Peabody, MA: Hendrickson, 2000), 853–854.
12 Swinton writes, "In terms of the actual attention given to it within the Scripture, the idea that human beings are made in the image of God would not appear to be of great import to the biblical writers." Swinton, *From Bedlam to Shalom*, 18.
13 Specifically, a segment of Genesis traceable to the Priestly writings. See Swinton, *From Bedlam to Shalom*.
14 Quoted in Swinton, *From Bedlam to Shalom*.

15 Barth, *Church Dogmatics III.2*, 72.

16 Oliver D. Crisp, *The Word Enfleshed: Exploring the Person and Work of Christ* (Grand Rapids, MI: Baker Academic, 2016), 55.

17 Marc Cortez, *Theological Anthropology: a Guide for the Perplexed* (New York: T&T Clark, 2010), 20.

18 Cortez, *Theological Anthropology*, 16.

19 Cortez, *Theological Anthropology*, 37.

20 Cortez, *Theological Anthropology*, 35.

21 Cortez, *Theological Anthropology*.

22 "It is the image of God which constitutes the possibility and the actuality of human response to God." Anderson, *Historical Transcendence and the Reality of God*, 136.

23 Thomas Aquinas, *Summa Theologica* (New York: Benzinger Brothers, 1947), I, 15.

24 Gregory of Nyssa, *Of the Making of Man* (n.p.: Aeterna Press, 2016), 8.8.

25 Swinton observes that theologians Edmond Hill and Carl F. H. Henry centralize the importance of rationality as the defining trait of human beings. Swinton quotes Hill, echoing Gregory of Nyssa, "Man [sic] is a rational animal; being human means being rational . . . it is only in the rational activity of intelligence and mind that man and woman can properly represent God and realize His [sic] image in themselves." Quoted in Swinton, *From Bedlam to Shalom*, 23.

26 Swinton, *From Bedlam to Shalom*, 24.

27 Hans Reinders, *Receiving the Gift of Friendship* (Grand Rapids, MI: Eerdmans, 2008), 8.

28 Reinders, *Receiving the Gift of Friendship*, 119.

29 Frederick Buechner, *Wishful Thinking: A Theological ABC* (New York: Harper & Row, 1973), 6.

30 Swinton, *From Bedlam to Shalom*, 26.

31 See Root, *Faith Formation in a Secular Age*.

32 Mary Aquin O'Neill, "The Mystery of Being Human Together," in Catherine Mowry LaCugna, ed. *Freeing Theology: The Essentials of Theology in Feminist Perspective* (New York: HarperCollins, 1993), 148.

33 Elaine L. Graham, *Transforming Practice: Pastoral Theology in an age of Uncertainty* (Eugene, OR: Wipf and Stock Publishers, 1996), 4.

34 O'Neill, "The Mystery of Being Human Together," 149.

35 David Arthur Auten, *Eccentricity: A Spirituality of Difference* (Eugene, OR: Cascade, 2014), 30.

36 Auten, *Eccentricity*.

37 Auten, *Eccentricity*, 50.

38 For more on delight and difference, see Wesley W. Ellis and Kinda Creasy Dean, "Friendship: The Joy of Befriending Youth," in David F. White and Sarah F. Farmer, eds., *Joy: A Guide for Youth Ministry* (Nashville: Wesley's Foundary Books, 2020), 79–81.

39 Auten, *Eccentricity*, 32.

40 Auten, *Eccentricity*, 42.

41 James K. A. Smith, *Desiring the Kingdom: Worship, Worldview, and Cultural Formation* (Grand Rapids, MI: Baker Academic, 2009), 18.

42 Smith, *Desiring the Kingdom*, 41.

43 Smith, *Desiring the Kingdom*, 41, 43.

44 Smith, *Desiring the Kingdom*, 46.
45 Smith, *Desiring the Kingdom*, 42–43.
46 Smith, *Desiring the Kingdom*, 43.
47 Smith, *Desiring the Kingdom*.
48 Smith, *Desiring the Kingdom*, 45.
49 Smith, *Desiring the Kingdom*, 46.
50 Smith, *Desiring the Kingdom*, 50–51.
51 Smith, *Desiring the Kingdom*, 51.
52 Smith, *Desiring the Kingdom*, 47.
53 Erikson, *Identity*, 136
54 Swinton, *From Bedlam to Shalom*, 31
55 Qvortrup, *Studies in Modern Childhood*, 5.
56 See Capps, *Life Cycle Theory and Pastoral Care*, 17.
57 Fowler, *Becoming Adult, Becoming Christian*, 28.
58 Balswick, King, and Reimer, *The Reciprocating Self*, 27.
59 Balswick, King, and Reimer, *The Reciprocating Self*, 30.
60 James and Prout, *Constructing and Reconstructing Childhood*, 10.
61 See Jenks, *Childhood*, 33.
62 Jenks, *Childhood*, 19.
63 Jenks, *Childhood*.
64 Jenks, *Childhood*.
65 See Ellis, "Human Beings and Human Becomings," 129.
66 Alisdair MacIntyre, *Dependent Rational Animals: Why Human Beings Need the Virtues* (Chicago: Open Court, 1999), 56.
67 MacIntyre, *Dependent Rational Animals*.
68 MacIntyre, *Dependent Rational Animals*, 82.
69 MacIntyre does not dispute the rationalist argument that cognitive ability is essential to humanity so much as he argues that this essentially human trait is also shared among other nonhuman animals, particularly dolphins. His contention is not that humans are *not* essentially cognitive, but that so are other animals. This does not help us shift the vantage point of anthropology to the theological any more than Smith's philosophical anthropology does. MacIntyre, *Dependent Rational Animals*, 12–13.
70 Hall, *Professing the Faith*, 281.
71 See Ecclesiastes 9:2.
72 Reinders, *Receiving the Gift of Friendship*, 117.
73 "The ultimate end of human life is clearly not dependent on them, but is a gift—an unexpected and undeserved gift." Reinders, *Receiving the Gift of Friendship*, 97.
74 Reinders, *Receiving the Gift of Friendship*, 314
75 Reinders, *Receiving the Gift of Friendship*, 217.
76 Hall, *Professing the Faith*, 323.
77 See Balswick, King, and Reimer, *The Reciprocating Self*.
78 Balswick, King, and Reimer, *The Reciprocating Self*, 273.
79 According to Chris Jenks, "the conflation of development with ideas of growth and progress builds a competitive ethic into the process of development itself which supports the ideology of possessive individualism at the root of industrialized capitalist cultural formations." Jenks, *Childhood*, 37.
80 Capps, *Life Cycle Theory*, 30.

81 Moltmann, *Theology of Hope*, 42. Moltmann goes on to say that "the Christian doctrine of the revelation of God must explicitly belong neither to the doctrine of God—as an answer to the proofs of God . . . nor to anthropology. . . . It must be eschatologically understood . . ." *Theology of Hope*, 43.

82 Moltmann, *The Coming of God*, 25.

83 Kathryn Tanner, *Jesus, Humanity, and the Trinity: A Brief Systematic Theology* (Minneapolis: Fortress Press, 2001), 99.

84 Tanner, *Jesus, Humanity, and the Trinity*, 34.

85 Moltmann, *The Coming of God*, 25.

86 Douglas John Hall, *Imaging God: Dominion as Stewardship* (Grand Rapids, MI: Eerdmans, 1986), 3.

87 Hall, *Imaging God*.

88 Moltmann, *The Coming of God*, 28.

89 "How is it that the risen One is future . . .? We must be careful not to formulate the answer in a way which would give to this final coming and consummation any other necessity than that of the free grace of God." Karl Barth, *Church Dogmatics IV.1* (Edinburgh: T&T Clark, 1960), 324.

90 Moltmann, *Theology of Hope*, 32.

91 Keen, *After Crucifixion*, 49.

92 Reinders, *Receiving the Gift of Friendship*, 249.

93 Keen, *After Crucifixion*, 49.

94 Keen, *After Crucifixion*, 64

95 Moltmann, *Theology of Hope*, 32.

96 "A theology in Christ remembers and hopes. Memory is for what is hoped; hope is for what is remembered." Keen, *After Crucifixion*, 48.

97 Jürgen Moltmann, *Hope for the Church: Moltmann in Dialogue with Practical Theology* (Nashville: Abingdon Press, 1979), 11.

98 Hall, *Imaging God*, 3.

99 Dean et al., *Delighted*, 67.

100 See Root, *Revisiting Relational Youth Ministry*.

101 W. H. Vanstone, *The Stature of Waiting* (New York: Morehouse, 1982), 83.

102 Vanstone, *The Stature of Waiting*, 102.

103 The pietist movement "represented a protest against the formalism in doctrine, worship, and life into which churches and their members had fallen after the original impulses of the Reformation had dissipated." Theodore G. Trappert, "Introduction," in Philip Jacob Spener, ed., *Pia Desideria* (Eugene, OR: Wipf and Stock, 1964), 1.

104 Trappert, "Introduction," 37.

105 Trappert, "Introduction."

CHAPTER EIGHT

1 Dietrich Bonhoeffer, *Life Together* (New York: Harper & Row, 1954), 27.

2 While I was there, I was reading a new book that I had just received in the mail called *Relationships Unfiltered* (Grand Rapids: Zondervan, 2009) by Andrew Root. Root's main argument, as I took it, was that I should stop trying to *influence* people and instead try to be *with* people and "share their place." With the combination of

Campolo's persuasive communication and Root's deep theological rationale, I left that retreat with a different vision for ministry than the one I had brought with me.

3 Mother Theresa's often quoted as saying, "Not all of us can do great things. But we can do small things with great love."

4 Bart Campolo, "College Briefing" at Forest Home in Forest Falls, California, September 3–6, 2010. The links to those presentations have since been deleted, but I documented the experience on my personal blog, where I wrote, "If we live only for success … if all of our relationships are about influence and 'changing lives' then we're sure to think that we suck at ministry." From "Story of Love," Wes Ellis, September 16, 2010, http://www.wesleywellis.com/2010/09/story-of-love.html, accessed June 14, 2021.

5 Bonhoeffer, *Life Together*, 27.

6 Bonhoeffer, *Life Together*, 27.

7 See Andrew Root, *The End of Youth Ministry?* (Grand Rapids, MI: Baker Academic, 2020).

8 Charles Taylor, *Human Agency and Language. Philosophical Papers 1* (Cambridge, UK: Cambridge University Press, 1985), 23.

9 Root, *Bonhoeffer as Youth Worker*, 5.

10 See Root, *The End of Youth Ministry?*, 20.

11 See Melinda Lundquist Denton and Richard Flory, *Back-Pocket God: Religion and Spirituality in the Lives of Emerging Adults* (New York: Oxford University Press, 2020).

12 See figure 27.1 in Dave Rahn, "Assessing Honestly: Continuous Improvement," in Dean, Clark, and Rahn, eds., *Starting Right*, 370.

13 Rahn writes, "Paying proper attention to the right results can actually guide us to greater faithfulness!" Rahn, "Assessing Honestly," 371.

14 Rahn, "Assessing Honestly."

15 Rahn, "Assessing Honestly," 372.

16 Rahn, "Assessing Honestly," 371.

17 Root, *Christopraxis*, 171.

18 See Root, *Christopraxis*, 154.

19 The impulse of reducing God to a function or an object has been strong throughout history, under a variety of epistemic regimes. Take, for example, the trinitarian heresy of "modalism" (Sabellianism and Patripassianism), wherein the persons of the trinity are understood as three modes or forms of activity rather than as three unified and differentiated persons within the godhead. It was corrected by the Athanasian and, eventually, Nicene creeds, and it has been important for theologians to correct this heresy wherever it becomes operative in order not only to maintain the divinity of the Father, Son, and Holy Spirit, and of revelation through Christ and the Spirit as well as our acknowledgment of God's freedom by maintaining the ontological reality of personal relationship in God, but also to keep from reducing our relationship with God to the reception of a "mode" of God's functioning, similar to the way we reduce human beings to functions when we interact with them only, for example, as a "teller" or a "waiter."

20 Take, for example, the Youth Specialties Conference, where they have begun to offer theological content but only as a sort of elective alongside the more core curriculum of the more pragmatic or "practical" approaches to youth ministry.

21 Take, for example, the Log College Project, http://iym.ptsem.edu/the-log-college-project/, accessed March 3, 2020.

22 According to Andrew Root, "A person can only be known and, more importantly, *shared in* through narrative discourse." Root, *The End of Youth Ministry?*, 166.

23 Eberhard Jüngel, *God as the Mystery of the World: On the Foundation of the Theology of the Crucified One in the Dispute between Theism and Atheism* (Eugene, OR: Wipf and Stock, 1983), 303.

24 Tillich, *On the Boundary*, 51.

25 Tillich, *On the Boundary*, 246.

26 As Kant proposed, it "cannot be made known publicly, that is, shared universally." Immanuel Kant, quoted in Jüngel, *God as the Mystery of the World*, 250.

27 Jüngel, *God as the Mystery of the World*, 251.

28 James D. G. Dunn writes, "Language of image and metaphor [i.e., mystery] retains its tantalizing capacity both to indicate what is to be believed and to point to a reality beyond words. The reality being experienced and expressed . . . always escapes formal far less final definition. And yet the experience and the hope ever strive to express that reality afresh, drawing on tradition but ever finding it necessary to find fresh expression." James D. G. Dunn, *New Testament Theology: An Introduction* (Nashville: Abingdon Press, 2009), 96.

29 James B. Nickoloff, ed., *Gustavo Gutiérrez Essential Writings* (Minneapolis: Fortress Press, 1996), 61.

30 Samuel Wells, *Improvisation: The Drama of Christian Ethics* (Grand Rapids, MI: Baker Academic, 2004), 67.

31 Douglas John Hall, *Has the Church a Future?* (Minneapolis: Fortress Press, 2007), 96.

32 Wells, *Improvisation*, 16

33 Amanda Hontz Drury, *Saying Is Believing: The Necessity of Testimony in Adolescent Spiritual Development* (Downers Grove, IL: InterVarsity Press, 2015), 19.

34 See Raffety and Ellis, "Disruptive Youth," 5–24, at 22.

35 Allison James, "Giving Voice to Children's Voices: Practice and Problems, Pitfalls and Potentials," *American Anthropologist* 109, no. 2 (2009): 261–272, at 266.

36 P. Christensen and M. O'Brien, eds., "Working with Ethical Symmetry in Social Research with Children," *Childhood* 9, no. 4 (2003): 477–497, at 481.

37 Amy E. Jacober, "From Experience to Ethics: The Shaping Impact of Narrative on Youth Ministry and Disability," in Ellis and Langford, *Embodying Youth*, 105.

38 See Osmer, *Practical Theology*.

39 Dykstra, *Vision and Character*, 33.

40 Dykstra, *Vision and Character*, 33–34.

41 Douglas John Hall, *The Cross in Our Context* (Minneapolis: Fortress Press, 2003), 201.

42 See Ellis, "Human Beings and Human Becomings."

43 Root, *The End of Youth Ministry?*, 185.

44 Root, *The End of Youth Ministry?*, 175.

45 Root, *The End of Youth Ministry?*, 162, n22.

46 Root, *The End of Youth Ministry?*, 162. Italics mine.

47 Rian Johnson, "Director Rian Johnson Breaks Down a Scene from 'Knives Out,'" *Vanity Fair*, YouTube, February 25, 2020, https://www.youtube.com/watch?v=69GjaVWeGQM 2:52-3:21, accessed May 4, 2020.

48 Wells, *Improvisation*, 60.

49 Raffety and Ellis, "Disruptive Youth," 23–24.

50 "According to the mechanistic theory, things are primary, and their relations to one another are determined secondarily, through 'natural laws'. But in reality relations are just as primal as the things themselves. 'Thing' and 'relation' are complementary modes of appearance, in the same way as particle and wave in the nuclear sector. For nothing in the world exists, lives and moves *of itself*. Everything exists, lives and moves *in others*, in one another, with one another, for one another, in the cosmic interactions of the divine Spirit." Moltmann, *God in Creation*, 11.

51 I am indebted to Marcus Hong for exposing me to improvisation as a lens for interpretation in his workshop entitled "Crash Helmets and Cultivation: Engaging Youth in Worship," at the Institute for Youth Ministry's Forum on Youth Ministry at Princeton Theological Seminary, spring 2015.

52 Jacober, "From Experience to Ethics," 105.

53 Tina Fey, *Bossypants* (New York: Little, Brown, 2011).

54 Improv Encyclopedia, "5 Basic Improv Rules," http://improvencyclopedia.org /references/5_Basic_Improv_Rules.html, accessed June 15, 2021.

55 Wells, *Improvisation*, 106.

56 For a constructive critique of the latter, see Root, *Faith Formation in a Secular Age*.

57 As quoted in Peter Bayer, LinkedIn, "Tina Fey's Rules for Brainstorming," https:// www.linkedin.com/pulse/tina-feys-rules-brainstorming-peter, accessed June 6, 2023.

58 "If the cosmic Spirit is the Spirit of God, the universe cannot be viewed as a closed system. It has to be understood as a system that is open—open to God and for his future." Moltmann, *God in Creation*, 103.

59 See Anderson, *The Soul of Ministry*, 43–51.

60 Ziegler, *Militant Grace*, 200.

61 Andrew Root, *The Congregation in a Secular Age* (Grand Rapids, MI: Baker Academic, 2021), 196.

62 See Rosa, *The Uncontrollability of the World*.

63 Rosa, *The Uncontrollability of the World*.

64 Rosa, *The Uncontrollability of the World*. Italics mine.

65 Rosa, *The Uncontrollability of the World*.

66 Bonhoeffer, *Life Together*, 27.

Bibliography

Almagno, Romano Stephen, and Conrad L. Harkins, eds. *Studies Honoring Ignatius Charles Brady, Friar Minor*. St. Bonaventure, NY: Franciscan Institute, 1976.

Anderson, Ray S. *Historical Transcendence and the Reality of God*. Grand Rapids, MI: Eerdmans, 1975.

———. *The Shape of Practical Theology: Empowering Ministry with Theological Praxis*. Downers Grove, IL: InterVarsity Press, 2001.

———. *The Soul of Ministry*. Louisville, KY: Westminster John Knox Press, 1997.

Augustine. *The City of God*. New York: The Modern Library, 1950.

Auten, David Arthur. *Eccentricity: A Spirituality of Difference*. Eugene, OR: Cascade, 2014.

Balogh, E. P., B. T. Miller, and J. R. Ball, eds. *Improving Diagnosis in Health Care*. Washington, DC: The National Academies Press, 2015.

Balswick, Jack O., Pamela Ebstyne King, and Kevin S. Reimer. *The Reciprocating Self: Human Development in Theological Perspective*. Downers Grove, IL: InterVarsity Press, 2005.

Barth, Karl. *Church Dogmatics I.1*. New York: T&T Clark, 1936.

———. *Church Dogmatics III.2*. Edinburgh: T&T Clark, 1960.

———. *Church Dogmatics IV. 1*. Edinburgh: T&T Clark, 1960.

Bauckham, Richard, ed. *God Will Be All in All: The Eschatology of Jürgen Moltmann*. Minneapolis: Fortress Press, 2001.

———. *The Theology of Jürgen Moltmann*. New York: T&T Clark, 1995.

Bender, Kimlyn J. *Karl Barth's Christological Ecclesiology*. n.p.: Taylor & Francis, 2017.

Bergler, Thomas E. *From Here to Maturity: Overcoming the Juvenilization of American Christianity*. Grand Rapids, MI: Eerdmans, 2014.

———. *The Juvenilization of American Christianity*. Grand Rapids, MI: Eerdmans, 2013.

Berkhof, L. *Systematic Theology*. Grand Rapids, MI: Eerdmans, 1939.

Berman, Marshall. "Erik Erikson, the Man Who Invented Himself." *New York Times*, March 30, 1975. https://archive.nytimes.com/www.nytimes.com/books/99/08/22/specials/erikson-history.html. Accessed May 26, 2021.

Blos, Peter. *The Adolescent Passage: Developmental Issues*. London: International Universities Press, 1979.

Bonhoeffer, Dietrich. *Christ the Center*. New York: Harper & Row, 1978.

———. *Life Together*. New York: Harper & Row, 1954.

Borgman, Dean. *Foundations for Youth Ministry*. Grand Rapids, MI: Baker Academic, 2013.

Brown, Francis, Emil Roediger, S. R. Driver, Charles A. Briggs, Edward Robinson, and Wilhelm Gesenius. *The Brown-Driver-Briggs Hebrew and English Lexicon*. Peabody, MA: Hendrickson, 2000.

Brunner, Emil. *Dogmatics, Vol 1: The Christian Doctrine of God*. London: Lutterworth Press, 1949.

———. *Man in Revolt*. Philadelphia: Westminster, 1939.

Buechner, Frederick. *Wishful Thinking: A Theological ABC*. New York: Harper & Row, 1973.

Burman, Erica. *Deconstructing Developmental Psychology*. New York: Routledge, 2007.

Burns, Jim, and Mike DeVries. *The Youth Builder*. Ventura, CA: Gospel Light, 2001.

Calvin, John. *Institutes of the Christian Religion, Vol.1*. Louisville, KY: Westminster John Knox Press, 1960.

Cannister, Mark. *Teenagers Matter: Making Student Ministry a Priority in the Church*. Grand Rapids, MI: Baker Academic, 2013.

Capps, Donald. *The Depleted Self: Sin in a Narcissistic Age*. Minneapolis: Fortress Press, 1993.

———. *Life Cycle Theory and Pastoral Care*. Eugene, OR: Wipf and Stock, 1983.

Christensen, P., and M. O'Brien, eds. "Working with Ethical Symmetry in Social Research with Children." *Childhood* 9, no. 4 (2003): 477–497.

Clark, Chap. *Hurt: Inside the World of Today's Teenagers*. Grand Rapids, MI: Baker Academic, 2004.

Cobb, John B., Jr. "Theology and the Philosophy of Science." *Religious Studies Review* 3, no. 4: 213–215.

Coles, Robert. *Erik H. Erikson: The Growth of His Work*. Boston: Atlantic Monthly Press, 1970.

Cone, James H. *A Black Theology of Liberation*. New York: Lippincott, 1970.

———. *The Cross and the Lynching Tree*. New York: Orbis, 2011.

Conner, Benjamin T. "Disabled Adolescents, Enabling Youth Ministry." *Journal of Disability and Religion* (2018). https://doi: 10.1080/23312521.2018.1521765.

Cortez, Marc. *Theological Anthropology: A Guide for the Perplexed*. New York: T &T Clark, 2010.

Crisp, Oliver D. *The Word Enfleshed: Exploring the Person and Work of Christ*. Grand Rapids, MI: Baker Academic, 2016.

Culpepper, R. Allan. "The Gospel of Luke." In *The New Interpreter's Bible: A Commentary in Twelve Volumes*, vol. 9. Nashville: Abingdon Press, 1995.

Dean, Kenda Creasy. "Are You Leaving Youth Ministry?" *Ministry Incubators,* August 14, 2015. https://ministryincubators.com/are-you-leaving-youth-ministry/. Accessed May 26, 2021.

———. "Pointing the Finger in the Wrong Direction: Thomas Bergler's *The Juvenilization of American Christianity*." *Theology Today* 70, no. 1 (2013): 79–81.

———. *Practicing Passion: Youth and the Quest for a Passionate Church*. Grand Rapids, MI: Eerdmans, 2004.

———. "Spiritual Entrepreneurship: It's a Full-Blown Movement Now." Ministry Incubators. https://ministryincubators.com/spiritual-entrepreneurship-its-a-full-blown-movement-now/. Accessed May 27, 2021.

———. "Why Churches Should Be Talking More about Social Entrepreneurship." *Caring*, August 31, 2017. https://caringmagazine.org/churches-talking-social -entrepreneurship/. Accessed June 6, 2023.

Dean, Kenda Creasy, ed. *OMG: A Youth Ministry Handbook*. Nashville: Abingdon Press, 2010.

Dean, Kenda Creasy, Chap Clark, and Dave Rahn, eds. *Starting Right: Thinking Theologically about Youth Ministry*. Grand Rapids, MI: Zondervan, 2001.

Dean, Kenda Creasy, Wesley W. Ellis, Justin Forbes, and Abigail Visco Rusert. *Delighted: What Teenagers Are Teaching the Church about Joy*. Grand Rapids, MI: Eerdmans, 2020.

DeJonge, Michael P. *Bonhoeffer's Theological Formation: Berlin, Barth, and Protestant Theology*. Oxford: Oxford University Press, 2012.

Denton, Melinda Lundquist, and Richard Flory. *Back-Pocket God: Religion and Spirituality in the Lives of Emerging Adults*. New York: Oxford University Press, 2020.

DeVries, Dawn. "Toward a Theology of Childhood." *Interpretation* 55, no. 2 (2001): 161–173.

DeVries, Mark. *Family-Based Youth Ministry*, Second Edition. Downers Grove, IL: InterVarsity Press, 2004.

———. *Sustainable Youth Ministry: Why Most Youth Ministry Doesn't Last and What Your Church Can Do about It*. Downers Grove, IL: IVP Books, 2008.

Dillenberger, John, ed. *Martin Luther: Selections from His Writings*. New York: Anchor Books, 1962.

Drury, Amanda Hontz. *Saying Is Believing: The Necessity of Testimony in Adolescent Spiritual Development*. Downers Grove, IL: InterVarsity Press, 2015.

Dunn, James D. G. *New Testament Theology: An Introduction*. Nashville: Abingdon Press, 2009.

Dykstra, Craig. *Vision and Character: A Christian Educator's Alternative to Kohlberg*. Eugene, OR: Wipf and Stock, 1981.

Ellis, Wesley W. "Diagnosing Adolescence: From Curing Adolescents to Caring for Young People." *Journal of Disability and Religion* 22, no. 4 (2018): 390–407.

———. "Human Beings and Human Becomings." *Journal of Youth and Theology* 14, no. 2 (2015): 119–137.

Ellis, Wesley W., and Michael D. Langford, eds. *Embodying Youth: Exploring Youth Ministry and Disability*. New York: Routledge, 2020.

Elman, Julie Passanante. *Chronic Youth: Disability, Sexuality, and US Media Cultures of Rehabilitation*. New York: NYU Press, 2014.

Epstein, Robert. *The Case against Adolescence: Rediscovering the Adult in Every Teen*. Sanger, CA: Quill Driver Books, 2007.

Erikson, Erik H. "Autobiographic Notes on the Identity Crisis." *Daedalus* 99, no. 4 (1970): 730–759.

———. *Childhood and Society*. New York: W. W. Norton, 1963.

———. *Identity: Youth and Crisis*. New York: W. W. Norton, 1968.

———. *Identity and the Life Cycle*. New York: W. W. Norton, 1980.

Fey, Tina. *Bossypants,* Enhanced Edition. New York: Little, Brown, 2011.

Flagler College Youth Ministry. "The Missing Voices Project." https://missingvoices .flagler.edu/. Accessed May 26, 2021.

Fowler, James W. *Becoming Adult, Becoming Christian: Adult Development and Christian Faith*. New York: Harper & Row, 1984.

———. *Stages of Faith: The Psychology of Human Development and the Quest for Meaning*. New York: HarperCollins, 1981.

Friedman, Lawrence J. *Identity's Architect: A Biography of Erik H. Erikson*. Cambridge, MA: Harvard University Press, 1999.

Fromm, Erich. *To Have or To Be*. New York: Bloomsbury, 1976.

Fuller Youth Institute. "Sticky Faith." https://fulleryouthinstitute.org/stickyfaith. Accessed May 26, 2021.

Gogarten, Friedrich. *Christ the Crisis*. Richmond, VA: John Knox Press, 1970.

Going, Nancy. "The Way of Jesus: Adolescent Development as Theological Process." *Journal of Youth Ministry* 9, no. 2 (2011): 49–66.

González, Justo L. *The Story of Christianity, Volume 2: The Reformation to the Present Day*. New York: HarperOne, 1985.

Graham, Elaine L. *Transforming Practice: Pastoral Theology in an Age of Uncertainty*. Eugene, OR: Wipf and Stock, 1996.

Gregory of Nyssa. *On the Making of Man*. n.p.: Aeterna Press, 2016.

Grenz, Stanley J. *Theology for the Community of God*. Grand Rapids, MI: Eerdmans, 2000.

Hall, Douglas John. *Confessing the Faith: Christian Theology in a North American Context*. Minneapolis: Fortress Press, 1996.

———. *The Cross in Our Context*. Minneapolis: Fortress Press, 2003.

———. *Has the Church A Future?*. Minneapolis: Fortress Press, 2007.

———. *Imaging God: Dominion as Stewardship*. Grand Rapids, MI: Eerdmans, 1986.

———. *Professing the Faith: Christian Theology in a North American Context*. Minneapolis: Fortress Press, 1993.

———. *Thinking the Faith: Christian Theology in a North American Context*. Minneapolis: Fortress Press, 1991.

Hay, David, and Rebecca Nye. *The Spirit of the Child*. Philadelphia: Jessica Kingsley Publishers, 2006.

Heath, Elaine A. *The Mystic Way of Evangelism*. Grand Rapids, MI: Baker Academic, 2017.

Heschel, Abraham Joshua. *The Sabbath*. New York: Farrar, Straus and Giroux, 1951.

Hockey, Jenny, and Allison James. *Social Identities across the Life Course*. New York: Palgrave, 2003.

Hong, Marcus. "Crash Helmets and Cultivation: Engaging Youth in Worship." Paper presented at the Forum on Youth Ministry at Institute for Youth Ministry, Princeton Theological Seminary, Princeton, NJ, Spring 2015.

Hunsinger, Deborah Van Deusen. *Theology and Pastoral Counseling: A New Interdisciplinary Approach*. Grand Rapids, MI: Eerdmans, 1995.

Hunsinger, George. *Conversational Theology: Essays on Ecumenical, Postliberal, and Political Themes, with Special Reference to Karl Barth*. New York: Bloomsbury, 2014.

Hunter, James Davidson. *The Death of Character: Moral Education in an Age without Good or Evil*. New York: Basic Books, 2000.

Jacober, Amy. *The Adolescent Journey: An Interdisciplinary Approach to Practical Youth Ministry*. Downers Grove, MI: InterVarsity Press, 2011.

James, Allison. "Giving Voice to Children's Voices: Practice and Problems, Pitfalls and Potentials." *American Anthropologist* 109, no. 2 (2009): 261–272.

James, Allison, and Alan Prout. *Constructing and Reconstructing Childhood*, Second Edition. New York: RoutledgeFalmer, 1997.

Jenks, Chris. *Childhood*, Second Edition. New York: Routledge, 2005.

Johnson, Rian. "Director Rian Johnson Breaks Down a Scene from 'Knives Out.'" *Vanity Fair*, YouTube, February 25, 2020. https://www.youtube.com/watch?v =69GjaVWeGQM2:52-3:21. Accessed May 4, 2020.

Jüngel, Eberhard. *God As the Mystery of the World*. Eugene, OR: Wipf and Stock, 1983

Keen, Craig. *After Crucifixion: The Promise of Theology*. Eugene, OR: Cascade, 2013.

Keener, Craig S. *The IVP Bible Background Commentary: New Testament*. Downers Grove, IL: IVP Academic, 1993.

Kessen, William. "The American Child and Other Cultural Inventions." *American Psychologist* 34, no. 10 (1979): 815–820.

———. *The Child*. New York: Wiley, 1965.

Keuss, Jeff. *Blur: A New Paradigm for Understanding Youth Culture*. Grand Rapids, MI: Zondervan, 2014.

Keuss, Jeff, and Rob Willett. "The Sacredly Mobile Adolescent: A Hermeneutic Phenomenological Study toward Revising of the Third Culture Kid Typology for Effective Ministry Practice in a Multivalent Culture." *Journal of Youth Ministry* 8, no. 1 (2009): 7–24.

King, Mike. *Presence-Centered Youth Ministry: Guiding Students into Spiritual Formation*. Downers Grove, IL: InterVarsity Press, 2006.

Kirgiss, Crystal. *In Search of Adolescence*. San Diego, CA: The Youth Cartel, 2015.

Kleinman, Arthur. *Rethinking Psychiatry: From Cultural Category to Personal Experience*. New York: The Free Press, 1988.

LaCugna, Catherine Mowry, ed. *Freeing Theology: The Essentials of Theology in Feminist Perspective*. New York: HarperCollins, 1993.

Leiter, Robert. "The Corrosive Nature of Fame." *Jewish World Review*. http://www .jewishworldreview.com/on/media112999.asp. Accessed May 26, 2021.

Lightfoot, Cynthia. *The Culture of Adolescent Risk-Taking*. New York: The Guilford Press, 1997.

Luhrmann, T. M. *When God Talks Back: Understanding the American Evangelical Relationship with God*. New York: Vintage, 2012.

Luther, Martin. *Three Treatises from the American Edition of Luther's Works*. Minneapolis: Fortress Press, 1970.

MacIntyre, Alasdair. *Dependent Rational Animals: Why Human Beings Need the Virtues*. Chicago: Open Court, 1999.

Mandal, Ananya. "Down Syndrome History." *News Medical Life Sciences*. https://www .news-medical.net/health/Down-Syndrome-History.aspx. Accessed May 26, 2021.

Marty, Martin E. *The Mystery of the Child*. Grand Rapids, MI: Eerdmans, 2007.

Mashable. "At the Google Hearing, Congress Proves They Still Have No Idea How the internet Works." https://mashable.com/article/google-hearing-congress-no-idea -about-internet- search/#VM1T1fmsCSqg. Accessed February 14, 2019.

McDonnell, Thomas P., ed. *A Thomas Merton Reader*. New York: Image Books, 1974.

Mercer, Joyce Ann. *Welcoming Children: A Practical Theology of Childhood*. St. Louis: Chalice Press, 2005.

Miller-McLemore, Bonnie J. "Childhood Studies and Pastoral Counseling."
Sacred Spaces: e-Journal of the American Association of Pastoral Counselors 6 (2014): 7–52.

Moltmann, Jürgen. *The Church in the Power of the Spirit*. Minneapolis: Fortress Press, 1993.

———. *The Coming of God: Christian Eschatology*. Minneapolis: Fortress Press, 1996

———. *The Crucified God: The Cross of Christ as the Foundation and Criticism of Christian Theology*. Minneapolis: Fortress Press, 1993.

———. *God for a Secular Society: The Public Relevance of Theology*. Minneapolis: Fortress Press, 1999.

———. *God in Creation: A New Theology of Creation and the Spirit of God*. Minneapolis: Fortress Press, 1993.

———. *Hope for the Church: Moltmann in Dialogue with Practical Theology*. Nashville: Abingdon Press, 1979.

———. *In the End—the Beginning*. Minneapolis: Fortress Press, 2004.

———. *The Power of the Powerless*. London: SCM Press, 1983.

———. *The Spirit of Hope: Theology for a World in Peril*. Louisville, KY: Westminster John Knox Press, 2019.

———. *Theology and Joy*. London: Hymns Ancient and Modern, 2013.

———. *Theology of Hope: On the Ground and the Implications of a Christian Eschatology*. Minneapolis: Fortress Press, 1993.

———. *Theology of Play*. London: Harper & Row, 1972.

———. *The Trinity and the Kingdom*. Minneapolis: Fortress Press, 1993.

———. *The Way of Jesus Christ*. Minneapolis: Fortress Press, 1993.Myers, Jeremy Paul. *Liberating Youth from Adolescence*. Minneapolis: Fortress Press, 2018.

Nakkula, Michael J., and Eric Toshalis. *Understanding Youth: Adolescent Development for Educators*. Cambridge, MA: Harvard Education Press, 2006.

Newsom, Carol A., Shaon H. Ringe, and Jacqueline E. Lapsley, eds. *Women's Bible Commentary*, Third Edition. Louisville, KY: Westminster John Knox Press, 2012.

Nickoloff, James B., ed. *Gustavo Gutierrez Essential Writings*. Minneapolis: Fortress Press, 1996.

Nixon, Rob. *Slow Violence and the Environmentalism of the Poor*. Cambridge, MA: Harvard University Press, 2011.

Nouwen, Henri J. M. *In the Name of Jesus: Reflections on Christian Leadership*. New York: Crossroad, 1989.

———. *Spiritual Formation*. New York: HarperOne, 2010.

Osmer, Richard Robert. *Practical Theology: An Introduction*. Grand Rapids, MI: Eerdmans, 2008.

———. *The Teaching Ministry of Congregations*. Louisville, KY: Westminster John Knox Press, 2005.

Osmer, Richard Robert, and Friedrich L. Schweitzer, eds. *Developing a Public Faith: New Directions in Practical Theology*. St. Louis: Chalice Press, 2003.

Pannenberg, Wolfart. *Jesus—God and Man*. Philadelphia: Westminster, 1975.

———. *Theology and the Philosophy of Science*. Philadelphia: Westminster, 1976.

Pew Research Center. "In US, Decline of Christianity Continues at Rapid Pace." https://www.pewforum.org/2019/10/17/in-u-s-decline-of-christianity-continues-at-rapid-pace/. Accessed May 26, 2021

Powell, Kara, Jake Mulder, and Brad Griffin. *Growing Young: 6 Essential Strategies to Help Young People Discover and Love Your Church*. Grand Rapids, MI: Baker Academic, 2016.

Powell, Kara E., and Chap Clark. *Sticky Faith*. Grand Rapids, MI: Zondervan, 2011.

Princeton Institute for Youth Ministry. "The Log College Project." http://iym.ptsem .edu/the-log-college-project/. Accessed May 26, 2021.

Qvortrup, Jens, ed. *Studies in Modern Childhood: Society, Agency, Culture*. New York: Palgrave, 2005.

Qvortrup, Jens, William A. Corsaro, and Michael-Sebastian Honig, eds. *The Palgrave Handbook of Childhood Studies*. New York: Palgrave, 2009.

Raffety, Erin, and Wesley W. Ellis. "Disruptive Youth: Toward an Ethnographic Turn in Youth Ministry." *Ecclesial Practices* 4, no.1 (2017): 5–24.

Reinders, Hans S. *Receiving the Gift of Friendship: Profound Disability, Theological Anthropology, and Ethics*. Grand Rapids, MI: Eerdmans, 2008.

Rice, Wayne. *Junior High Ministry: A Guide to Early Adolescence for Youth Workers*, Updated and Expanded. Grand Rapids, MI: Zondervan, 1998.

Richards, Lawrence O. *Youth Ministry: Its Renewal in the Local Church*. Grand Rapids, MI: Zondervan, 1991.

Rolt, Clarence Edwin. *The World's Redemption*. New York: Longmans, Green, 1913.

Root, Andrew. "Being a Pastor within the Secular Frame Means Teaching People How to Pray." *Christian Century*, June 25, 2019. https://www.christiancentury.org/article /critical-essay/being-pastor-within-secular-frame-means-teaching-people-how-pray. Accessed May 26, 2021.

———. *Bonhoeffer as Youth Worker*. Grand Rapids, MI: Baker Academic, 2014.

———. *Christopraxis: A Practical Theology of the Cross*. Minneapolis: Fortress Press, 2014.

———. *Churches and the Crisis of Decline*. Grand Rapids, MI: Baker Academic, 2022.

———. *The Congregation in a Secular Age*. Grand Rapids, MI: Baker Academic, 2021.

———. *The End of Youth Ministry?* Grand Rapids, MI: Baker Academic, 2020.

———. *Exploding Stars, Dead Dinosaurs, and Zombies: Youth Ministry in the Age of Science*. Minneapolis: Fortress Press, 2018.

———. *Faith Formation in a Secular Age*. Grand Rapids, MI: Baker Academic, 2017.

———. *The Pastor in a Secular Age*. Grand Rapids, MI: Baker Academic, 2019.

———. *Relationships Unfiltered*. Grand Rapids, MI: Zondervan, 2009.

———. *Revisiting Relational Youth Ministry: From a Strategy of Influence to a Theology of Incarnation*. Downers Grove, IL: InterVarsity Press, 2007.

———. "Youth Ministry as a Magical Technology: Moving toward the Theological." *Catalyst* 40, no. 1 (2013): 1–3. http://www.catalystresources.org/youth-ministry-as-a -magical-technology-moving-toward-the-theological/. Accessed June 6, 2023.

Root, Andrew, and Kenda Creasy Dean. *The Theological Turn in Youth Ministry*. Downers Grove, IL: InterVarsity Press, 2011.

Rosa, Hartmut. *The Uncontrollability of the World*. Medford, MA: 2020.

Schleiermacher, Frederick. *Brief Outline of the Study of Theology*. Eugene, OR: Wipf and Stock, 2007.

Schmidt, Morgan. *Woo: Awakening Teenagers' Desire to Follow in the Way of Jesus*. San Diego, CA: The Youth Cartel, 2014.

Schrag, Calvin O. *The Resources of Rationality: A Response to the Postmodern Challenge*. Indianapolis: Indiana University Press, 1992.

Schwatrz, Kelly D. "Adolescent Brain Development: An Oxymoron No Longer." *Journal of Youth Ministry* 6, no. 2 (2008): 85–93.

Schweitzer, Friedrich, and Johannes A. van der Ven, eds. *Practical Theology—International Perspectives.* New York: Peter Lang, 1999.

Siegel, Daniel J. *The Developing Mind, Second Edition: How Relationships and the Brain Interact to Shape Who We Are.* London: Guilford Publications, 2012.

Slate. "Google's Web of Confusion." https://slate.com/technology/2018/12/google -congress- hearing-sundar-pichai-confusion-regulation.html. Accessed February 14, 2019.

Smith, James K. A. *Desiring the Kingdom: Worship, Worldview, and Cultural Formation.* Grand Rapids, MI: Baker Academic, 2009.

———. *How (Not) to Be Secular: Reading Charles Taylor.* Grand Rapids, MI: Eerdmans, 2014.

Soelle, Dorothee. *Thinking about God.* Eugene, OR: Wipf and Stock, 2016.

Sölle, Dorothee, and Shirley A. Cloyes. *To Work and to Love: A Theology of Creation.* Philadelphia: Fortress Press, 1984.

Spener, Philip Jacob. *Pia Desideria.* Eugene, OR: Wipf and Stock, 1964.

Stivers, Richard. *Technology as Magic: The Triumph of the Irrational.* New York: Continuum, 2001.

Stucky, Nathan T. *Wrestling with Rest: Inviting Youth to Discover the Gift of Sabbath.* Grand Rapids, MI: Eerdmans, 2019.

Swinton, John. *Becoming Friends of Time: Disability, Timefullness, and Gentle Discipleship.* Waco, TX: Baylor University Press, 2018.

———. "The Body of Christ Has Down Syndrome." *Journal of Pastoral Theology* 13, no. 2 (2003): 66–78.

———. *Finding Jesus in the Storm: The Spiritual Lives of Christians with Mental Health Challenges.* Grand Rapids, MI: Eerdmans, 2020.

———. *From Bedlam to Shalom: Towards a Practical Theology of Human Nature, Interpersonal Relationships, and Mental Health Care.* New York: Peter Lang, 2000.

———. *Raging with Compassion: Pastoral Responses to the Problem of Evil.* Grand Rapids, MI: Eerdmans, 2007.

———. *Spirituality and Mental Health Care: Rediscovering a "Forgotten" Dimension.* Philadelphia: Jessica Kingsley Publishers, 2001.

———. "Who Is the God We Worship? Theologies of Disability; Challenges and New Possibilities." *International Journal of Practical Theology* 14, no. 2 (February 2011): 273–307.

Swinton, John, and Harriet Mowat. *Practical Theology and Qualitative Research.* London: SCM Press, 2006.

Tanner, Kathryn. *Christ the Key.* Cambridge, UK: Cambridge University Press, 2010.

———. *Jesus, Humanity, and the Trinity: A Brief Systematic Theology.* Minneapolis: Fortress Press, 2001.

Taylor, Charles. *The Explanation of Behavior.* New York: The Humanities Press, 1964.

———. *Human Agency and Language. Philosophical Papers 1.* Cambridge, UK: Cambridge University Press, 1985.

———. *A Secular Age.* Cambridge, MA: The Belknap Press, 2007.

———. *Sources of the Self.* Cambridge, MA: Harvard University Press, 1989.

Taylor, Mark Kline. *Paul Tillich: Theologian of the Boundaries*. Minneapolis: Fortress Press, 1991.

Thomas Aquinas. *Summa Theologica*. New York: Benzinger Bros., 1947.

Tillich, Paul. *On the Boundary: A Autobiographical Sketch*. Eugene, OR: Wipf and Stock, 1966.

———. *The Protestant Era*, trans. James Luther Adams. Chicago: University of Chicago Press, 1948.

———. *The Shaking of the Foundations*. Eugene, OR: Wipf and Stock, 1948.

———. *Systematic Theology, Volume 1*. Chicago: University of Chicago Press, 1951.

———. *Systematic Theology, Volume 2*. Chicago: University of Chicago Press, 1957.

van Huyssteen, J. Wentzel. *The Shaping of Rationality: Toward Interdisciplinarity in Theology and Science*. Grand Rapids, MI: Eerdmans, 1999.

Vanstone, W. H. *The Stature of Waiting*. New York: Morehouse, 1982.

Ward, Pete. *Introducing Practical Theology: Mission, Ministry, and the Life of the Church*. Grand Rapids, MI: Baker Academic, 2017.

Washington Post. "Transcript of Mark Zuckerberg's Senate Hearing." https://www.washingtonpost.com/news/the-switch/wp/2018/04/10/transcript-of-mark-zuckerbergs-senate-hearing/?utm_term=.d4a3c312f47b. Accessed May 27, 2021.

———. "Transcript of Zuckerberg's appearance before House Committee." https://www.washingtonpost.com/news/the-switch/wp/2018/04/11/transcript-of-zuckerbergs- appearance-before-house-committee/?utm_term=.1dc38558d106. Accessed May 27, 2021.

Weber, Otto. *Foundations of Dogmatics, Vol. 1*. Grand Rapids, MI: Eerdmans Publishing, 1981.

Webster, J. B. *Eberhard Jüngel: An introduction to His Theology*. New York: Cambridge University Press, 1986.

Wells, Samuel. *Improvisation: The Drama of Christian Ethics*. Grand Rapids, MI: Baker Academic, 2004.

Whaling, Frank, ed. *John and Charles Wesley: Selected Prayers, Hymns, Journal Notes, Sermons, Letters and Treatises*. New York: Paulist Press, 1981.

White, David F., and Sarah F. Farmer, eds. *Joy: A Guide for Youth Ministry*. Nashville: Wesley's Foundary Books, 2020.

Wilber, Ken. *No Boundary: Eastern and Western Approaches to Personal Growth*. Boulder, CO: Shambhala, 2001.

Yaconelli, Mark. *Contemplative Youth Ministry: Practicing the Presence of Jesus*. Grand Rapids, MI: Zondervan, 2006.

Ziegler, Philip G. *Militant Grace*. Grand Rapids, MI: Baker Academic, 2018.

Zirschky, Andrew. *Beyond the Screen: Youth Ministry for the Connected but Alone Generation*. Nashville: Abingdon Press, 2015.